REPAIRING BRITISH POLITICS

The constitutional crisis of 2009, sparked by the 'expenses scandal', led rapidly to the questioning of our entire political order. This book presents a major new constitutional analysis of the way we are governed.

At t   ment.
Repair   **ONE WEEK LOAN**   cused
around   tional
suprem   ıbility
more c

A w   ıritain
is to h   ter by
definin   more
rationa   ıthout
a clear   refore
essenti   ıebate
might l

Wri   *airing*
British   with a
profess   favour
of a w   ents a
workin   ıs and
explan   model
Consti   urther
discuss   ution.
Part 3   ce any
form o

We   ıs the
govern

Repairing British Politics

A Blueprint for Constitutional Change

Richard Gordon

·HART·
PUBLISHING

OXFORD AND PORTLAND, OREGON
2010

Published in the United Kingdom by Hart Publishing Ltd
16C Worcester Place, Oxford, OX1 2JW
Telephone: +44 (0)1865 517530
Fax: +44 (0)1865 510710
E-mail: mail@hartpub.co.uk
Website: http://www.hartpub.co.uk

Published in North America (US and Canada) by
Hart Publishing
c/o International Specialized Book Services
920 NE 58th Avenue, Suite 300
Portland, OR 97213-3786
USA
Tel: +1 503 287 3093 or toll-free: (1) 800 944 6190
Fax: +1 503 280 8832
E-mail: orders@isbs.com
Website: http://www.isbs.com

© Richard Gordon 2010

Richard Gordon has asserted his right under the Copyright, Designs
and Patents Act 1988, to be identified as the author of this work.

British Library Cataloguing in Publication Data
Data Available

ISBN: 978-1-84946-049-1

Edited and typeset by www.textcollective.co.uk
Printed and bound in Great Britain by
TJ International Ltd, Padstow, Cornwall

Civilization is a thin and precarious crust, erected by the personality and will of a very few, and only maintained by rules and conventions skilfully put across and guilefully preserved.

John Maynard Keynes ('My Early Beliefs', 1938)

Our generalised feeling that the House of Commons is unfit to discharge its responsibilities, and our particular rage over MPs' expenses arises not because we think democracy doesn't matter, but because we know it does.

Matthew Parris (*The Times*, 7 November 2009)

Contents

3. THE CONSTITUTION OF BRITAIN (REFERENDUMS) ACT

Acknowledgements

I should like to thank a number of people for their help.

Professor Swati Jhaveri, Associate Professor at the Chinese University of Hong Kong, provided illuminating insights with regard to the text generally and on comparative constitutional law in particular. Glen Davis, barrister, made several characteristically incisive comments on drafting and a number of very helpful points on the text.

My old history teacher, Patrick Tobin, came out of retirement to give me a masterly history lesson which saved me from many mistakes. David Walter, former political correspondent for ITN, Channel 4 News and the BBC, made penetrating observations from an 'insider' perspective on the political sections of the draft Constitution. Professor Stuart Weir has provided invaluable assistance on aspects of proportional representation. Special thanks to Mark Hofman, who suggested the idea of second-past-the-post and tested my theories in a number of stimulating discussions.

A helpful paper prepared by a number of constitutional lawyers, still in draft, entitled *Towards a Codified Constitution* was shown to me at proof stage. I have benefited greatly from reading it and have made specific acknowledgement in the text where appropriate. My thanks go to its authors Stephen Hockman QC, Professor Vernon Bogdanor, Professor Sir David Edward, Professor Andrew Le Sueur, Professor Brice Dickson, Rabinder Singh QC, Jemima Stratford, Noemi Byrd, Sarah Naylor and Christopher Knight.

My publisher, Hart Publishing, has given out of the ordinary support in terms of planning and content. My thanks go to Richard Hart, Jo Ledger, Jane Parker and Mel Hamill.

The team at Spada, especially Gavin Ingham Brooke, Joanna Tudor and Dillon Mann, has supported the project from an early stage and helped to make the finished product more like Tom Paine than Edmund Burke.

Others who have read part of the text and made helpful comments include the financial analyst Miles Saltiel, journalist Edward Fennell, and my editor Ruth Massey.

Finally, my wife Jane and children Edmund and Adam have each inspected the text critically (sometimes very critically) and removed as much over-statement as I would allow.

It goes without saying that any errors of law or fact are attributable to no one other than myself.

Glossary of Essential Terms

Accountability

In the context of this book, this embodies the concept of **responsibility** of either executive government or of the **judiciary** for their acts and omissions. In electoral terms this is usually taken to mean accountability to voters but the **executive** is also accountable to **Parliament** and the judiciary is subject to control by the Legal Services Ombudsman.

Act of Parliament

A law passed as primary **legislation** by **Parliament**.

Address by Parliament

A statement of the wishes or opinions of one or both of the Houses of Parliament delivered to the sovereign. It is a necessary prerequisite for the removal of a senior judge from office.

Amending Constitutions

The process of changing the terms of a written Constitution. It is usually set at a high threshold so that provisions of a written Constitution are often said to be 'entrenched' compared to the ability of **Parliament** to make and unmake laws by simple majority vote.

Attorney-General

The main legal adviser to the government.

Bill of Rights

A statement of fundamental rights and privileges considered essential to afford protections to citizens of a state.

Domestic Bill of Rights

A Bill of Rights that is the product of an **Act of Parliament** and does not depend on **international treaties** such as the ECHR, part of which has still not been **incorporated** into domestic law. Like any piece of domestic **legislation**, a domestic Bill of Rights can be repealed by **Parliament** at any time, under the doctrine of **parliamentary sovereignty**, unless it is 'entrenched' in a written Constitution.

By-election

An election that is held to fill a political office that has become vacant between general elections.

Cabinet

The committee of senior government ministers at the heart of executive government and the supreme decision-maker in government.

Citizens' Branch

One of the branches of government contained in a written Constitution reflecting citizen power. Mention of a Citizens' Branch in written Constitutions is, however, unusual.

Civil Service

A branch of public service entrusted with the administration of the state and for providing advice to government but which does not form part of the three traditionally recognised arms of government—**executive**, **legislature** or **judiciary**.

Constituency

An electoral area that elects an **MP** to the House of Commons.

Single-member constituency

A constituency that returns one elected candidate to **Parliament**.

Two-member constituency

A constituency that returns two elected candidates to **Parliament**.

Multi-member constituency

A constituency that returns more than two elected candidates to **Parliament**.

Constituency link

The link between an individual **MP** and electors in a particular **constituency**. This link is broken by most if not all forms of **proportional representation**.

Constitution

A device setting out the role and functions of the branches of government. Constitutions may be written or unwritten but all modern democracies (the UK, New Zealand and Israel excepted) have written Constitutions.

Codification

The process of reducing a constitution to a single written document.

Dignified constitution

A term coined by the political theorist Walter Bagehot (1826–77) to denote those parts of the UK's unwritten constitution which inspired reverence (notably, the **monarchy**) rather than performing efficient functions.

Efficient constitution

A term coined by the political theorist Walter Bagehot (1826–77) to denote those parts of government playing a functional role in the day-to-day business of government (most notably, the **executive** and **Parliament**).

Unspoken Constitution

A satirical account, published by Democratic Audit in 2009, of the current rules by which we are governed in the form of a mock written Constitution.

Unwritten constitution

As used in this book, the term means a constitution where the rules by which society is organised, including the institutions of government, have not been codified. In this sense the UK can certainly be said to have an unwritten constitution since the roles and functions of government are contained in various different sources including informal **constitutional conventions**. However, the absence of a written Constitution means that the doctrine of **parliamentary sovereignty** survives intact. Conversely, a written Constitution by reference to which the powers of the branches of government would be constrained, is incompatible with the retention of parliamentary sovereignty.

Contractarian theories of government

Theories of government which postulate a theoretical **social contract** between people and government. Generally, such theories (espoused by, amongst others, Thomas Hobbes (1588–1679) and John Rawls (1921–2002)) do not suggest any legal 'contract' but, rather, a rationale for the existence of such a contract.

(Constitutional) convention

In the constitutional context, a convention is a set of agreed or generally accepted political standards or practices which are in practice treated as binding. The full term 'constitutional convention' is used to denote a gathering for the purposes of drafting a written Constitution.

Salisbury Convention

A constitutional convention preventing the House of Lords from vetoing the second or third parliamentary reading of any government **legislation** promised in its election manifesto.

Sewel Convention

A constitutional convention that the Westminster **Parliament** will only legislate on reserved matters (ie matters reserved to the Westminster Parliament) and will not legislate on devolved matters (ie matters delegated to the Scottish Parliament) without first seeking the consent of the Scottish Parliament.

Constitutional documents

A term sometimes used to denote the documents that make up the informal and uncodified constitution of the United Kingdom. The documents often referred to in this phrase include Magna Carta (1215), the Bill of Rights (1689), the Act of Settlement (1701), the Acts of Union 1707 and 1800, the Great Reform Act 1832, the Parliament Acts 1911 and 1949, the European Communities Act 1972 and the Human Rights Act 1998.

Constitutional moment

A point of national crisis which prompts a state to draft a written, codified Constitution.

Constitutional monarchy

This term has been used in a variety of ways. However, here it means a **monarchy** in which the power of the monarch is limited by a written Constitution. In a wider sense the term is sometimes used to denote a form of constitutional government where the monarch does not wield autocratic power and is the sole source of political power. In the first sense, the United Kingdom does not have a constitutional monarchy; in the second sense it does.

Counter-majoritarian dilemma

The dilemma arising where laws are made by judges without popular mandate. The term was coined by the jurist Robert Bork (1927–).

Declaration

A legal remedy whereby a court states (declares) what the law is.

Democracy

A system of government in which citizens govern directly or, more commonly, which is conducted by elected representatives of the people.

Deliberative democracy

A mixture of direct democracy and representative democracy in which popular consultation is used to formulate political policy.

Direct democracy

A system of government in which the process of government is undertaken directly by the citizens. It is often said to derive from ancient Athens.

Representative democracy

A system of government in which citizens elect individuals to represent them in government. It is to be distinguished from direct democracy in which the citizens participate directly in the business of government. It is argued here that a representative democracy underpinned by **parliamentary sovereignty** is necessarily less 'representative' than one underpinned by constitutional or popular sovereignty, since only in the latter is power conferred by the people as opposed to being imposed on the people.

Devolution

The granting of power by central government to government at a local level. In the United Kingdom there have been significant devolution reforms leading to the establishment of the Scottish Parliament and the Welsh and Northern Irish Assemblies, which exercise, in different ways, power ('devolved power') formerly attaching to central government in Westminster.

Election primaries

An adaptation by UK **political parties** of the US system of primaries whereby potential candidates for election are voted on by the public in the **constituency** rather than being chosen by the party machine. A **by-election** was conducted by the Conservative Party in Totnes using this procedure in 2009.

Elective dictatorship

A graphic phrase used by the former Lord Chancellor, Lord Hailsham (LC 1970–4), to describe the dominance of the **executive** over **Parliament** reflecting the fact that once elected on a general political manifesto the government of the day will usually be able to pass whatever **legislation** it wishes.

Emergency powers

Powers of central government to act outside its normal powers in an emergency such as war or armed rebellion.

European Charter of Fundamental Rights

An international document which introduces many economic and social rights that do not appear in the **ECHR**. It is referred to in the Treaty of Lisbon, which came into force on 1 December 2009. However, the Charter applies only to the implementation of EU law and is not a general charter of rights.

European Convention on Human Rights (ECHR)

An **international treaty** to protect human rights and fundamental freedoms. Many of its provisions have been **incorporated** into domestic law by the Human Rights Act 1998, which came into force on 2 October 2000. However, the existence of **parliamentary sovereignty** in the UK means that Parliament may violate fundamental rights protected by the ECHR if it chooses to do so using clear language.

European Union (EU)

A group of 27 Member States regulated by a number of **international treaties** which are designed to ensure primarily economic integration. EU law is a system of law operated directly by the institutions of the EU (EU Commission, EU Parliament and European Court of Justice sitting in Luxembourg) and was **incorporated** into UK law by the European Communities Act 1972. It has supremacy in each of the Member States (including the United Kingdom). The effect of this is that **parliamentary sovereignty** is powerless to resist EU law overriding laws enacted by **Parliament**. The only way parliamentary sovereignty could assert itself in an EU context would be by complete withdrawal from the EU.

Executive

A constitutional organ of government that is responsible for the daily administration of the state.

Expenses crisis

The name given to the political scandal triggered in 2009 when it was discovered, following disclosures under the Freedom of Information Act, that **MPs** had in a great many cases misused their permitted allowances and expenses. The crisis came to light when the *Daily Telegraph* leaked on a day-by-day basis the names of particular MPs who had apparently exaggerated their expenses claims.

First-past-the-post (FPTP)

The electoral system currently used for **general election**s in the United Kingdom whereby the candidate with a simple majority (ie more than 50 per cent) of votes in each **constituency** is elected to **Parliament**.

Fixed term parliament

A regime whereby **general election**s are called within a stipulated time, as opposed to the situation at present where the Prime Minister is free to decide the date of a general election under prerogative powers.

Fusion of powers

The political theorist Walter Bagehot (1826–77) distinguished the fusion of powers in the unwritten United Kingdom **constitution** from the traditional **separation of powers** doctrine because of the fact that one arm of government—the **executive**—was selected from another arm—the **legislature** (**Parliament**) and so instead of being separate they were inextricably fused.

General election

In a general election **MPs** are elected to the House of Commons in each of the constituencies of the United Kingdom. General elections are required to take place every five years but are usually held earlier, on a date decided by the Prime Minister.

Hereditary peer

A person who is a member of the Peerage by inheritance. Only 92 hereditary peers (out of 700) sit in the House of Lords, being elected from their number.

Incorporation / incorporated

The process by which an obligation of the state in international law is enacted into domestic law.

International treaties

International treaties are not part of national law unless **incorporated** into national law by **Act of Parliament**. This is as true of EU treaties and the **ECHR** as it is of any other international treaty. Unincorporated international treaties do not present any challenge to the doctrine of **parliamentary sovereignty**.

Interregnum

In this book, this term describes the period of parliamentary and military rule under the Commonwealth of England following the English Civil War and the ascent to power of Oliver Cromwell.

Judicial independence

The idea that judges should be free from interference by the other organs of government.

Judiciary

The system of judges and courts charged with interpreting and applying the law.

Legislation

Laws passed by a legislature or other governing body.

Primary legislation

Laws passed by **Parliament** in the form of Acts of Parliament. Prior to being enacted (following the formality of Royal Assent by the monarch) the draft law is called a Bill.

Secondary legislation

Sometimes called subordinate or delegated legislation, secondary legislation is a law made under authority contained in primary legislation.

Legislature

The law-making body in a state. In the United Kingdom, **Parliament** is the relevant law-making body.

Bicameral legislature

The practice of having two legislative bodies. In the United Kingdom there is a bicameral legislature consisting of the (elected) House of Commons and the (currently unelected) House of Lords.

Unicameral legislature

The practice of having only one legislative body.

Member of Parliament (MP)

A person elected to the House of Commons to represent his or her **constituency**.

Monarch

Hereditary Head of State. Referred to in the text of the Constitution as 'Sovereign'. See also **Constitutional monarchy**.

Parliament

The legislative body (the **legislature**) of the United Kingdom, consisting of the House of Commons and the House of Lords.

Parliament Acts

These are the generic name for two Acts of Parliament (1911 and 1949) which limited the former legislative veto of the House of Lords and the ability of the House of Lords to delay Bills passing into law.

Sovereignty

Government free from external control.

Constitutional sovereignty

Under constitutional sovereignty (used interchangeably with 'popular sovereignty'), the legitimacy of a government is determined by the consent of the people in a written Constitution. This doctrine is the antithesis of parliamentary sovereignty, which (see below) is conferred either by unelected judges or is derived from the claims of the English **Parliament** as reflected in the Bill of Rights 1689.

Parliamentary sovereignty

A constitutional doctrine that, as outlined by the Victorian jurist AV Dicey (1835–1922) provides for the absolute legislative supremacy of **Parliament**. The effect of this is that Parliament may, with no constitutional restraint at all, make whatever laws it chooses, and may change or repeal earlier Acts of Parliament. It has also been taken to mean that the validity of Acts of Parliament cannot be challenged in the domestic courts. The origins of the doctrine are obscure. Although the claims of Parliament to rule without royal interference were made in the Bill of Rights 1689, many believe that the doctrine of parliamentary sovereignty is judge-made.

Political party

A body that seeks to attain and maintain political power in government consistently with a published political manifesto.

Proportional representation (PR)

An electoral system designed to ensure a close approximation between the percentage of votes cast and the number of seats allocated. Most forms of PR break the **constituency link**.

Alternative vote (AV)

Not a form of proportional representation but is often confused with it. AV is an electoral system designed for single-winner elections in which voters rank candidates in order of preference. A candidate with over 50 per cent of the votes wins. If there is no such candidate, the second-preference votes of the candidate finishing last are redistributed. This process continues until there is a candidate with more than 50 per cent of the votes. Some maintain that AV is less proportional than **first-past-the-post** (see below).

Alternative vote plus (AV+)

A combination of AV and diluted proportional representation. It involves electing most **MPs** from constituencies in the normal way (albeit under AV rather than **first-past-the-post**). However, constituents also elect 15–20% of MPs from regions containing 'top-up' lists of parties determined by the vote share of the parties. AV+ was recommended in the 1998 Jenkins Report but was never implemented.

Party list

A form of proportional representation in which a list of candidates is prepared by each of the political parties in a multi-member **constituency** with seats being allocated to each party in proportion to the number of votes received, which may, depending on the type of list system employed, be cast for a party, for candidates or for a list.

Single transferable vote

A system of proportional representation used in multi-member constituencies in which voters have only one vote but can rank the candidates in order of preference. Their vote may be transferred to another candidate (their second preference) when their first preference candidate has too few votes to be elected or where their first choice candidate does not need their vote.

Originalism

The theory that the interpretation of a written Constitution should be consistent with the intentions of those drafting the Constitution and that its meaning depends on the meaning ascribed to it at the time of drafting. Justice Scalia (1936–) and Robert Bork (1927–) are often associated with this view.

Preamble

An introductory or explanatory statement in a document (such as a Constitution) that explains the document's purpose and underlying philosophy.

Private Member's Bill

A Bill introduced into **Parliament** by backbench **MPs** or peers. Such Bills have very little prospect of becoming law because of the inadequate parliamentary time devoted to debating them.

Queen in Parliament

A term referring to the Crown in its legislative capacity acting with the advice and consent of **Parliament**.

Recall

A means of removing an **MP** from office by a vote when a certain threshold of dissatisfaction has been reached.

Referendum

A vote by the electorate on a specific proposal, usually of a significant or constitutional nature. Sometimes called a plebiscite.

Republic

A state without a **monarch**.

Responsibility

The obligations, whether legal or moral, owed by citizens to each other or to the state. There is an issue as to which, if any, civic responsibilities should be inserted in a domestic **Bill of Rights**.

Royal prerogative

The formal powers of the **monarch** such as declaring war or appointing ministers. The powers are non-statutory and many are outside the control of the courts. In modern times the prerogative powers have been delegated to central government but are still exercised on a non-statutory basis. Many consider that all prerogative power should now be placed on a statutory footing and brought within the control of the courts.

Rule of law

A principle that all are subject to the law and that the law is publicly and prospectively promulgated and publicly administered in the courts.

Second ballot

A run-off electoral system whereby a single vote is cast. If no candidate receives an absolute majority of votes only the two candidates with the most votes go forward and a second round of voting takes place.

Second-past-the-post

An electoral system in which the first two candidates securing the most votes are elected to **Parliament**. This is not a system currently practised in the United Kingdom and would require two-member **constituencies**.

Select committee

A committee composed of parliamentary members appointed to deal with specific issues.

Separation of powers

The constitutional doctrine that divides governmental power into separate organs of state so that no one branch acquires a monopoly of power over another. In the United Kingdom it is sometimes thought that there is a separation of powers as between the **executive, legislature** and **judiciary**. However, in reality, the United Kingdom has a fused system in which the executive and legislative branches of government are not truly separate and in which, increasingly, central government (the executive) dominates the legislature from which it is selected (**Parliament**).

Social contract

A key notion in much political theory. Its premise is a theoretical agreement between the people leading to the surrender of autonomy in return for governmental protection. Social contract theory cannot be used to justify **parliamentary sovereignty** because whereas the former presupposes legislative power coming from the people, the latter is incompatible with any superior constraint on the powers of Parliament.

Statute of Westminster 1931

This Act established legislative equality between the self-governing dominions of the British Empire and the United Kingdom. It sets the basis for the continuing constitutional relationship between the Commonwealth States and the Crown.

Statutory instrument

The main form in which secondary **legislation** is made in the United Kingdom.

Supreme Court

The highest court possessing final jurisdiction to hear appeals. In many countries, such as the US, the Supreme Court exercises constitutional power and may strike down **legislation**. A Supreme Court was established in the UK in October 2009, to replace the former judicial jurisdiction of the House of Lords. Currently, it possesses no powers comparable to that of the US Supreme Court although some have suggested that it will develop such powers incrementally.

West Lothian question

An apparent anomaly whereby Scottish **MPs** can vote on issues affecting England, whereas English MPs cannot vote on issues affecting Scotland.

Whip

A role in party politics designed to ensure control over attendance by **MPs** at votes and compliance with the wishes of the Party as to the vote cast on pain of sanction.

1

Setting the Scene

STARTING FROM SCRATCH

IN HIS *RIGHTS of Man*, published in 1791, Thomas Paine argues for a radical brand of republicanism that will sweep away the old order; the dead hand of hierarchical authority embodied in the autocracy of George III. His target is the conservative Edmund Burke, the defender of tradition, experience and precedent as guardians of an unwritten constitution.

Paine wants to start again with a *tabula rasa*. With the examples of the American and French revolutions fresh in his mind, and as a direct participant in many of the dramatic events that were unfolding in those countries, his approach is uncompromising:

> Man has no property in man; neither has any generation property in the generations which are to follow ... I am contending for the rights of the *living*, and against their being willed away by the manuscript assumed authority of the dead.[1]

It may be thought that we need some of Paine's iconoclasm today as the United Kingdom seeks to extricate itself from its most significant constitutional crisis since 1945.[2] The events that led in 2009[3] to a perceived disintegration of the political order started with something as seemingly banal as MPs trying to compensate for relatively low salaries by swelling their allowances with morally dubious claims. They were able to do so in a culture that encouraged greed by fostering secrecy.

Misleadingly dubbed as an 'expenses' scandal,[4] it led to a knee-jerk clamour for constitutional reform from politicians and to a more general questioning of our entire political setup by the media.

---

[1] Thomas Paine, *Rights of Man* (1791–92) (Oxford, Oxford World's Classics, 2008) 92.

[2] I acknowledge that many will prefer Edmund Burke over Thomas Paine as a standard-bearer. Paine's values certainly influenced the Declaration of Independence, but the leaders of the American Revolution rejected Paine's ideals as the rule of 'the worst over the best'. John Maynard Keynes was a fervent admirer of Burke, of whom Keynes observed, 'He does not think of the race as marching through blood and fire to some great and glorious good in the distant future': see Robert Skidelsky, *John Maynard Keynes: Volume 1, Hopes Betrayed* (Harmondsworth, Penguin, 1994) 154–57. However, as will be seen, *Repairing British Politics* has strong Burkean elements in seeking to preserve the continuity of the most valuable elements of our existing institutions.

[3] 2009 marked the two hundredth anniversary of Thomas Paine's death.

[4] See Jonathan Raban, 'Trouble at the Fees Office' *London Review of Books*, 11 June 2009.

The Guardian launched its 'A New Politics' series, featuring pundits and celebrities weighing in with piecemeal (if often inconsistent) proposals for change. Other papers and periodicals quickly followed suit. The hapless speaker of the House of Commons, Michael Martin, who had resisted information disclosure in the fashion of a shop steward opposing wage cuts and redundancies, was despatched to the House of Lords when the information on bogus claims came pouring out anyway through embarrassing leaks to the *Daily Telegraph*.

With an election looming, the Government and Opposition started to bang the drum of constitutional reform. As *The Times* put it, 'an intense race to shake up the political system has begun as Gordon Brown and David Cameron compete to look more radical than each other in the wake of the expenses scandal'.[5] Yet, appearances can be deceptive. On Andrew Marr's breakfast show the Liberal Democrat leader Nick Clegg claimed that despite the rhetoric, 'an elaborate establishment stitch-up' was taking place and that the major parties were 'colluding', having failed to understand the depth of public anger and 'the breadth of reform that is now necessary to clean up British politics for good'.[6]

Whether Clegg is right or not about collusion, politics has become the art of understanding how short the public's attention span can be. The most successful politicians are those who find ways of spinning news to distract. It can hardly be doubted that without intense pressure being brought to bear on central government—of the kind it suffered in the aftermath of the expenses fiasco—little will happen.[7]

In this book I argue that inertia should not be allowed to take over. If it is, the moment for significant change will have passed. It may not arise again for several hundred years. For a few, fleeting months in the summer of 2009 it looked as if the sun was breaking through to light up the opacity that is our glorious, unwritten British constitution. Yet, even as these words are written, the shadows are threatening to descend.

WHY WE NEED A WRITTEN CONSTITUTION[8]

The central idea driving *Repairing British Politics: A Blueprint for Constitutional Change* is that of triggering a public debate focused on a draft written Constitution

---

[5] Phillip Webster and Francis Elliott, *The Times*, 27 May 2009.

[6] *The Andrew Marr Show*, BBC, 21 June 2009.

[7] Even in the context of expenses it is unclear how deep any reforms will go. The Kelly Report was published on 4 November 2009 with sweeping recommendations for cleaning up MPs' allowances. However, Sir Ian Kennedy, the head of the new expenses watchdog (the Independent Parliamentary Standards Authority (IPSA)), is reported to have said that he may not implement all of the proposals advocated by the Standards Committee headed by Sir Christopher Kelly (see *The Telegraph*, 8 November 2009). The IPSA launched a five-week consultation period on 7 January 2010 on the new system for managing MPs' expenses.

[8] The non-specialist reader may find it helpful at this stage to consult the Glossary of Essential Terms, beginning on p xi, for a brief explanation of some of the most important terms used in the book.

for the United Kingdom, underpinned by a new principle of constitutional (or popular) sovereignty in place of the traditional principle of parliamentary sovereignty.

Although my own preferences are clear, I stress that the book is not a campaign advocating a written Constitution; rather, the intention is to initiate a debate as to whether we should have one.

We cannot avoid the fact that we are living through a period of acute national misgiving. Our vaunted national autonomy seems precarious in the face of European diktat and global capitalism. Many of our politicians appear as ineffectual as they have demonstrated themselves to be self-interested. Time-honoured institutions such as the House of Lords, the banks and the police appear increasingly unfit for purpose.

This book has a specific thesis. It suggests that our profound disillusionment with politics can only get worse with the 'constitution' we have; a 'constitution' which is out of touch with the reality of the modern world. Our disaffection with politics is exacerbated by a constitutional settlement in which the spoils of victory following the power struggle between a monarchy claiming absolute power and Parliament all went to Parliament but in which the people were left out. It is argued that a written Constitution is not merely a desirable objective; it is in fact a constitutional necessity if true representative democracy is to be achieved in Britain.

Despite this, I should make it clear at the outset that I do not advocate that 'the people' should simply be able to vote on anything and everything affecting the process of government. That would be unrealistic. Any constitution needs checks and balances, and an unrestrained system of public voting would not provide this. My argument is that the constitutional principles that govern our informal, unwritten constitution have themselves got out of control and have ceased to provide the best mechanism for good and effective government.

Repairing British Politics asks what a written Constitution based on constitutional (in substance popular) sovereignty might look like and how it might be brought into being. It contains a possible model in the form of a draft Constitution, to which are attached Observations and Explanatory Notes. There, the main issues are discussed alongside a presentation of arguments for and against the various proposals that are set out.

However, this 'Constitution' is merely intended as the first stage in a public debate rather than as a series of suggested set-in-stone reforms. Even if—which is by no means obvious[9]—there were in principle strong support for a written Constitution, the drafting begun here (without professional drafting input) and most, if not all, of the 'answers' that appear in *this* (sacrificial lamb) Constitution would be likely to be torn apart during the course of that public debate. But such debate has

---

[9] There is, for example, support for the opposite premise, articulated in works such as Adam Tomkins' *Our Republican Constitution* (Oxford, Hart Publishing, 2005), namely that parliamentary sovereignty is alive and kicking and has a contemporary constitutional basis (albeit a weak one). For further discussion of some practical arguments against a written Constitution see Stephen Sedley, 'No Ordinary Law' *London Review of Books*, 5 June 2008, 20–23.

not happened. It will *never* happen without a clear focal point around which certain threshold questions can be confronted.

What are these questions? I suggest that there are three:

- Should we, as a people, endorse the *principle* of a written Constitution?
- (If so,) what should be the *content* of that Constitution?
- What *process* should be undertaken to answer these two questions?

A practical starting point for thinking about whether we want a written Constitution is likely to be whether (and if so, how) it would affect our lives. The institutions that have developed in the UK over time and that, as a whole, make up most of our unwritten 'constitution' reflect, in part, a characteristic British pragmatism. They have evolved organically and in that way we have been able to distance ourselves from the revolution and social unrest that characterise our European neighbours' constitutional histories. After a fashion our constitution—haphazard as it may be—'works'. To move from an informal arrangement of that kind to a formal written Constitution, itself usually the product of a crisis in national affairs, may seem at best pointless and at worst threatening.

But there is another side to this. The current apathy that seems to have triggered rapidly declining electoral voting patterns is part of a more general malaise in which we, as citizens, feel powerless to affect events about which we feel strongly but over which we have no control (the Iraq war is a notable recent example); a malaise in which the top-down government that we have—itself the legacy of our history of absolute monarchy—leaves us politically disillusioned and at times ('expenses' being a notable recent example) profoundly mistrustful of the good intentions of those who exercise power over us.

The argument advanced in *Repairing British Politics* is that a written Constitution for the UK would change our lives for the better in a number of practical ways. Underlying the constitutional shift advocated in these pages is an empowerment of the people. As a doctrine, parliamentary sovereignty has taken us a long way from the successive eras of feudal monarchy, Henrician despotism, and botched Stuart absolutism (though the ruling monarch, in theory at least, continues to hold a measure of power over Parliament).[10] But parliamentary sovereignty, in constitutional terms, should be viewed as but one stage in the course of society's development, rather than as a necessary end-point.

---

[10] From a practical point of view parliamentary sovereignty works best when the constitution is balanced and where none of the organs of government is dominant. This was the position in the nineteenth century. But things changed with the weakening of the House of Lords by the Parliament Acts and by the growth of the modern party system (see The Hon Mr Justice Beatson, 'Reforming an Unwritten Constitution', 31st Blackstone Lecture (2010) 126 *Law Quarterly Review* 48). Tellingly, the lecture cites Andrew Adonis, *Making Aristocracy Work: The Peerage and the Political System in Britain 1884–1914* (Oxford, Oxford University Press, 1993) 278: 'Only once since the Napoleonic wars—the great Reform Act of 1832—has far reaching constitutional change come as a direct response to popular pressure …'

Implicit in the thesis presented here is that with a written Constitution defining our over-arching values we would become a more responsible, more accountable society, and that with greater citizen involvement in the form of a Citizens' Branch of government we would also be more inclusive.

If the changes suggested in this book are to escape the fate of merely providing food for thought at middle-class dinner parties, the ideas of 'responsibility', 'accountability' and 'inclusiveness' (political buzz words at the present time, often used to secure electoral advantage) need to be made real; things to which people as a whole can relate on a personal level. We are not individually *responsible* if we play no part in political decisions. MPs are not *accountable* if they can simply hide behind the notion of parliamentary sovereignty to resist strict controls over their expenses claims or to prevent us having at least a measure of control over the other ways in which they exercise power over us. As a society we are not *inclusive* if we break off into atomistic groups (criminal gangs, bankers, MPs) driven to different degrees (depending on the group) by herd instinct and self-interest.

A written Constitution would not immediately change these things, but it would contribute to improving them by giving people more power in terms of how they are governed. A blueprint for constitutional change of the kind found in a written Constitution is designed to remedy the apathy and indifference that fester like a cancer within British politics at the present time.

We are not an oppressed society like those—at least at the time—in South Africa or India that had to devise their own written Constitutions more or less from scratch. But it is in a climate of apathy and indifference that freedoms come to be sacrificed. A climate in which things which seem to work and so are tolerated can change into much more hostile and threatening weather which, overcome by a kind of creeping paralysis, we are powerless to resist. Today it might be prolonged detention of terror suspects without charge or draconian libel laws—which do not affect most people. But tomorrow it could be wholesale invasion of our privacy (a national DNA database) or abandonment of the rule of law[11] as we have come to recognise it (scrapping the presumption of innocence in criminal trials).

Power corrupts, and absolute power corrupts absolutely. Parliamentary sovereignty entails a claim to absolute power on the part of Parliament. The logic of those who defend it is to resist the situation whereby MPs surrender control over their expenses claims to unelected civil servants (such as Sir Christopher Kelly) because to do so is, it is suggested, to violate parliamentary sovereignty. The same logic would resist a UK Supreme Court having stronger powers to protect fundamental rights on the basis that this would offend parliamentary sovereignty by offering 'its own subtle challenges to constitutional norms'.[12]

---

[11] It is impossible to give any comprehensive definition of the term 'rule of law.' In his 2006 Sir David Williams lecture entitled 'The Rule of Law' (2007) 66 *Cambridge Law Journal* 67 Lord Bingham suggested that the term connotes that 'all persons and authorities within the state, whether public or private, should be bound by and entitled to the benefit of laws publicly and prospectively promulgated and publicly administered in the courts'.

[12] Colin Kidd, 'The Irresistible Itch' *London Review of Books*, 3 December 2009.

A written Constitution of the kind proposed here would move in the opposite direction, by creating new institutional checks and balances, including the establishment of a Citizens' Branch to engage citizens directly for the first time in the business of government.[13]

Yet, even if there were to be widespread support for a written Constitution *in principle*, its detailed content would present another, entirely different set of issues. Should we simply catch up with the organic unwritten constitution that is modern Britain and put it in writing?[14] Or should we strike out boldly in new directions, and, if so, what new areas should a written Constitution encompass? In this book I suggest that the time is ripe for us to chart a new course. External 'constitutional moments' in which momentum for change exists are extremely rare. Further, no written Constitution can co-exist with parliamentary sovereignty. The two are mutually exclusive because the institutions of government are bound by the terms of such Constitution and, therefore, no single institution can possess potentially unlimited sovereignty. Under a written Constitution the *people* are sovereign. So, charting a new course is inevitable once it is accepted that there should be a written Constitution. By the very act of adopting such a Constitution, we cast ourselves into a new constitutional settlement in which the over-arching principles affecting government are different.

These, then, are the shapes of the main *arguments*. But obtaining any consensus on the principle and possible content of a written UK Constitution will take much time. There is bound to be disagreement along the way.

OUTLINE OF THE BOOK

This book seeks to kick-start the debate and to suggest a framework within which it might usefully be conducted. It is divided into three Parts. In this Part, *Setting the Scene*, I briefly present some of the ideas that might drive and be included in a written Constitution, as well as a short background analysis which puts these ideas in context. The core of the analysis is that despite its original virtues in effecting a transfer of power from absolute monarch to Parliament, the doctrine of parliamentary sovereignty is responsible for perpetuating a hierarchical, top-down system of government in Britain that obstructs rather than reflects representative

[13] There is a subtle but important difference between one the one hand a written Constitution with a Citizens' Branch which may, subject to appropriate constitutional safeguards, participate to a limited extent but distinctively in the process of government and, on the other hand, the notion of deliberative polling by which a sample of the population is polled on specific issues in order to elicit a list of proposed democratic reforms which are then put to MPs. Deliberative polling—which draws on the work of Professor James Fishkin (Stanford University)—is a sophisticated technique espoused by, amongst others, Power 2010, which on 9–10 January 2010 conducted a deliberative poll with a view to lobbying MPs before the 2010 election with a number of democratic reforms identified by the poll.

[14] For a brilliant lampoon of what our present 'constitution' might look like reduced to writing, see *The Unspoken Constitution* (Democratic Audit, October 2009).

democracy, or, impedes giving (to use the more demotic phrase) *power to the people*. Baroness Williams, speaking recently in a television interview, went so far as to say that 'It's a huge revolution in the wings if we're going to save representative democracy'.[15]

I have already accepted that the simple replacement of one constitutional norm (parliamentary sovereignty) by another (constitutional sovereignty) will not, at a stroke, change the nature of the institutions by which we are governed. However, what I argue it will do, by engendering a proper separation of powers and much greater citizen participation in politics, is to promote greater trust in the democratic process and to create a number of policing mechanisms which will make each of the organs of government (including the citizenry itself) more responsible and more accountable.

The meat of the book is to be found in Part 2 (A Draft Constitution for the United Kingdom). In devising a prototype Constitution the taking of positions at least some of which may, to some, appear extreme is probably inescapable. But care has been taken to preserve our main institutions, including the monarchy (as a constitutional monarchy), to as great an extent as is logically compatible with the ideas behind the new Constitution.

That there is a need for continuity alongside change is undeniable. Continuity is essential both from a jurisprudential point of view (the incremental development of the common law) and from a practical perspective. Political mechanisms and institutions (and, as importantly, the people behind the institutions) require time and space to catch up with the changes introduced by a new system.

Therefore, the aim has been to collate in written form much of our existing informal constitution but to add a number of possible changes for which there is some currently unfocused momentum and which would, taken as a whole, have the effect of altering the underlying basis of our constitutional arrangements which have lasted for several hundreds of years with passive acquiescence but without any obvious popular endorsement. In many cases the pros and cons of particular proposals are canvassed in the Observations and Explanatory Notes.

Cosmetic, short-term tinkering of the kind set out in the Government's long-awaited 2009 Constitutional Reform and Governance Bill (still not, at the time of writing, on the statute book and now lacking many of the originally intended reforms such as reform of the Attorney-General's functions) and the Parliamentary Standards Act 2009 (rushed through in indecent haste and victim of appalling drafting in a frenzied response to the clamour over expenses) is not the answer. What is needed is public discussion of the ground rules by which we want to live and be governed. There has never been encouragement for, or proposed organisation of, such public discussion. *Repairing British Politics* is intended as a modest first step in that process.

---

[15] Baroness Williams, *The Andrew Marr Show*, BBC, 20 September 2009. In the same interview Baroness Williams described the House of Commons as 'an excessively exclusive place'.

Finally, Part 3 contains a working draft of the Act of Parliament that would be needed to introduce any form of constitutional change. The Constitution of Britain (Referendums) Act sets out a step-by-step approach for (if necessary) *two* national referendums. The first referendum would, in the absence of any clear commitment to introduce a written Constitution, canvass opinion as to the idea of such a Constitution in principle.[16] If the idea of a written Constitution were approved, there would be a second referendum to approve content. On the safe hypothesis that the model Constitution drafted in this book would not itself be approved, it could at least serve to mark the start of a process of drafting a new written Constitution with the widest possible public participation. The Act also contains a requirement for public education and debate preceding the first referendum so that those voting on whether we should have a written Constitution are as well informed as possible about the issues involved.

The timing of the 2010 election is relatively predictable. An election campaign could provide a useful opportunity to debate aspects of constitutional reform in terms of policy (including questions such as whether we should have fixed-term Parliaments). But the subject is too important to be left to the 2010 election manifestos. Whichever party takes office in 2010, the questions raised in *Repairing British Politics* will still need to be debated.

I now want to revisit some of the ground just covered in order to sketch a little more finely the main themes that led me to write this book.

POWER TO THE PEOPLE

In his penetrating nineteenth century study of American society, *Democracy in America*, Alexis de Tocqueville complained that, in reality, Britain had no constitution.[17] He was wrong. For centuries Britain has had an uncodified constitution but it is old-fashioned, top-down and—as far as the rest of the free, democratic world is concerned—of a fast-disappearing kind.

However, nearly all democratic states have a *written* (in the sense of a properly codified) Constitution. Only Israel and New Zealand join us in relying on a nebulous body of rules, some contained in Acts of Parliament, some in constitutional conventions, others scattered around in the most diverse sources. In addition, the British constitution is underpinned by a doctrine of parliamentary sovereignty, which, I suggest here, should be replaced by constitutional supremacy even though

[16] From the point of view of the arguments advanced in *Repairing British Politics*, it would of course be preferable if the election manifestos of the various parties accepted the idea of a written Constitution, thus bypassing the need for a first referendum. If that were done, the structure of the Act proposed here would be different. The two-step approach is suggested on the basis that *as a minimum* each of the parties campaigning for office should make a commitment to hold a referendum on the idea of a written Constitution for the UK.

[17] Alexis de Tocqueville, *Democracy in America* (Harmondsworth, Penguin Classics, 2003) vol 1 pt 1 ch 6, p 118.

the powers of Parliament itself would, in relation to executive government, be strengthened under the proposals set out in the draft Constitution.

Written Constitutions necessarily embody the idea of constitutional supremacy, which is something quite different from parliamentary sovereignty and usually comes from the people. The term *constitutional supremacy* (interchangeable, in the sense intended here, with *popular sovereignty*) expresses the idea that the Constitution is the supreme law of the land, is derived from the people, and cannot, at least in its fundamental features, be altered save (if at all) by wide popular consent. This means that in principle the Constitution 'trumps' any laws that are inconsistent with it. A Constitution in this sense has the effect of *entrenching* its provisions so that they cannot simply be repealed by Parliament, as happens with existing laws. This general constitutional principle, adopted by almost all democratic states, is one that I argue should now be established in the United Kingdom in place of parliamentary sovereignty.

Before moving to popular sovereignty's antithesis—parliamentary sovereignty—I should make clear what I do not include as part of 'popular sovereignty' in the context of a written Constitution. I am not advocating mere plebiscitary consent by majority vote without controls in the form of constitutional checks or balances. Although the exact nature of such controls will need to be debated, there are obvious dangers in simply leaving the fundamentals of political decision-making to a popular vote.

A written Constitution must contain control mechanisms that ensure a broad separation of effective power among the institutions of government. The nature of those control mechanisms should not, I believe, be decided by a simple majority vote; if it were, there could be no practical guarantee that a constitutional settlement was being devised that would best protect minority interests and secure an enduring moral and ethical dimension to our constitutional arrangements.[18] Both the initial control mechanisms and provisions for amendment that are laid out here are based on the premise that there are fundamental values in a western liberal democracy that need to be entrenched. They include, but are not limited to, the rule *of* law (as opposed to rule *by* law) and respect for and enforcement of fundamental rights. These values are not to be voted on as they form the fabric of the society in which we live.

But none of this is incompatible with a greatly enhanced role for public participation in deciding how we are governed and, subject to the necessary constitutional checks and balances, with explicit recognition that power is conferred by the people on government rather than government simply imposing its authority on the people.

If this form of constitutional supremacy replaced parliamentary sovereignty, the focus would (because a written Constitution would compel greater institutional balance) shift rather more to a true separation of powers as the organising consti-

---

[18] Unrestrained decision-making by 'the people' could otherwise be used to subvert democracy and promote extremism if a cause were sufficiently populist in nature.

tutional principle used to explain the division of power among the various branches of government (currently executive, legislative and judicial). Without such a Constitution we have, as Bagehot recognised,[19] not a *separation* of powers in the UK but a *fusion* of powers, by which, in reality, the executive—essentially selected by the Prime Minister from the governing political party in Parliament—controls Parliament. The move towards increased separation of powers would involve both strengthening Parliament in its relations with executive government and providing enhanced checks from a stronger judiciary as well as from a new Citizens' Branch of the Constitution.

Parliamentary sovereignty is quite different. In theory at least it admits of no superior authority and does not achieve a true separation of powers. A written Constitution that retained parliamentary sovereignty could be repealed by Parliament at any time. This is because the idea underpinning parliamentary sovereignty, as articulated most clearly by the great Victorian lawyer AV Dicey,[20] is that Parliament can make (and change at any time) whatever laws it pleases. This would appear to be the position however unjust, however arbitrary those laws may be. It is at both first and second sight terrifying. Its origins are controversial and the source of its supposed authority is wholly unclear. Its consequences in the twenty-first century are, anyway, belied by the political reality that it is not Parliament (one part of which—the House of Lords—is still wholly unelected[21]) but, with the rise of the first-past-the-post electoral system, executive government (and—to some extent included in that—unelected special advisers) which holds real and potentially arbitrary power. A former Lord Chancellor, Lord Hailsham, accurately stigmatised this in his celebrated 1976 Dimbleby Lecture as *elective dictatorship*.

Any idea of *legislative* sovereignty—whether that of Parliament or executive government—is at odds with the notion of *constitutional* supremacy, which provides by far the strongest foundation for representative democracy. Put shortly, constitutional supremacy makes it clear that power resides in the people and that they have delegated a defined measure of that power to government. This type of popular sovereignty is usually forgotten in this country until elections are imminent. Exceptionally, in the wake of the mistrust engendered by the expenses furore, it was given voice by leading politicians, who, with (it may be thought) a practised alacrity for vocalising anodyne aspirations, suggested that, as Parliament's role is to represent the people, more power should be given to the people.[22]

In fact, the slogan *Power to the People* is probably better known as the title of a John Lennon song than as a real political aspiration in Britain. Yet it is the logical

---

[19] Walter Bagehot, *The English Constitution* (Oxford, Oxford World's Classics, 2009) 11.

[20] See *Introduction to the Study of the Law of the Constitution* (London, Macmillan, 1855). Although a strong advocate of parliamentary sovereignty, it is worth recording that Dicey's opposition to Home Rule for Ireland led him to support the use of the referendum (though not until the eighth edition of his magisterial work and then only in the Introduction).

[21] Only the 'new' hereditary peers are elected from among their dwindling number. But, of course, they were never elected in the first place.

[22] See eg David Cameron, *Giving Power Back to the People* (speech, Imperial College London, 25 June 2009, www.conservatives.com).

result of representative government. As will be suggested later, it is not merely an aspiration but represents the essence of modern constitutionalism. It was also, for the briefest of periods, the express basis on which we were governed.

But as a concept constitutional supremacy is still-born if parliamentary sovereignty survives. It is therefore extremely odd that popular sovereignty is often suggested as a justification for parliamentary sovereignty when it is actually its antithesis.

In approaching constitutional reform, the first task is to show that there is nothing axiomatic in the idea that Parliament can do anything it chooses. The seeds of parliamentary sovereignty were sown when the sovereignty of the 'King in Parliament' was established in the 1530s with savage penalties for those who demurred. In more recent times, parliamentary sovereignty has gained passive acceptance as the prevailing constitutional orthodoxy. And this provides the foundation of the unwritten constitution that we currently have. But it has never been endorsed by the people. Crucially, therefore, it has nothing whatsoever to do with an expression of popular sovereignty and cannot be justified on that basis.

There is nothing self-evidently true in the idea that Parliament has an unfettered right to govern us or to make any laws it chooses and impose them on the people. To quote again from Thomas Paine's *Rights of Man*:

> Sovereignty, as a matter of right, appertains to the Nation only, and not to any individual; and a Nation has at all times an inherent indefeasible right to abolish any form of Government it finds inconvenient, and establish such as accords with its interest, disposition and happiness.[23]

We have accepted for too long that the Emperor is wearing clothes when the truth is otherwise.

Power-sustaining Devices

Laws and government did not, in general, spring up because of any social contract or collective agreement. Political theories that postulate such models are not usually describing an asserted historical event; rather, they are seeking to justify a set of political arrangements by reference to normative ideas. Thus, for example, John Rawls[24] relies on a social contract which is negotiated under a 'veil of ignorance' under which the individuals negotiating the contract do not know what their position in society—stemming from the terms of the contract—will be. Rawls is not suggesting that such a contract was ever made. It is a purely hypothetical construct designed to suggest a formulation for the content of justice.

Political theories of this kind are, though, divorced from the reality of government. At best they serve as myths to suggest how we should live, rather than reflecting how we actually live.

---

[23] Paine (n 1) 193.
[24] John Rawls, *A Theory of Justice* (Oxford, Oxford University Press, 1999).

A different type of myth or social narrative lies in using ideas to legitimate the existing power of government. Governments and the institutions of government have often originated from the brute fact of plunder and conquest. Those who were stronger ended up as tribal chieftains and later (with the development of the nation state) as monarchs or emperors. Those who lost out were (assuming they were lucky enough to survive) enslaved and made subjects. If those who conquered were to retain power, it was convenient to devise associative ideas that would suggest or reinforce the legitimacy of their authority. This association might be a ritual or a doctrine, or even a symbol. It would, necessarily, change over time but would be extremely potent in particular societies. Examples of such legitimating devices include the crowning of Charlemagne as Emperor by the Pope in AD 800 and notions of the divine right of kings in Europe in the sixteenth century.

In his 1919 Vocation Lectures Max Weber suggested that mechanisms of these kinds were designed solely to legitimate acts of violence,[25] but it is equally possible to view what might be termed *power-sustaining devices* more broadly. Political ideology is strewn with *concepts* serving the ends of those seeking to exercise power in specific ways. Thatcher's and Blair's use of social narrative (market forces, the third way) to explain the sudden rise of their respective visions of the social good is different in degree but not perhaps in kind from Marx's narrative of the dictatorship of the proletariat.

THE ORIGINS OF PARLIAMENTARY SOVEREIGNTY

Parliamentary sovereignty has come to form the bedrock of our political constitution today. However, it is, I suggest, no more than another power-sustaining device. Valuable though it has proved in marking a transition from monarchical absolutism to a relatively weak form of democracy, it should reflect the middle rather than the end of the constitutional story. In order to see its weaknesses, we need to understand its origins.

The result of the conflict between the common law and the royal prerogative (judge-made law against king-made law) with the judges emerging victorious is usually portrayed as Britain's gift to the civilised world—constitutional liberty.[26] Viewed in this light, the story is one of glowing triumphalism.

But there is another, I suggest more realistic, way of analysing how we have come to be where we are.

---

[25] Max Weber, *The Vocation Lectures: Science as a Vocation, Politics as a Vocation* (Indianapolis, Hackett, 2004).

[26] See, generally, Peter Kellner, *Democracy: 1,000 Years in Pursuit of British Liberty* (Edinburgh, Mainstream, 2009). The Foreword by John Humphreys is worth reading as a model of the traditional and somewhat self-satisfied take on the merits of our current constitutional arrangements with no hint that they might be less than adequate. It was, however, written before the expenses scandal and might not be drafted in the same way now.

Anglo-Saxon England was in some respects a brutal and bloody place. It was a world in which a triumvirate of superstition, magic and religion held sway.[27] There were published laws, but they were made by the King and there was, save for the reciprocity intrinsic in feudalism, no limit to his power. This remained the position for several hundred years.

Magna Carta (1215) is often regarded as our first constitutional document. But in truth, it was the result of a stand-off between King John and his rebellious barons. Its contents were rooted in a specific historical conflict and, side by side with a few general sound-bites about justice being neither denied nor delayed, were many more detailed clauses dealing with a number of vested interests such as those of the barons themselves and the Church.

To view Magna Carta as our first charter of rights is therefore fundamentally misleading (although it did make reference to limited rights which would later be used in the development of more general theories of rights in Britain). However, its undoubted significance lies in the fact that it was the product of historical events which made it necessary to find new ways of explaining governmental power. For the first time the power of the King had been directly challenged. This meant that, although the source of the concessions made in Magna Carta came from the King and could in theory be withdrawn, absolutist notions of kingship had to give way to different power-sustaining devices.

Over the course of the next several hundred years there evolved our current power-sustaining device—the doctrine of parliamentary sovereignty. Before discussing its defects it is important to trace the main elements in its story; along the way, this country was given not one but two written Constitutions.

Much of the essential story of the transition from royal to parliamentary power is there in the history we were fed at school. After Magna Carta there was Simon de Montfort and, in 1258, the Provisions of Oxford. Just a few years later, in 1264, came the first rudimentary Parliament, and (albeit sporadically) many others followed. They were not Parliaments as we know them today and, at least to start with, there was not even a suggestion that they were there to represent the people. Nonetheless, even though they were the King's Parliament and therefore, in one sense, a manifestation of royal authority, they also acted increasingly as a curb on royal power.

From about the middle of the thirteenth century claims to absolutist monarchy were gradually whittled away. As early as 1341 a statute made during the reign of Edward III required annual meetings of Parliament. In 1471 Sir John Fortescue, a former Chief Justice of the Court of King's Bench, published *The Difference Between an Absolute and Limited Monarchy as it more particularly regards the English Constitution*[28] in which he extolled the virtues of limited monarchy in England as compared with the absolute power held by the French kings.

---

[27] This is to over-simplify. Many of the Anglo-Saxon Kings, such as Athelstan and Edgar, were enlightened men who had a strong sense of ruling under 'God'.

[28] It was later published as *The Governance of England*.

However, there were no effective curbs on royal power until the seventeenth century. It was not until the accession of James I that theory itself became divisive in competing claims for power. James lacked the political skill to avoid conflict; in his case it came by resurrecting the (by then) absurd doctrine of the divine right of kings. It drove him into conflict with Sir Edward Coke, the supreme lawyer and judge (Lord Chief Justice) of the day.

Coke sided with the Parliamentarians, first by upholding the supremacy of the common law over the royal prerogative; secondly by discovering a source of legal constraint over the King in Magna Carta; and finally by arguably single-handedly inventing the doctrine of parliamentary sovereignty when he observed in his *Institutes* (1644) (he said many contradictory things too)[29] that Parliament possessed a 'transcendent and abundant' authority which could not be 'confined ... within any bounds'.[30] This short statement has been used to buttress the notion of parliamentary sovereignty ever since.

The Parliamentarians' increased strength led to a confrontation with the King. Following growing dissatisfaction with his autocratic behaviour Charles I was removed from power and executed in January 1649. Under Cromwell, we became a republic.

Yet the potential significance of what followed the execution of the King is skated over in most school history lessons.

The usual version has it that as both the Restoration and so-called Glorious Revolution of 1688 show, the execution of Charles I by no means heralded the end of faith in the office of King. After a short spell of republicanism with Cromwell the status quo was restored and, unlike the radical constitutional revolutions that took place in France and the USA in the eighteenth century, the British constitution never witnessed a revolution. What happened instead—over the next few centuries—was a gradual evolution, helped along by voting reform, into the popular model of representative democracy that we enjoy today. Parliamentary sovereignty, recognised by Coke, developed into an over-arching principle following the Bill of Rights 1689 and the Act of Settlement 1701.

Whatever its precise origins, the context in which parliamentary sovereignty emerged as a constitutional doctrine was a power struggle between King and Parliament. But the assertion of parliamentary power over the King tells us little about the role of the people in such a constitutional settlement. Importantly, it was not at all obvious at the time that the institution of monarchy would survive and that Britain would cease to be a republic. The events that saw the possibility of a republic vanish were driven more by personality than by anything else. As Jenny Uglow puts it in her recent study of Charles II:

---

[29] For example, his judgment in *Dr Bonham's Case* (1610) suggested that the common law could control Acts of Parliament and render them void.

[30] *The Fourth Part of the Institutes of the Laws of England: Concerning the Jurisdiction of the Courts* (London, W Clarke & Sons, 1817) 36.

[Charles II's] return in May 1660 was a crucial turning point and although the Stuart dynasty would soon lose the crown, the way that Charles played his hand is part of the reason that Britain is still a monarchy today: we call the Commonwealth and Protectorate the 'Interregnum', as if it was a gap in an accepted sequence.[31]

It is surprising that so little is made of the fact that in the mid-seventeenth century Britain became a republic and that we had a written Constitution which purported to grant legislative power to Parliament from the people. Certainly, the process was incomplete, but a royal (top-down) source of authority was for the first and only time in our history expressly replaced by a popular (bottom-up) one.[32] That could have continued. Indeed, it is how democracy progressed to the next stage in most countries, even if (as in the USA and France) it took revolutions to achieve it. It is certainly true that the execution of Charles I dealt at least a temporary body blow to any royal pretensions to absolute power or divine right to rule. But it also resulted in at least the initiation of a process by which power could be transferred to the people. The tearing up of the Constitution and the restoration of royal power in 1660 made it impossible for that process to continue.

Once royal power was restored it was inescapable that, as a matter of constitutional theory, the King was the ultimate source of authority. We were no longer a republic. Just as Magna Carta was a mixed bag of concessions granted by the Crown, so too was the Bill of Rights in 1689, despite its references to an elected Parliament and despite the increasing power of that Parliament.

It is at precisely this point that we need to pause and ask one of the great *what ifs?* of history. What if Britain's spell of 'republicanism' had actually taken root?

CROMWELL AND THE UK'S TWO WRITTEN CONSTITUTIONS

It comes as a surprise to many to learn that we have already had two written Constitutions in this country.[33] We are surprised because we have grown so used to swallowing the comfort fodder which tells us that the merits of our informal constitutional arrangements are to be preferred to a codified Constitution such as that adopted in the USA. The British constitution, as JAG Griffith once suggested with characteristic realism,[34] is 'what happens'.

Curiously, it occurs to few to look back—only a little over three hundred and fifty years—to the world's first written Constitution , which was actually British. In 1653 the Instrument of Government established Cromwell as Lord Protector of

---

[31] Jenny Uglow, *A Gambling Man* (London, Faber and Faber, 2009) 2.

[32] It must be conceded that Cromwell himself was constantly improvising between 1649 and 1658 and would have preferred to become King but was deterred from this by the objections of his army.

[33] Our second Constitution was called the Humble Petition and Advice and was drawn up in 1657 to replace the Instrument of Government. It was an attempt to limit Cromwell's power and is not relevant to the argument I am advancing here.

[34] JAG Griffith, 'The Political Constitution' (1979) 42 *Modern Law Review* 1, 19.

the Commonwealth of England, Scotland and Ireland (and on an elective rather than hereditary basis). Power was vested in the Lord Protector, who was assisted by a Council (of between 13 and 21). The Instrument made provision for a triennial Parliament which would sit for five months (Article X provided for 400 persons to be chosen 'within England, Wales, the Isles of Jersey, Guernsey and the town of Berwick-upon-Tweed' and 30 each for Scotland and Ireland as well as a property-based franchise). The Instrument of Government set out a short but comprehensive written framework for how Britain was to be governed, which (somewhat obscurely) separated legislative and executive power. Crucially, it substituted for the authority of the King in Parliament that of the people. Article 1 expressly provided that supreme authority resided not only in the Lord Protector but also in 'the people assembled in Parliament'.

These were paradigm shifts which—had they lasted—would have led to popular sovereignty as it is preached but not practised today. As mentioned earlier, popular sovereignty is a political theory which embraces the notion that power resides in the people but the people delegate power to a government in order to avoid confronting the practical impossibility of making and enforcing laws themselves.

The Instrument of Government did not give voice to the idea of popular sovereignty by accident. In late 1647, in similar fashion to the way the USA Declaration of Independence came to be drafted a century or so later, a series of extended debates on England's constitutional future (the Putney debates) took place, during which, amongst other profound topics, the concept of popular sovereignty and the idea of replacing the monarchy were analysed by leading players, rather in the manner of a modern constitutional convention of the good and the great.

In Cromwell's time, then, popular sovereignty was becoming a strong political ideology.[35] Had it taken root we might have been living in a very different society today, with a properly codified written Constitution. Instead, we are governed by reference to a constitutional principle—that of parliamentary sovereignty—which is not the product of popular sovereignty and which has never received popular endorsement. Worse still, to the extent that Parliament is in thrall to the executive, it is *not* in practice sovereign, even if in terms of prevailing constitutional theory it is supposed to be.

I want, next, to consider how the notion that *parliamentary* sovereignty is justified by *popular* sovereignty is likely to have come about, and then to suggest why it is incorrect.

---

[35] It was not, however, the prevailing orthodoxy. Levellers who espoused popular sovereignty were themselves viewed as political threats by Cromwell, who was determined not to tolerate Leveller democracy. Poor John Lilburne had his ears nailed to the pillory for such excesses.

NO-ONE EVER VOTED FOR PARLIAMENTARY SOVEREIGNTY

Theories have a habit of catching fire. They then endure as a means of labelling events and, as I have already suggested in the context of politics, are sometimes used as power-sustaining devices. This is exemplified by the attempt to link parliamentary and popular sovereignty.

There are at least two reasons why it appears that popular sovereignty is used as the basis for propping up parliamentary sovereignty. The first is that without it there would be no obvious *democratic* justification for the assertion of parliamentary sovereignty at all. Put another way, it would raise the question, 'Who gave Parliament authority to legislate as it chose?'—to which there could, without popular consent, be no answer that would withstand democratic scrutiny. As suggested in this section, there has never been any endorsement of the doctrine of parliamentary sovereignty by the people.[36]

The second reason why popular sovereignty is used to defend parliamentary sovereignty is that the idea of consensual endorsement of the Government by the people fits in with the contract-based political theory that developed from the seventeenth century in the ideas of Hobbes, Locke, Rousseau and others. This is not the place for a detailed account of such theories. However each of them, in their own way, advances a theory of government that presupposes a voluntary cession of rights in exchange for governmental power exercised for the public good—albeit with different views of that aspect of human nature which compels such action. On the basis of such a pact it is an easy (if misplaced) assumption that parliamentary sovereignty represents the fruits of that exchange.

But if there is in fact no popular consent to parliamentary sovereignty, this type of reasoning becomes circular and suffers from the fact (as suggested above) that contract-based theories of government are (save, perhaps, in exceptional cases) hypothetical constructs divorced from the reality of government rather than a description of how governmental power has come to be exercised over time.

The fact that we are allowed to vote at the ballot box for a political party with specific policies is completely different from endorsement by the people of the way in which power may be exercised by any government that is voted in. Thus, the fact that our present electoral system (including the limitation on the powers of the unelected House of Lords) can be traced back to the elections of 1910 and the subsequent Parliament Act of 1911 or the fact that, since 1928, there has been universal adult suffrage is neither here nor there. The simple point is that we have never been invited to vote on whether we should be ruled by a principle of parliamentary sovereignty.

---

[36] A point implicitly endorsed by Thomas Paine in his *Rights of Man* (n 1) 140: 'The Parliament in England, in both its branches, was erected by patents from the descendants of the Conqueror. The House of Commons did not originate as a matter of right in the people to delegate or elect, but as a grant or boon.' Not only did Parliament not originate from popular election; the proposition that Parliament is sovereign is claimed as a creation of the judges (see below).

The American colonists looked back to Locke and other radical English thinkers for inspiration when drafting the Declaration of Independence and the USA Constitution. They were right to do so. What the proponents of consensus as the underlying basis of government tell us is that popular sovereignty is a necessary rationale for good government. They neither state not imply, however, that a doctrine such as parliamentary sovereignty is in any way to be derived from some form of social contract.

It is clear that in England the electoral franchise was not reformed even as a matter of theory until the Great Reform Act of 1832. The reform itself also needs to be put in perspective. Once the 1832 Act came into force it had the effect of enfranchising only around one in five *males* (women were still almost a century away from getting the vote on equal terms to men—that only happened with the passing of the Representation of the People Act in 1928). The difficulty, therefore, with seeking to locate a doctrine of parliamentary sovereignty in popular sovereignty is that—given that, as we have seen, Sir Edward Coke was bandying the idea around nearly two hundred years before the Great Reform Act Act in 1644 as if it were an axiomatic truth—no-one had ever bothered to seek the endorsement of the people to its establishment.

Since parliamentary sovereignty has never been voted on, neither its origins nor its survival has anything to do with an expression of popular will.[37] As explained above, no solace can be taken in political theorists such as Locke or Rawls who provide at best a general rationale for government rather than any specific doctrinal basis on which the people have consented to be governed.

In reality, a doctrine of parliamentary sovereignty was probably the reflection of gradual institutional changes[38] that came about as a consequence of the conflict between King and Parliament. This was facilitated by the dissolving of religious or charismatic notions of governmental authority into secular ones[39] which made it possible for the judges to start setting limits on the scope of royal authority by reference to the superior authority of Parliament. But popular sovereignty has never had anything to do with the origins or continuation of parliamentary sovereignty. We are therefore left with a doctrine that is said to underpin our unwritten constitution but which, in fact, lacks any representative democratic foundation.

In the absence of any democratic foundation for the doctrine of parliamentary sovereignty, attempts to justify it must be found elsewhere.

If parliamentary sovereignty is not an expression of the popular will, it can only reflect the claims of an assertive but undemocratic Parliament, as enacted in the Bill

---

[37] This is not to say that it would be impossible for profound constitutional change to be foreshadowed in an election manifesto. Even though it served the interests of the executive, the erosion of the House of Lords' power to veto proposed legislation was set out in the 1911 Parliament Act. It was a was a very explicit and radical constitutional change preceded by two general elections in which the proposals were foreshadowed.

[38] Many abstract political ideas appear to develop in this way: see generally Raymond Geuss, *Philosophy and Real Politics* (Princeton NJ, Princeton University Press, 2008).

[39] See eg John Neville Figgis, *The Divine Right of Kings* 2nd edn (Bristol, Thoemess Press, facsimile (March 1997) of 1914 edition).

of Rights 1689, to legislate as it chose without royal interference[40] or it is a creation of the common law by unelected judges.

The latter is indeed what the judges are starting to say. In a recent case in the House of Lords[41] Lord Steyn made these comments:

> The classic account given by Dicey of the doctrine of the supremacy of Parliament, pure and absolute as it was, can now be seen to be out of place in the modern United Kingdom. Nevertheless, the supremacy of Parliament is still the general principle of our constitution. It is a construct of the common law. The judges created this principle. If that is so, it is not unthinkable that circumstances could arise where the courts may have to qualify a principle established on a different hypothesis of constitutionalism.

What Lord Steyn is saying (and he is not alone)[42] is that parliamentary sovereignty was created by the judges and could as easily be abolished by the judges. This is truly alarming as it suggests that it is the unelected judges who lay down the ground rules of our constitution.[43]

The suggestion that unelected judges may create new and binding constitutional principles under the umbrella of the common law is as unfathomable in terms of representative democracy as the proposition enshrined in parliamentary sovereignty (whoever created it) that Parliament can make and unmake any laws it wants because it is sovereign.

Whether created by the judges or not, parliamentary sovereignty as a doctrine is profoundly undemocratic (because it is divorced from popular sovereignty). If our judges have the power both to invent and to change that principle with a wave of their common law wands this compounds the problem, for in that event all of our constitutional principles are at the mercy of the judges. This is, since we do not elect judges, even less democratic than the assertion of unlimited power by Parliament. Some form of 'countermajoritarian difficulty'[44] cannot ultimately be evaded,

---

[40] A particular historical difficulty arises in relation to Scotland. When the Bill of Rights was enacted in 1689, Scotland had its own distinct Parliament. The Acts of Union were not enacted until 1707, some 18 years later. There is no clear evidence that parliamentary sovereignty was being asserted by the Scottish Parliament.

[41] *Jackson v Attorney-General* [2006] 1 AC 262.

[42] See eg Lord Hope's speech in the same case at para 107; H Woolf, 'Droit Public—English Style' [1995] *Public Law* 57; J Laws, 'Law and Democracy' [1995] *Public Law* 80. Lord Justice Sedley, writing extra-judicially, suggests that 'It is now widely accepted ... that the doctrine of parliamentary supremacy is itself an artefact of the common law, growing out of the historic compromise between the three limbs of the crown—legislative, judicial and executive—which was reached in the course of the 17th century and has been developed in modern concepts of the rule of law': Stephen Sedley, 'On the Move' *London Review of Books*, 8 October 2009, 3–5. For a directly contrary view which expressly disagrees with Lord Steyn and Lord Hope, see Tom Bingham, 'The Rule of Law and the Sovereignty of Parliament' (2008) 19(2) *King's Law Journal* 223.

[43] This alarming consequence may also be the position as far as the US Constitution is concerned if Chief Justice Charles Evans Hughes was right when he observed that 'the Constitution is what the judges say it is'.

[44] This phrase was coined by the American scholar Robert Bork to defend the thesis of originalism, which, put shortly, is the notion that, consistent with the requirements of democracy, constitutional adjudication by the judiciary may only take place by reference to the understanding of those who originally drafted the US Constitution.

in that no power should be unfettered and there must be a need for at least some judicial checks and legal norms if governmental absolutism is to be curbed. However, judges should not have unrestricted freedom to select our constitutional norms as and when they choose.

Constitutionally, we are in a muddle. We claim to be a democracy and yet the touchstone of our constitutional arrangements (parliamentary sovereignty) has no democratic foundation or even clear historical starting point. That does not deprive it of any status as a constitutional principle. Nor does it mean that if it is a sound principle, we should not retain it. But it does mean that we should not be inhibited from trying to find a better principle and one more in tune with the nature of a representative democracy as the starting point for a new constitutional settlement.

But the stumbling block in searching for that settlement may be parliamentary sovereignty itself. Taken at face value, it seems to inhibit any entrenched changes as well as failing to confront the reality of modern politics. I will briefly suggest why.

WHY PARLIAMENTARY SOVEREIGNTY DOESN'T WORK

A codified Constitution is one that contains, amongst other features, at least some entrenched provisions of a fundamental kind that are incapable of being changed without invoking a specific amendment procedure set out in the Constitution itself.[45]

Taking the US Constitution as an illustration of how popular sovereignty works in practice, the starting point is a formal delegation of power by the people by reference to particular ground rules (the Constitution). This is made clear in the Preamble:

> We the People of the United States, in Order to form a more perfect Union, establish Justice, insure domestic Tranquility, provide for the common defence, promote the general Welfare, and secure the Blessings of Liberty to ourselves and our Posterity, do ordain and establish this Constitution for the United States of America.

There follows a series of Articles which lay down both the scope and, as importantly, the limits of legislative, executive and judicial power under the Constitution. Also encompassed in a number of Amendments at the end of the main provisions is a Bill of Rights containing important fundamental rights.

---

[45] See eg Art V of the US Constitution: 'The Congress, whenever two thirds of both Houses shall deem it necessary, shall propose Amendments to this Constitution, or, on the Application of the Legislatures of two thirds of the several States, shall call a Convention for proposing Amendments, which, in either Case, shall be valid to all Intents and Purposes, as part of this Constitution, when ratified by the Legislatures of three fourths of the several States, or by Conventions in three fourths thereof, as the one or the other Mode of Ratification may be proposed by the Congress; Provided that no Amendment which may be made prior to the Year One thousand eight hundred and eight shall in any Manner affect the first and fourth Clauses in the Ninth Section of the first Article; and that no State, without its Consent, shall be deprived of its equal Suffrage in the Senate.'

This structure exemplifies the essence of most written Constitutions. It can immediately be seen that the structure is inconsistent with parliamentary sovereignty in two important respects.

First, parliamentary sovereignty rejects all constraints on the exercise of legislative power. It follows that no constitutional provision can ever be entrenched because the effect of entrenchment is to fetter Parliament's absolute right to make and unmake laws as it pleases. Secondly, parliamentary sovereignty is incompatible with popular sovereignty for the reasons already given.

These are insuperable obstacles to constitutional reform only if parliamentary sovereignty is elevated from its true status as a constitutional principle of the moment to one that can be treated by those who wield the ultimate source of power (the people) as an immutable yardstick against which all constitutional reform must be assessed. For many hundreds of years we have wrongly treated parliamentary sovereignty as sacrosanct when it is merely a constitutional principle of undemocratic origin which can be changed.

There are several indicators which suggest that—despite the benefits it once had—parliamentary sovereignty is now outmoded as a doctrine. First, even as a concept it threatens to obstruct, and certainly does not facilitate, important national changes.[46] Secondly, because of the dominance of the two major parties, not only does parliamentary sovereignty serve no practical purpose, it actually weakens representative democracy by enabling executive government to pass whatever legislation it wishes, often in defiance of the pluralism that should be intrinsic in any democracy. Thirdly, if, as I argue, a written Constitution would be a distinct improvement on what we have now, the survival of parliamentary sovereignty is incompatible with a written Constitution for the reasons already discussed.[47]

I shall address each of these objections to the retention of parliamentary sovereignty in the paragraphs that follow. When coming to the third reason I will focus on the subsidiary question that is thrown up—is a written Constitution better than the system we have?

When a constitutional principle which is designed to enhance legislative supremacy threatens instead to subvert it, something has gone badly wrong. This is certainly what has been happening with parliamentary sovereignty in the context of Europe.

---

[46] In addition to the difficulties encountered in reconciling the idea of parliamentary sovereignty with our membership of the EU (see below), Britain's loss of empire presents further problems. How, for example, could Parliament legitimately pass laws with any effect over any independent Commonwealth country?

[47] This incompatibility can take an extreme form. It is sometimes suggested that parliamentary sovereignty cannot be 'repealed' by Act of Parliament because, by its very nature, Parliament cannot legislate to destroy its own legislative competence. If correct, that would prevent any written Constitution from ever being drawn up. But the fallacy is to treat parliamentary sovereignty as binding merely because of its own precepts. For an illuminating discussion of the academic issues see Michael Gordon, 'The Conceptual Foundations of Parliamentary Sovereignty: Reconsidering Jennings and Wade' [2009] *Public Law* 519.

Our entry into the European Union (EU) in 1972 was, in all but name, a surrender of parliamentary sovereignty to Brussels. It is no part of my argument here to debate the pros and cons of joining Europe. Whatever the merits or demerits of the decision, it was what the Government of the day wanted to do. The difficulty, as many opponents perceived, was that joining Europe meant that the EU institutions would control what future laws Parliament could enact; this was a direct affront to parliamentary sovereignty.

Following the enactment of the European Communities Act 1972, Parliament had no legislative power to do anything it wanted if it conflicted with EU law, *unless it pulled out of Europe*. By the very fact of doing what it wanted in joining Europe, legal constraints were placed on Parliament's own sovereignty in the future because in legal terms the EU's institutions pulled the strings. This change was the automatic result of the doctrine of the supremacy of EU law as laid down by the European Court of Justice in Luxembourg (a court whose rulings the UK courts are bound to follow). It means that EU law always prevails over inconsistent national law and that the UK must always prefer and apply EU law even when it conflicts with national law. As a principle EU legal supremacy is unequivocal and unyielding. In the words of one commentator, it has the effect that 'the most minor piece of technical Community legislation ranks above the most cherished constitutional norm'.[48]

A graphic illustration of EU law's supremacy over parliamentary sovereignty[49] was afforded by a case in the courts called *Factortame*.[50] At stake was the constitutionality of a law passed by Parliament which prevented foreign-owned vessels from fishing in British waters (the Merchant Shipping Act 1988). Before our entry into the EU, parliamentary sovereignty would have made it impossible for a law enacted by Parliament to be the subject of challenge in a domestic court. But the legality of a national law—the Merchant Shipping Act—was ultimately challenged before the European Court of Justice in Luxembourg and was held by that court to be materially incompatible with EU law. The result was that the House of Lords was required to dis-apply it even though Parliament had enacted it.

Unsurprisingly, attempts have been made to get round what is an insurmountable problem. For example, it has been suggested that Parliament can, if it so chooses, limit its own sovereignty. But this contradicts the essence of parliamentary

---

[48] S Weatherill, *Law and Integration in the European Union* (Oxford, Oxford University Press, 1995) 106.

[49] The extent to which joining the EU involved loss of sovereignty was not stressed at the time of the UK's entry, but the legal position was acknowledged in July 1990 by Hoffmann J: 'The EEC Treaty is the supreme law of this country, taking precedence over Acts of Parliament. Our entry into the European Economic Community meant that (subject to our undoubted but probably theoretical right to withdraw from the Community altogether) Parliament surrendered its sovereign right to legislate contrary to the provisions of the Treaty on the matters of social and economic policy which it regulated. The entry into the Community was in itself a high act of social and economic policy, by which the partial surrender of sovereignty was seen as more than compensated by the advantages of membership.' *Stoke-on-Trent City Council v B & Q plc* [1991] Ch 48.

[50] *R v Secretary of State for Transport, ex p Factortame* [1991] 1 AC 603.

sovereignty which is that Parliament can make and *unmake* whatever laws it chooses. What happens therefore if, in the future, Parliament wished to legislate contrary to EU law? Plainly it cannot do so while we remain a member of the EU. It will not have power to do so because the courts would be bound to dis-apply such a law. This is inconsistent with the notion of the unfettered constitutional freedom of Parliament, as expounded by Dicey, not only to make laws but also to unmake them at any time.

The ratification of the Lisbon Treaty, which came into force on 1 December 2009, illustrates the impotence of parliamentary sovereignty when opposed by the superior might of EU law.[51] David Cameron was thought to have offered a 'cast-iron guarantee' to hold a referendum on the Lisbon Treaty. But this 'guarantee' could never be honoured once Lisbon had been ratified by all Member States (as it was once the Czech Republic's President Klaus signed up to it). It then became part of EU law and, as such, superior to all national law (including the outcome of any national referendum). Without pulling out of Europe, David Cameron (whose fault is not lack of integrity but lack of knowledge of EU law) can no more honour his 'guarantee' than he can commit his party to pulling out of Europe.

In the wake of Lisbon, the Conservatives have suggested a UK Sovereignty Act as part of a new policy initiative which would seek to enshrine in quasi-constitutional form the supremacy of the British Parliament by holding national referendums in respect of possible future treaties that would have the effect, if ratified, of transferring powers away from Britain to the EU. To the extent that the proposed Sovereignty Act requires a people's mandate before new far-reaching international obligations are entered into *which are not themselves required by EU law* it is difficult to fault. But there is a danger in confusing that over which Parliament retains legitimate control with the assertion that parliamentary sovereignty can have any superiority over EU law while we remain a member of the EU. The following media report referring to the Conservative proposal (telling in its reference to a written Constitution) illustrates the scope for possible confusion:

'Unlike many other European countries, Britain does not have a written constitution,' said Mr Cameron. 'Given the increasing amount of EU law with which we have to deal, we would amend the law ... to make it explicit that ultimately Britain's parliament is sovereign.'[52]

It was, in fact, fear of usurpation of parliamentary sovereignty that prevented earlier incorporation of the European Convention on Human Rights (ECHR) into

---

[51] See Christopher Booker, 'The End of the Great Deception' *Sunday Telegraph*, 8 November 2009. It is true that the UK has negotiated certain opt-outs from the Lisbon Treaty. Their legal effect is not always clear. But an opt-out is weaker than a veto and, in any case, the negotiation of an opt-out has no relevance to the impotence of parliamentary sovereignty once confronted with the requirements of an existing treaty obligation governed by EU law after it has been entered into. In particular, an opt-out does not in any meaningful sense mean that British law overrides EU law.

[52] *Daily Telegraph*, 8 November 2009.

national law. The Convention was drafted as long ago as 1950 and was ratified by the UK in 1951. But it remained an international treaty that has not been incorporated into national law by Act of Parliament and was therefore not enforceable in our courts. It was not until 2 October 2000 with the passing of the Human Rights Act 1998 that the ECHR was, in substance, incorporated into national law.

Despite the backing of the judges who had been informally lobbying for incorporation for many years, a draft human rights bill introduced by Lord Lester of Herne Hill fell by the wayside in 1995. The fear was that a home-grown Bill of Rights would allow judges to strike down legislation which offended against fundamental rights as unconstitutional.[53] This could not, it was argued, be reconciled with parliamentary sovereignty.

The Human Rights Act 1998 tries to square the circle by, in essence, incorporating the ECHR into domestic law but then permitting primary legislation which breaches the ECHR to remain on the statute book with full legal validity, leaving it to Parliament to change the law only if it wishes to do so.

These contortions grapple with monsters that need not exist. The slogan 'Bringing Rights Home' was the name of the consultation document published before the 1997 general election, which advanced the case for the Human Rights Act. But a statute does not bring rights home in any meaningful sense if Parliament is free, with impunity, to breach the very rights that it has introduced.

At best, sustained adherence to the supposed sovereignty of Parliament in the European context produces laws whose effect when they conflict with it must be denied, and 'guarantees' which in those circumstances cannot be honoured, or else the conflict must allow sovereignty to triumph so that the law cannot do what is necessary. This can only produce bad law, even if (as appears to be the case with the Human Rights Act) Parliament complies with European Court rulings and changes laws when they offend against fundamental rights.[54]

At worst, though, purely domestic laws left at the mercy of a doctrine of unchecked parliamentary sovereignty may, in theory, be wholly unreasonable or— however fundamental in nature—may be changed at the whim of an incoming government. In a written, properly codified Constitution this could not happen because laws would be subject to the Constitution.[55]

---

[53] This fear was apparently shared in Hong Kong by the last Chief Justice under British rule, who warned the Chinese Government that the Hong Kong Bill of Rights would lead to chaos due to judges striking down legislation: see 'Chief's Warning over Hong Kong Bill' *Financial Times*, 19 November 1995.

[54] For an analogue, consider the law on assisted suicide, which, though still a crime, co-exists with the fact that conduct which assists suicide is in some circumstances (clarified recently by the Director of Public Prosecutions) very unlikely to be prosecuted. The logical position ought surely to be that in those circumstances the law should not stigmatise such conduct as a crime.

[55] It seems distinctly possible that, for example, a new Conservative Government would seek to repeal the Human Rights Act, replacing it 'with legislation that emphasises our "responsibilities" rather than our rights'. See Ross McKibbin, 'Will we Notice when the Tories have Won?' *London Review of Books*, 24 September 2009.

There is a further practical consequence of retaining parliamentary sovereignty in the UK with its combined brand of first-past-the-post voting and strong party discipline through the whips. Save in a hung Parliament, the majority party controls the House of Commons and usually implements its policies in full without fear of effective parliamentary opposition. It may be, as we are constantly told by the majority parties, that there are some virtues in strong government. But, whatever those virtues may be, strong government is *executive* sovereignty. It is not, even taking into account the independence but relative powerlessness of the unelected House of Lords, a manifestation of the sovereignty of *Parliament*. The two ought not to be confused. Whatever its other demerits, the notion that Parliament is elected to legislate and the executive to govern is one that lends some democratic legitimacy to the organic constitutional arrangements that we have which are, in theory at least, meant to reflect the separation of powers so admired by Montesquieu.

In reality, there is no true separation of powers in the UK. Indeed, it was only in October 2009 that a new Supreme Court was created in order to remedy a different issue over separation of powers—the judiciary, at its highest level (the Law Lords), being part of the legislature (the House of Lords) and entitled to vote on proposed laws.

The vice of executive sovereignty masquerading as parliamentary sovereignty is that an overly strong executive dominating Parliament weakens the pluralism that is intrinsic in representative democracy. It is emphasised that this is not so much a question of extreme policies dividing society; it is more one of policies reflecting the wishes of those in power rather than the wishes of the people.

As is explained more fully in the Notes to the Constitution, our current political system consists of, in essence, a struggle for power between the two main parties. The minority parties are squeezed out so that they lack any effective representative influence. The Conservative and Labour Parties are engaged not in *representative* politics but in *power* politics. Thus, the major parties may well agree on a number of policies. They may, though, not properly consider a policy—electoral reform being a case in point—which the electorate would almost certainly support.

So, even if—as proved to be the position during the expenses scandal—politicians are forced by the collective public anger at least to be seen to be doing *something*, that something in a first-past-the-post voting system need be very little indeed. This is because the only effective choice that the electorate has at a general election is to vote for one of the two main parties.[56]

In all but name, parliamentary sovereignty (because under our modern electoral system it tends to *elective dictatorship*) can wreak havoc on pluralism because, in order to work, pluralism involves choices that must at least be *available*. In modern

---

[56] It should, however, be noted that in his speech to the Labour Party Conference in 2009 Gordon Brown promised a national referendum should Labour win the 2010 general election on whether our current majority vote in constituencies—'first-past-the-post'—should be replaced by the 'alternative vote'. The nature of alternative vote and other types of electoral system are discussed further in the Notes to the Constitution in Part 2.

cast for a party rather than for a policy. It follows that voters may agree with some of the policies of one party and some of the policies of another but can only, in the end, vote for one party.

THE NEED FOR A PUBLIC DEBATE

As explained earlier, parliamentary sovereignty is incompatible with a written Constitution derived from the will of the people and imposing legal constraints on each of the institutions of government. Despite this, if a written Constitution offered nothing better than the doctrine of parliamentary sovereignty there would not seem to be much point in jettisoning that doctrine as the basis of our current constitutional arrangements.

If a referendum were to be held offering people the choice between parliamentary sovereignty and a written Constitution, it would be meaningful, in constitutional terms, for the people to reject a written Constitution and to embrace parliamentary sovereignty.[57] However, that has never happened. The fact that when presented with an electoral choice, the people vote by putting a cross beside a name on their ballot paper does not mean, and cannot be taken to mean, that they have endorsed any underlying principle of parliamentary sovereignty.

Unless, therefore, one subscribes to the view that the people should simply have no choice in the matter, parliamentary sovereignty cannot be defended on the basis of popular sovereignty unless and until the people have voted on it. It is not easy to see how democratic theory sits easily beside a view of parliamentary sovereignty that is not linked in some way to popular sovereignty since, if parliamentary sovereignty is not founded on popular sovereignty, it is founded on no clear constitutional doctrine at all.

The starting point is, therefore, that whether or not parliamentary sovereignty has advantages over a written Constitution, the issue should be put to the people in a referendum. There may be those who believe that a weakening of parliamentary sovereignty will also weaken executive power and so lead to less rather than more effective government.[58] In a representative democracy those views may prevail. However, that does not remove the need for a fully informed public debate as to how we should be governed.

---

[57] There would, though, as Thomas Paine pointed out in a different context, be some difficulty in saddling future generations with that choice (see Notes to the Constitution in Part 2).

[58] History provides examples of cases where the strongest forms of democratic government have been considered necessary. When, for example, De Gaulle emerged as the saviour of France it was on the understanding that the Fifth Republic would alter the constitutional balance in favour of a strong executive President after the inherently unstable Fourth Republic.

THE VIRTUES OF REPRESENTATIVE DEMOCRACY

Repairing British Politics advances the proposition that a written Constitution deriving its authority from the people and founded on principles of representative democracy based on popular sovereignty has incomparable advantages over our current organic constitutional arrangements.

That said, there is a potential difficulty inherent in the notion of 'power to the people'.[59] Letting the people decide is by no means always guaranteed to result in the most informed decision-making. It was for this reason that, according to Plato, Socrates, in his classification of governments, put democracy well down the list and below both the philosopher-kings and the oligarchs (ending up only just above the tyrants). The basis for this was that in a pure democracy (Socrates was considering the Greek brand of direct democracy whereby all citizens were required to participate in political decision-making) the people as a whole would be likely to become slaves to their own desires. In Plato's somewhat emotive words, such persons might spend their days 'winebibbing and abandoning [themselves] to the lascivious pleasures of the flute'.[60]

Although the dangers of excessive flute-playing could, no doubt, be borne with equanimity, from a twenty-first century perspective the risks of reaching uninformed decisions are potentially considerable. It might be considered unfortunate if decisions of this kind were made on the basis of less than fully informed public opinion. For example, debating whether the British armed forces should be withdrawn from Afghanistan requires a degree of specialist knowledge, including, most probably, some insider awareness of the strategies being deployed there by our military commanders. Without the benefit of any of these advantages, public opinion is heavily on the side of troop withdrawal. In November 2009, *The Guardian* reported that 'a ComRes poll for the BBC found 64% of the public felt that the [Afghan] war was unwinnable, up from 58% in July'.[61] It is hard to avoid forming the impression that, in relation to public hostility to the British Army remaining in Afghanistan, the public is understandably focusing more on the casualty body-count than on wider strategic considerations. Concern over war casualties on the scale we have witnessed in Afghanistan is understandable, but the media has tended to concentrate on this aspect without necessarily providing objective information about the finer points of war strategy. Although there is a compelling case to be made for leaving important decisions such as these to persons or bodies with greater specialist knowledge than the general populace, this is not inconsistent with

[59] Coming from another direction, a rather different issue with empowering the people lies in the fact that empowerment needs to distinguish between abstract measures such as more decentralisation and the need to account for the resources that people need to lead dignified lives. See Daniel Leighton, 'What Power the People?' *The Guardian*, 19 December 2009.

[60] *The Republic*, 561c. *The Collected Dialogues of Plato*, Edith Hamilton and Huntington Cairns (eds) (Princeton NJ, Princeton University Press, 1963) 789.

[61] Richard Norton-Taylor, 'Defence Chiefs Voice Anger at "Mixed Messages" on Afghanistan' *The Guardian*, 8 November 2009.

establishing a true separation of powers through a new principle of constitutional supremacy.

As suggested earlier, it is crucial to put in place constitutional mechanisms that entrench the protection of minority interests. The idea that those interests should be protected should not itself be a majority voting issue; it is simply a premise underlying civilised society. Similar considerations attach to the need to ensure that certain areas of decision-making are delegated to those who have the expertise to make such decisions. No civilised society could operate if every aspect of decision-making had to be taken by a majority vote. Constitutional supremacy would, however, make the exercise of political power more accountable by putting in place greater checks on its legitimacy and enabling citizens, in cases where the exercise of power was wholly out of kilter with the mood of the people, to prevent its continuation by recourse to constraining constitutional mechanisms such as referendums where triggered by a sufficiently large proportion of the electorate.

It is in the light of these considerations that Part 3 of *Repairing British Politics* sets out a mechanism whereby referendums can be held on whether we wish to continue with parliamentary sovereignty or embrace a new principle of constitutional supremacy (the first referendum)[62] and how—if we support constitutional supremacy—we should bring it into effect (the second referendum).

In seeking to devise a 'good' constitution (with a small 'c') we have few tools at our disposal other than the aggregation of individual reason directed towards finding *better* (not ideal, not even always the *best*) ways of solving our common predicament in the light of what we know about ourselves and each other.

I argue that one need only look to the theoretical alternatives to collective reason for the creation of effective constitutional arrangements to see how inadequate any other regulating principle would be. Any principle other than the collective wisdom of the people reflected in a representative democracy fails a threshold question, namely what is to happen when the interests of an authority accepted *outside* that collective wisdom conflicts with the interests of the people. Unquestioning obeisance to monarchical authority fails this test. Parliamentary sovereignty fails this test. No-one suggests that there is any other basis such as tyranny or oligarchy for our giving others power over us. The sleight-of-hand has been to equate parliamentary sovereignty with popular sovereignty. For the reasons set out earlier, that elision is a false one.

The fact that every other liberal democracy apart from Israel and New Zealand has a written and codified Constitution should give us pause for thought. All the more so, perhaps, when it is realised that New Zealand retains the Queen as Head of State and Israel is in the process of devising a written Constitution .

---

[62] There is, of course, a concealed danger here. If one generation votes against parliamentary sovereignty, why should the next generation not embrace it? The answer to this must be that provided that basic democratic values are preserved, the basis on which we are governed must be susceptible to review.

DRAFTING A WRITTEN CONSTITUTION: THE PRACTICALITIES

The difficulties inherent in devising a written Constitution founded on rational principles and reflecting a representative democracy lie, perhaps, not so much in selecting the appropriate constitutional theory as in the practice. It would be tempting to dismiss these difficulties, as de Tocqueville arguably did in describing the newly-minted United States republic as:

> ... the slow and tranquil action of society on itself. It is an orderly state truly founded in reality upon the enlightened will of the nation ... Republicans in the United States value customs, respect beliefs, recognize rights.[63]

However, even if the British collective popular will is 'enlightened', there are many different versions of enlightenment. It is here that the mechanism enabling, and the quality of, a public debate is so critical.

In offering a possible model for a Constitution in *Repairing British Politics* the approach has been first to adhere to the central principle that the Constitution is meant to reflect as strongly as possible a representative democracy. This entails a number of highly specific suggested changes discussed in the Observations and Explanatory Notes that accompany each Part of the Constitution.

Against that over-arching principle two further principles have been followed. First, given that the changes proposed here are not derived from some external precipitating event (a 'constitutional moment') but involve major changes to an existing, albeit 'organic', constitutional structure, they are tailored as far as possible to fit in with that existing structure. The most obvious example is that of the monarchy. Making a written Constitution the supreme law is, in theory, more compatible with a republic than with any form of monarchy. If one were starting with a blank piece of paper it is unlikely that a constitutional monarchy would be created.

But, if there is a sense in which the monarchy in modern Britain has arguably become anachronistic, it is an anachronism with which we are comfortably familiar. Even if the possible wisdom of Bagehot's warning not to 'let in daylight upon magic'[64] by ceasing to 'reverence' has been tested over the years by marital difficulties in the Royal Family and by caricature fictionalisation in films such as Stephen Frears' *The Queen,* the Crown—as a totemic symbol—still arguably forms part of our national identity. In some ways, along with red pillar boxes, the Union Jack and the traditional pint, the Royal Family is an emblem of Britain that, in an era of bland anonymity, provides distinctiveness and historical continuity. Some would go further and defend the monarchy as being essential as a protection against the dangers of social dislocation[65] or even tyranny.

---

[63] de Tocqueville (n 17) vol 1 pt 2 ch 10, pp 464–65.

[64] Walter Bagehot, *The English Constitution* (Oxford, Oxford's World Classics, 2009) 54.

[65] The position of the King of Thailand, the world's longest-reigning monarch, is a case in point.

It cannot be denied that our Queen is widely respected and a considerable asset in terms of our relations on the international scene, thus demonstrating that a monarch with no formal political role may yet wield considerable symbolic, even moral, authority and be widely revered as a unifying figure.[66] Provided, therefore, that the monarchy can, as an institution, be made to fit in with the principles of a representative democracy, there is considerable justification for retaining a constitutional monarchy with a clear symbolic rather than political function. That is the proposal suggested in the draft Constitution.

The final principle adhered to in devising this Constitution is more abstract and requires separate consideration. It is the need to search for pragmatic solutions to specific issues rather than for some ideal of a perfect Constitution.

Whatever else it does, a written Constitution should reflect the principles of a just society. That statement is unlikely to be controversial. It is when we start to think about what constitutes justice that we get into difficulties. It was clear to the framers of the US Declaration of Independence, drafted in 1776, what justice meant. Its declamatory second sentence asserts that:

> We hold these truths to be self-evident, that all men are created equal, that they are endowed by their Creator with certain unalienable Rights, that among these are Life, Liberty and the pursuit of Happiness.

From this it can immediately be seen that what may have been self-evident to those who drafted the US Declaration is not necessarily so obvious more than two centuries later. For one thing, the reference to a 'Creator' (in the French Declaration of the Rights of Man drafted in 1789 it was a *Supreme Being*) as the author of fundamental rights is, to put it neutrally, now very far from obvious. For another, though in the twenty-first century we would probably agree that the right to life is inalienable, we recognise certain constraints on the right to liberty, and the ECHR, at least, recognises the possibility of even derogating from Article 8 (right to respect for private and family life), which is the Convention right most directly linked to the pursuit of happiness.

Of course, if our supposed creator is *not* the source of fundamental rights, a second difficulty arises. Even if identifiable fundamental rights exist, where do they come from? To the renowned utilitarian Jeremy Bentham the answer was obvious:

> Right ... is the child of law; from real laws come real rights; from imaginary laws, from laws of nature, fancied and invented by poets, rhetoricians, and dealers in moral and intellectual poisons, come imaginary rights, a bastard brood of monsters.[67]

---

[66] Consider, for example, the words of General Dannatt, who observed in a recent debate that the British Army, with its mix of religions, works 'because we all owe our allegiance to Her Majesty The Queen and endeavour to live our lives by a core set of values that are themselves essentially British'. *It's Still Great to be British,* 27 July 2009, CLA Game Fair, www.countrylife.co.uk/debate.

[67] Jeremy Bentham, 'Anarchical Fantasies' in AI Melden (ed), *Human Rights* (London, Wadsworth, 1970) 28, 30–34.

To Bentham, therefore, it was clear that any idea of 'natural rights' amounted to 'rhetorical nonsense', or, in his more memorable phrase, 'nonsense upon stilts'. It is easy to become trapped by Bentham's logic into conceding that if divine natural law is an illusion, it follows that the only source of entitlement to fundamental rights is to be derived from law. This is a false dichotomy if we accept that certain moral events or situations are, at least at the present time, obviously wrong. For example, it is surely obvious that murder is morally wrong. It is certainly obvious now, and became increasingly so in the course of the nineteenth century, that slavery is morally wrong.

But certain things are not as clear. In fact they may not be clear at all. In his recent book *The Idea of Justice*[68] Amartya Sen provides a helpful illustration of this. In his example of three children who each claim entitlement to a flute on different grounds, Child A claims entitlement because she is the only one who can play the flute. Child B claims entitlement on the ground of poverty—he has no toys of his own. Child C claims entitlement because the flute is the product of her labour— she made it. As Sen points out, a Marxist would certainly incline to Child C's claim. The economic egalitarian would favour Child B. A utilitarian hedonist might support Child A.

The example illustrates perfectly the genuinely different views that reason—the 'goddess' that the French celebrated so enthusiastically at Notre Dame de Paris in 1793—might supply for the resolution of moral dilemmas for which there can be more than one answer.

Two consequences seem to flow from this. First, the fact that reason may come up with different answers to moral dilemmas means that the search for an 'ideal' formulation of fundamental rights, or other constitutional obligations and responsibilities, is probably doomed to fail. Amartya Sen's principal criticism of the so-called 'original position' of the liberal thinker John Rawls is precisely that Rawls appears to imagine that there is only one liberal solution to justice,[69] and that his contractarian model of political thought (shared with others such as Hobbes and Locke) ignores the practical objection that it may not—even in theory—be easy to persuade sufficient numbers to add their names to the contract.

The second consequence of reason providing not one but a number of possible resolutions to moral dilemmas is that it supports, rather than negates, the propo-

[68] Amartya Sen, *The Idea of Justice* (London, Allen Lane, 2009) 12 ff. For a treatment of justice that makes this point in different and illuminating ways see Michael Sandel, *Justice: What's the Right Thing to Do?* (London, Allen Lane, 2009). Sandel argues, amongst other things, that contemporary western reliance on the free market credo has tended either to obscure the necessity of making moral judgements about justice or has detrimentally informed some of the moral judgements that have been made. The conclusion to which Sen and Sandel implicitly subscribe is that philosophies such as those of the free market or libertarianism or utilitarianism or communitarianism are meta-principles none of which can authoritatively determine how a just constitution should be ordered. Indeed, they may well be in conflict one with another—for example, economic freedom versus social justice.

[69] Sen's argument is more complex than this and he acknowledges a huge debt to Rawls, but the essence of his critique is that Rawls fails to address the many different ways in which the search for just solutions may be resolved.

sition that reason is a valuable aid for examining these issues. How else could such examination be conducted? Nonetheless, it is equally consistent with the societal truth that, ultimately, decisions are made in a social context rather than in some philosophical vacuum.

The power of ideas fuelled by reason but needing to be accepted in the social marketplace before they acquire more than transient validity was recognised by Justice Oliver Wendell Holmes in his strong dissenting opinion in *Abrams v United States*.[70] He said this:

> Persecution for the expression of opinions seems to me perfectly logical. If you have no doubt of your premises or your power and want a certain result with all your heart you naturally express your wishes in law and sweep away all opposition ... But when men have realized that time has upset many fighting faiths, they may come to believe even more than they believe the very foundations of their own conduct that the ultimate good desired is better reached by free trade in ideas ... that the best test of truth is the power of the thought to get itself accepted in the competition of the market, and that truth is the only ground upon which their wishes safely can be carried out. That at any rate is the theory of our Constitution.

Holmes' reference, in the context of free expression, to free trade in ideas being 'the theory of our Constitution' (by which he means *underlying* theory) is also the necessary theory behind *any* written Constitution. A debate reflecting Holmes' 'free trade in ideas' must be the starting point for considering how best to draw up a written Constitution. Some ideas will fall by the wayside; others will triumph in the marketplace of ideas.[71]

In order to triumph in that context, it seems clear that ideas must be practical and attract a consensus. If they are impractical they will attract little consensus, and if they do not attract consensus they will never be generally accepted. In a representative democracy those kinds of ideas will not find their way into a written Constitution.

That is the reasoning underpinning my third and final drafting principle. This is not to suggest that *any* of the ideas set out in this Constitution will find acceptance. But the drafting focuses, for the most part, on ideas which have found some support from various groups in the past. They are put forward for further debate, following which the best ideas may survive.

The methodology followed, then, in drafting this Constitution for the UK has been to start from the central premise of representative democracy and to advance a personal statement of how, informed by reason but respecting the traditions that have developed over the centuries, this might be achieved in the post-millennium UK.

---

[70] (1919) 250 US 616.

[71] Holmes' market in ideas can, however, be carried too far and could never be used to justify eroding fundamental values such as the protection (and advancement) of minority interests.

REPAIRING BRITISH POLITICS: THE PROPOSALS

The draft Constitution contains a Preamble and 14 Parts. It consists of a 17-point blueprint for constitutional reform as follows:

- The creation of a sovereign, democratic, secular state with power conferred by the people according to the terms of a written, codified Constitution and dis-establishment of the Church of England.

- Making that written Constitution the supreme law with a duty on all the organs of state (including the courts and a newly-created Citizens' Branch) to apply and to implement its provisions.

- The scrapping of parliamentary sovereignty as a constitutional doctrine applicable to the UK and its replacement with a doctrine of constitutional supremacy.

- Renaming the Houses of Parliament the House of Representatives (formerly the House of Commons) and the Senate (formerly the House of Lords) and re-forming the Senate by making it 70 per cent elected and 30 per cent appointed.

- Fixed-term Parliaments of four years with major electoral reform from first-past-the-post to a system of proportional representation or alternative vote and with a constitutional requirement that there should, as far as possible, be an equal number of elected men and women in Parliament.

- Tight control of MPs' financial interests and conduct with strict consequences for breaches of the rules including mandatory loss of seat and provision for the recall of MPs if a sufficient number of their constituents are dissatisfied with their performance.

- Transferring most prerogative power from the Crown to executive government and subjecting those powers to control by both Parliament and the courts.

- Converting the Crown into a constitutional monarchy with recognition of the symbolic authority the monarch wields as Head of State but with a duty to swear an oath of allegiance to the Constitution as a condition of assuming office.

- Strengthening Parliament in its relations with executive government by enabling Parliament to veto the exercise of certain executive powers, including the appointment of special advisers, reforming the system for membership of select committees, and empowering Parliament to initiate legislation and public inquiries.

- Empowering the Supreme Court with major new constitutional responsibilities, including power to declare laws that violate the Constitution to be unconstitutional with the effect that such laws are invalid, except in the case of EU law which the Supreme Court may, nonetheless, declare to be incompatible with the Constitution.

- Creating a Bill of Rights for the UK which strengthens the existing protections, including those contained in the Human Rights Act 1998, and introduces a number of 'third generation' social and economic rights.
- Introducing the notion of civic responsibilities under the Constitution.
- Creating a clear regime for the exercise of emergency powers which may not be used to derogate from a wide range of fundamental rights.
- Introducing state funding of political parties but also permitting the Supreme Court in certain circumstances to declare parties which threaten to subvert democracy to be unconstitutional and, in certain cases, making temporary banning orders.
- Creating a new Citizens' Branch of the Constitution selected annually at random from the electoral register and the election by the Citizens' Branch of a small Citizens' Council to initiate legislation and public inquiries (where a referendum shows sufficient support) and to make applications direct to the Supreme Court on questions of constitutional interpretation.
- Making important changes to the civil service, the army, the police and local authorities, including the principle of progressive strengthening of local authority power and self-financing.
- Creating a mechanism for the holding of citizens' referendums to determine important constitutional and legislative developments.

TOWARDS THE FUTURE

The bitterest argument will be whether we should change anything at all. This is amply illustrated by the furore that arose over the creation of a Supreme Court in the UK in October 2009.

We simply cannot have anything like a separation of powers without a Supreme Court. Other countries with written Constitutions have a Supreme Court which can pronounce laws to be constitutionally invalid. That is one of the very points of separating judicial power from legislative power. There is something quaint and very British about having our top judges sitting in a legislative body (the House of Lords). But it is constitutionally inept. The fact that the system has creaked along over the centuries is neither here nor there in terms of what a modern constitution in a modern state should contain.

Yet the fears that surfaced shortly before the opening of the Supreme Court show how little prepared we are for change. Lord Neuberger of Abbotsbury, the new Master of the Rolls, had this to say about the new Court:

The danger is that you muck around with a constitution like the British constitution at your peril because you do not know what the consequences of any change will be.[72]

That is, of course, true. But if it were applied literally, our constitution could never change. If an inbuilt fear of change had deterred, say, the 13 colonies, there would have been no USA Constitution or, indeed, any constitutional progress of any kind, anywhere.

In *Great Expectations* the wealthy spinster Miss Havisham will never remove her wedding dress nor move her wedding cake—leaving it uneaten on the table—nor change the clocks from the time of her betrayal at the altar. She lives alone in a decaying mansion in a doomed attempt to reverse history by denying what actually happened. Resistance to the idea of change would lead to a fate little different on the national scale from that of the individual fate of Miss Havisham. Sadly, it is obvious that without a written Constitution Britain will be driven increasingly to supporting the fiction of parliamentary sovereignty by more and ever greater subterfuges as the reality of a global, secular and multicultural society discredits it more and more openly.

Although Gordon Brown personally supports the idea of a written Constitution that would embed the constitutional changes of the past with further reform of all our institutions from local government to the House of Lords,[73] it seems unlikely that the policies of either the Conservative or Labour Parties will, without considerable popular pressure, contain any meaningful proposals in this respect or that, therefore, the British people will ever be given the opportunity to consider them.

Yet, what the expenses crisis of 2009 shows is that the fabric of our so-called constitution could easily unravel. It is like the proverbial house of cards. Unlike the USA Constitution, no-one has ever drawn up plans, commissioned an architect or even taken a step back to consider what the house might look like.

But the expenses crisis also shows us that it is when things go wrong that a space is opened up for change. As suggested earlier, due to the strong disillusionment generated by the expenses crisis, during the summer of 2009 we were presented with a rare opportunity for a debate on constitutional change. It should not be lost.

One of our deepest intuitions as far as the process of government is concerned is the idea of the social contract. It has never come to fruition. Political philosophers have suggested theoretical models for what might go into such a contract, were one ever to be concluded. But these models lag behind reality because, without a movement for change, there is no sensible prospect of the people ever being offered a contract for government. We will have to be content with what we have. And what we have is the outmoded doctrine of parliamentary sovereignty; the palest of shadows of the popular sovereignty to which we are entitled if we want it.

---

[72] Joshua Rozenberg, 'Fear Over Supreme Court Impact', BBC News Channel, 8 September 2009.
[73] See Gordon Brown, 'What I Believe', *Prospect*, October 2009, www.prospectmagazine.co.uk.

2

A Draft Constitution for the United Kingdom

CONTENTS

PREAMBLE

WHEREAS the peoples who have come to these islands over the centuries share a common belief in and aspiration towards principles of liberty, fairness, tolerance and economic well-being for all;

Whereas the Constitution of the United Kingdom of Great Britain[1] and Northern Ireland has developed piecemeal and has, in particular, evolved without systematic review of the effectiveness of its institutions or of its constitutional and democratic principles;

Whereas, in particular, the principle of parliamentary sovereignty[2] has not proved sufficiently effective to continue to protect fully the interests of the people of the United Kingdom and other persons residing in or otherwise living in the United Kingdom;

Whereas the nature of society in the United Kingdom has undergone many social and political changes such that it is now multicultural and its citizens practise a variety of faiths, as well as having decentralised legislative bodies in Northern Ireland, Scotland and Wales,[3] with the result that its different backgrounds, cultures, faiths and beliefs are no longer best reflected in the present constitutional arrangements;

---

[1]   There is often confusion as to the exact meaning of the terms 'Britain', 'Great Britain' and 'the UK'. The United Kingdom ('the United Kingdom of Great Britain and Northern Ireland') was formed as a union of England and Wales (Laws in Wales Act 1536) with Scotland, forming Great Britain (Union with Scotland Act 1707) and Northern Ireland (Union with Ireland Act 1800, Government of Ireland Act 1920). It does not include the Crown Dependencies (the Channel Islands and the Isle of Man). In legislation, 'United Kingdom' means 'Great Britain and Northern Ireland' (Schedule 1 to the Interpretation Act 1978) and 'British Islands' means the United Kingdom, the Channel Islands and the Isle of Man (ibid). Although Gibraltar is not part of the UK for most purposes, the UK is responsible for its external relations and for the purpose of voting in European elections it forms part of the South West England constituency. In popular usage 'Britain' and 'the UK' are interchangeable terms and include England, Scotland, Wales and Northern Ireland. However, Great Britain should be used to encompass only England, Scotland and Wales.

[2]   The doctrine of parliamentary sovereignty is expressed by AV Dicey in his *Introduction to the Study of the Law of the Constitution* (London, Macmillan, 1855): 'Parliament ... has ... the right to make or unmake any law whatever; and further ... no person or body is recognised by the law of England as having a right to override or set aside the legislation of Parliament. Parliament is not bound by its predecessor.' Thus, parliamentary sovereignty and the supremacy intrinsic in a written Constitution are incompatible. This incompatibility is discussed further in the Notes immediately below and in *Setting the Scene*.

[3]   There are, as a result of specific devolution reforms, many detailed issues that could become relevant in drafting a written Constitution. Some of them are relevant to the drafting of a domestic Bill of Rights (see Part 9). Such issues could arise as the result of devolving certain matters to the respective legislative bodies of Scotland, Wales and Northern Ireland while at the same time reserving certain matters to the Westminster Parliament. The final detail of a written Constitution may therefore, as a matter of practicality, have to make allowance for this division of functions. See further below in the Notes to Part 2 (under the sub-heading Devolution).

Whereas it is now necessary that the United Kingdom adopts a new written Constitution[4] to remedy these and other concerns so as to establish clear constitutional and representative democratic principles for the exercise of legislative, executive, judicial and citizen power and, thereby, to ensure the fullest protection of the human, political, legal, social and economic rights and general welfare of all the people of the United Kingdom and all those otherwise subject to its laws;

We the People of the United Kingdom[5] therefore establish and adopt this Constitution for the United Kingdom.

OBSERVATIONS AND EXPLANATORY NOTES

Nature of a preamble   The preamble to a Constitution usually sets out its main principles and purposes and can often serve as a mission statement or set of values for what follows.

However, there is no necessity for such a statement and there are even some dangers in including one. The risk of stating values in any detail is that other equally important values may be overlooked.[6]

There is also a danger of ambiguity if that which appears in the preamble does not find its way expressly into the main body of the Constitution and is in tension with it. It is often thought that preambles have no legal force. However, in some countries the courts have held that the preamble operates as a general framework within which the Constitution is to be interpreted.[7]

These dangers are sought to be avoided by keeping the drafting simple, by not stating a set of values other than by reference to certain categories of rights and interests which will be elaborated upon in the Constitution itself, and by emphasising the need for clear constitutional and democratic principles which are reflected in the Constitution.

Why a preamble?   There is scope for disagreement over whether there should be a preamble at all. The reasons for including one are twofold. Each is related

---

[4]   The word 'new' is inserted before 'written Constitution' to anticipate the critique that the UK already has a written, albeit not a codified, Constitution (see n 8 below). For an earlier (pre-devolution and pre-Human Rights Act 1998) attempt to draft a codified Constitution see Robert Blackburn, *A Written Constitution for the United Kingdom*, Institute of Public Policy Research (London, Mansell Publishing, 1993). John Macdonald QC drafted a written Constitution which was included in the Liberal Democrat Report *We the People: Towards a Written Constitution* (London, Liberal Democrat Policy Unit, 1991). An altogether more radical proposal involving amongst other things abolition of the monarchy and House of Lords to be embodied in a Commonwealth of Britain Bill has also been advanced by Tony Benn: see Tony Benn and Andrew Hood, *Common Sense—A New Constitution for Britain* (London, Hutchinson, 1993).

[5]   The expression 'the People of the United Kingdom' means those persons who are entitled to vote in UK parliamentary elections (see Part 14).

[6]   Nor is agreeing a statement of values an easy task: see eg 'In Search of British Values: 1', *Prospect*, October 2007, www.prospectmagazine.co.uk.

[7]   For example, the courts of South Africa and India rely heavily on the mention of equality in the preambles to their constitutions when adjudicating constitutional questions. But the values set out in the preambles have also been used by the courts to define the spirit or nature of the society they govern (for example, they are used to define the identity of the jurisdiction/society concerned).

to a premise that fundamental changes are needed; hence the need for a new written Constitution.

First, it was relevant to identify at the outset that the concept that underpins our present constitutional arrangements (parliamentary sovereignty) is no longer sufficiently effective as a constitutional principle (see *Setting the Scene*). It is certainly true that parliamentary sovereignty—a doctrine that enables Parliament to make and unmake laws as it chooses because it is 'sovereign'—has led to some considerable benefits. It has, for example, inspired trust in the legislature; a trust which the legislature has not, in the main, sought to abuse. It has also been influential in 'shaping' the early constitutions that were set up in many common law jurisdictions such as India, Canada and Australia. However, the development of rights-based cultures and recognition of the dangers of a purely statistical democracy have led to an almost universal principle of constitutionalism in which a perceived need to protect the rights and values entrenched in a codified, written Constitution places significant legal constraints on the legislature.

Parliamentary sovereignty is thus inconsistent with this type of written Constitution[8] because it permits a legislature, unrestrained by a Constitution, simply to legislate as it chooses.[9] Since one of the principal reasons for adopting a written Constitution in the sense used above is to substitute constitutionalism for sovereignty, there is good reason to foreshadow this in a preamble.

The second justification for having a preamble is to make it clear that the social fabric of British society (including the changes wrought by devolution) has altered so much in modern times that a written Constitution is needed to reflect these important developments.

This last factor also encompasses Britain's growing multiculturalism, which is an important root cause of an increasing disaffection with politics. It is perhaps especially important that a post-millennium Constitution is seen to be the common heritage of everyone and not the exclusive preserve of a privileged or indigenous section of society. In the wake of the real prospect of such growing disaffection it is important at least to consider including explicit recognition of the fact that this Constitution accepts that as a society we have changed and are

---

[8] In a limited sense the *United Kingdom* already has a *written* Constitution because it has written laws some of which are of a constitutional nature. It lacks only a *codified* Constitution. But this distinction ignores the logic underlying parliamentary sovereignty, which is that written laws (whether codified or not) may be unmade at any time and are not in any meaningful sense entrenched. Even if an Act of Parliament contained entrenchment provisions, such provisions could easily be repealed. It is the entrenchment of constitutional provisions that creates the dividing line between a written Constitution as envisaged in this book and an organically evolving set of laws that may be written down but can be repealed by a majority (over 50%) vote in Parliament.

[9] A Constitution expresses and determines the reality of exercise of public power. The scope of that power is reflected in the language of the Constitution. Some maintain that parliamentary sovereignty is merely a political theory and that it is what Parliament can do in practice that matters. But theory mirrors power. It is the theory of parliamentary sovereignty that is said, for example, to prevent Parliament from being bound by a written Constitution and the courts from being able to strike down legislation that violates fundamental rights.

no longer exclusively Christian. We may or may not be a 'broken society' but our Constitution at least must seek to promote inclusion, not separation.[10]

These social changes pose enormous challenges for the legislature. Much of the symbolism of a state reflects the strength of its component parts.[11] There are dangers of alienating minority values or regions in the choice of (for example) a national flag or anthem, or in the selection of an official language or languages, or in the development of citizenship values. For the most part the Constitution does not attempt to deal with the detail of such matters but the strong recognition in the Preamble of the fact of social change lays a foundation for future development in these areas.

Under the Constitution those who are entitled to vote in UK elections possess sovereignty rights since the expression *the people* includes British citizens and other persons entitled to vote in UK general elections (see Article 2 and Part 14). It should also be noted that most of the fundamental *protections* provided by the Constitution (see generally Part 9) are not confined to such persons but are available to all. In principle, this Constitution is intended in terms of its values and protections to be a charter for all the people.

Other preliminary questions   The inclusion of a preamble is but one of numerous threshold issues that arise in attempting to draft a written Constitution for the UK. Other questions, as identified in a draft paper entitled *Towards a Codified Constitution* (see Acknowledgements), include: (i) What should a Constitution say about sovereignty? (ii) Should principles such as separation of powers and independence of the judiciary be explicitly set out in the Constitution or merely reflected in its provisions? (iii) Should the Constitution be for the whole of the UK or should there—as in a federal state—be separate documents for its component parts (England, Scotland, Wales and Northern Ireland)? (iv) How should a Constitution reflect the interaction between 'the people' and the various institutions of government? These are but examples of dilemmas which drafting a written Constitution is likely to entail. Various 'choices' have had to be made in this Constitution, the reasons for which are set out in the Parts of the Constitution that follow.

There is one final but important preliminary drafting question. Many—but by no means all—written Constitutions have title headings over each Article. This is the model adopted in statutory drafting in the United Kingdom. Should that method be adopted here?

---

[10] How inclusion is to be promoted is a more complex question and one probably more for political policy-making than for a Constitution, although entrenched constitutional protection of minority rights (see Part 9) must form part of the picture. Similarly, a Constitution must be flexible enough to ensure that group recognition or conferment of minority rights does not subvert democratic values. However, whether or not a concept of citizenship should be developed to seek progressively to integrate cultural minorities into the majority community or whether an older multicultural model of respecting different cultural and religious identities should prevail, or whether these two models can co-exist, is the subject of protracted debate and is probably better left to domestic law rather than be included in the Constitution, provided that such law is compatible with the Constitution.

[11] Consider, for example, the US flag with its 50 stars representing the 50 states of the USA.

The argument for title headings is that they are user-friendly. However, as is indicated by the title of Part 2 and the whole approach to producing a final written Constitution for the United Kingdom, this draft is, necessarily, incomplete. It is introduced as a working document rather than as the product of finely-tuned legislative drafting. It will be subject to considerable revision in subsequent versions if it is not jettisoned altogether. To say the least, the positioning of Articles can be expected to change and the content of some of the provisions in one Article may well be taken out and placed in another. For these reasons title headings for each separate constitutional provision do not appear in this draft written Constitution.

PART 1
THE STATE AND THE CONSTITUTION

1.   The United Kingdom is a sovereign, democratic, secular state consisting of the Nations of England, Scotland, Wales and Northern Ireland. Save as otherwise provided,[12] nothing in this Constitution shall affect the constitutional relationship between the Crown and those territories being set out in Schedule 1 to this Constitution which do not form part of the United Kingdom but which have either historical associations with the United Kingdom, or else are Crown dependencies or British Overseas Territories.[13]

2.   National sovereignty shall vest in the people,[14] who shall exercise that sovereignty through delegation of the powers as set out in this Constitution to their representatives and through the other provisions of this Constitution including the establishment of a Citizens' Branch[15] acting in exercise of powers conferred, and subject to obligations imposed, by this Constitution.

---

[12] Article 24 should be noted. This provides for Orders in Council (the legislation affecting the Commonwealth of Nations made by the Privy Council in the name of the Queen) to be brought in as Bills so as to ensure Parliament's involvement.

[13] Schedule 1 is not reproduced, as the detail of the Commonwealth territories that would be included is not for present purposes relevant to the drafting of the Constitution. It should, however, be borne in mind that 'the United Kingdom' (see also Part 14) is limited to England, Scotland, Wales and Northern Ireland. However, the reference to 'the people' in Article 2 does, at least at present, encompass citizens of certain other states provided that they are resident in the United Kingdom and fulfil other specific conditions that entitle them to vote (see Notes to Part 14). There is a constitutional convention that alterations to the constitutional relationship between the UK and the Commonwealth territories set up by the Statute of Westminster 1931 requires the consent of the Parliaments of those territories. But, a convention of that kind would not operate to prevent the proposals envisaged in this Constitution as they are confined to proposals affecting the UK as defined. It is inevitable that following the change in the status of the Crown the constitutional relationship between the Crown and Commonwealth territories would require some modification. But this is happening in any event as those countries become progressively detached from their ties to the Crown.

[14] The term 'the people' is defined in Part 14.

[15] See Part 10.

3.   This Constitution is the supreme law of the state and the exercise of power is only lawful if permitted by this Constitution. In particular, the Bill of Rights Act 1689 is to be read as subject to, and as amended by, the provisions of this Constitution.

4.   It shall be the duty of the Head of State, the Government, Parliament, the Judiciary and the Citizens' Branch to comply with this Constitution and use their best endeavours within their jurisdiction under this Constitution to secure and to safeguard the rights and interests protected by this Constitution.

5.   Subject to Article 7 any law that is contrary to this Constitution is invalid but only to the extent of the inconsistency. Where this Constitution is silent as to the method by which particular provisions of this Constitution shall be implemented, laws must provide for the method and detail of implementation and such laws must be compatible with this Constitution.

6.   In the interpretation and application of a provision of this Constitution—

   (i)   each and every provision of this Constitution shall be construed and applied in a manner compatible with the rights and interests protected by this Constitution and, in particular, consistently with the needs of a representative democracy in a modern and developing society, including where appropriate making use of the benefits of technological developments;

   (ii)   a construction that will promote the purpose or object underlying the provision taking into account the spirit of this Constitution as a whole is to be preferred to a construction that will not promote that purpose or object;

   (iii) regard must be paid to the context in which this Constitution was drafted and to the intention that constitutional interpretation pay particular regard to—

      (a) developments in the understanding of the content of particular rights mentioned in this Constitution, and

      (b) developments in the promotion of those rights;

   (iv)   without prejudice to Article 135 and to Part 9, regard may be had to the precedents of foreign jurisdictions including comparative materials and international treaties.[16]

---

[16] There are obvious arguments on both sides of the debate as to whether (and if so, how) courts should refer to foreign law in interpreting domestic constitutional provisions. For example, there is the view that domestic constitutional provisions should be interpreted using purely domestic values or norms. This can be contrasted with the view that there is a need to have an organic/global understanding of the content of rights so as to keep in line with international standards (this of course assumes that international standards are higher than domestic standards). These divergent views have fuelled the existential debate over whether or not courts have any power at all to refer to foreign law in constitutional

7.   Subject to Article 5 and to the rest of this Article, laws, whenever made, are to be interpreted and applied consistently with this Constitution and if they cannot be so interpreted and applied must be declared to be unconstitutional by the Supreme Court. Common law principles must be applied consistently with this Constitution and any principle of the common law which cannot be so applied must be disregarded. If and to the extent that a provision of European Union law will apart from its legal status as European Union law be incompatible with this Constitution, the Supreme Court must make a declaration[17] that such provision is incompatible with this Constitution. However, the law will remain valid for all purposes.[18]

8.   Without prejudice to Part 9 of this Constitution, laws made after the coming into force of this Constitution shall, in particular, promote equal access by women and men to elective offices and posts and public appointments as well as to professional and social positions.[19]

9.   This Constitution may not be wholly or partially suspended or abrogated.

OBSERVATIONS AND EXPLANATORY NOTES

Overview   This Part outlines the structure of the British state and sets out the role of the Constitution in that state. The first point to note is the description of the new state that is envisaged. A description of the state as *sovereign* and *democratic* is uncontroversial, although it will be necessary to consider more precisely what is meant by *democratic*.

adjudication (most notably in the US, as evident in the Scalia-Breyer debate in death penalty cases). There are different degrees to which constitutions can make reference to the courts' powers in using foreign/comparative law. The South African constitution *requires* courts to make reference to foreign law, whereas the Hong Kong Basic Law simply *permits* it. There is obvious scope for debate, but the solution proposed here is to permit such reference to be made. Other provisions in the Constitution contain stricter obligations on the courts in the context of fundamental rights (Part 9) and in the context of treaties that have been ratified but not incorporated into domestic law (Article 135). This provision is without prejudice to those other constitutional provisions.

[17] A declaration is simply a remedy granted by the court which states what the law is. See also Part 14 for definitions of particular types of declaration created by this Constitution.

[18] Not all will be convinced by this formulation. Why, it may be asked, do the people not have the power to undercut the proposition that the UK has conferred on the European Union (EU) by treaty the power to make laws which have direct effect? If an EU law is incompatible with the Constitution, why should it not be unenforceable and of no effect within the UK by operation of the Constitution? A law or a provision of a law which is declared to be incompatible with the Constitution could, on that basis, be unenforceable from the date of the Constitution. The formulation adopted here is, however, similar to that in the Human Rights Act 1998 which leaves Acts of Parliament with full legal validity even if they have been held to be incompatible with the European Convention on Human Rights (ECHR) (see Part 9). It is a compromise designed to preserve the supremacy of EU law, just as the Human Rights Act 1998 is a compromise designed to preserve parliamentary sovereignty. It is not easy to see how, if the supremacy of EU law were to be denied, we could continue to be a member of the EU. Continued membership of the EU is a controversial area and one—like separation of one or more parts of the United Kingdom—better addressed either as a matter of government policy or as the subject of a referendum (which could be triggered under the Constitution (see Part 13)).

[19] This provision could have been included in Part 9 (fundamental rights) but is positioned here as a distinct positive obligation on the state when applying the Constitution.

Establishing a secular state (Article 1)   A significant proposed change is the transition from a Christian-based society to a secular one. There is constitutional precedent for the express creation of a secular society (as, for example, in the 1958 French Constitution) but the enormity of the change and its social consequences should not be understated.

Crucially, the change reverses the effect of many hundreds of years of national history both by removing the constitutional relationship between the Crown and religion and, specifically, by effecting the disestablishment of the Church of England, which was created in 1534 when the English monarchy under Henry VIII broke away from the Roman Catholic Church. Creating a secular society reflects the fact that Britain has undergone profound social change in the last 50 years and that its first 'post-Cromwell' written Constitution should demonstrate recognition of that change. A written Constitution that simply assumed the continued hegemony of a property-based class either leisured or founded on Protestant ethics that has been our constitutional stereotype for so long would be stillborn in terms of achieving consensus, as it would be subject immediately to the critique that it is out of touch even before it has begun. Reflecting the reality of social change in this way is significant since a Constitution is an important means of forging a national identity.

Transition to a secular society would have a profound impact on the monarchy, although, as will be seen, this Constitution seeks a constitutional monarchy rather than abolition of the monarchy altogether. The Crown still serves a powerful cultural and totemic function in modern Britain and attracts considerable loyalty. In those circumstances abolition would, it is suggested, be a mistake.

However, many changes are likely to be needed if the approach advocated is to be adopted. The Queen is currently Head of the state Church and, following the Act of Settlement of 1701, is indissolubly bound to it. This is considered by many to be an historical anachronism and it is argued here that retention of the monarchy as constitutional Head of State carries with it the sensitive and difficult task of unpicking the strongest of ties between the Crown and the Church of England if the Crown is to survive as a credible institution in the modern age. It also requires a number of other changes to bring the monarchy up to date, including, most notably, repeal of the Royal Marriages Act 1772, changing rules of succession to allow males and females to succeed to the throne equally, and allowing royal marriages to (amongst others) Catholics.[20] These reforms, necessary if the premise of a secular state is accepted, are addressed in Part 5.

Those who oppose the concept of a secular state should ask themselves what, for the foreseeable future, is the alternative? It cannot be denied that society is both multicultural and consists of different denominational faiths. If that reality is ignored we could see the present strains and tensions that plainly exist explode into something far more dangerous.

---

[20] It is perhaps for consideration whether there should be any restrictions on an 'unsuitable' royal marriage (ie a marriage that tends to reduce the dignity of the Crown).

Operational rules (Articles 2–9)   Articles 2–9 set out clear and unambiguous ground rules for the operation of the Constitution. Three key ideas flow through these provisions. One (see Article 3) is that the Constitution is the supreme law of the land, which includes exercising supremacy over the common law (see Article 7) and, in an important sense, even over contrary European Union (EU) law.[21] This supremacy is often left implicit in constitutional provisions but is made explicit in some Constitutions (such as the 1970 Fiji Constitution abrogated by the President in somewhat unfortunate circumstances in 2009). Article 9 makes it clear that the Constitution may not be suspended or abrogated.

Importantly, Article 3 amends even 'constitutional' statutes. Express reference is made to the Bill of Rights 1689, which, amongst other things, limited the rights of the Crown and purported to define the rights of Parliament. Some see the Bill of Rights 1689 as establishing the doctrine of parliamentary sovereignty, although this is less than clear (see *Setting the Scene*). The Bill of Rights is regarded as one of the core constitutional documents of the UK's informal constitution (others include Magna Carta (1215), the Act of Settlement (1701), the Acts of Union (1707, 1800), the Great Reform Act 1832, the Parliament Acts of 1911 and 1949, the European Communities Act 1972 and the Human Rights Act 1998) and contains other important provisions including determining succession to the throne and, by virtue of Article IX, the doctrine of parliamentary privilege. Article IX will under this draft Constitution remain in force but will be subject to the Constitution so that it cannot be used to stifle the effect of the Constitution.[22] Any other provisions of the Bill of Rights (or any other core constitutional document) that conflict with the Constitution are similarly amended (or repealed) so as to give effect to the provisions of this Constitution.

The second key idea is that of *interpretation*. Non-lawyers need to be aware that there are two sets of provisions requiring principles as to how they should be interpreted. There is the Constitution itself, and then there are all the laws

[21] This is important if the Constitution is to be accorded absolute legal priority given the potential for an assertion of supremacy of the common law over even the Constitution, and given the doctrine of the supremacy of EU law over national law. There are, however, a great many legal complications that could be caused by the principle of constitutional supremacy in certain areas. Very careful consideration would therefore need to be given to its articulation as a principle and whether it should admit of exceptions, at least in EU cases where the UK has, by acceding to the EU, already accepted the doctrine of the supremacy of EU law as laid down by the European Court of Justice in Luxembourg. The solution proposed here is that the Supreme Court has jurisdiction to make declarations of incompatibility in relation to EU law provisions but cannot invalidate such provisions by declaring them to be unconstitutional. Any other solution would necessitate breaching the EU Treaties (see also Article 12). The practical effect of Article 4 would be to require executive government to negotiate a practical solution to any conflict between EU law and the Constitution. However, the tensions that arise from increasing EU centralism are likely to be exacerbated by the Treaty of Lisbon, which came into force on 1 December 2009. Negotiations to resolve a conflict with EU law could be made more difficult if a 'strong' President proved to be insensitive to concerns over national sovereignty. The Conservative Party proposes a new Sovereignty Act in response to concerns over an assertive EU encroachment on such sovereignty, but there are formidable difficulties involved (see *Setting the Scene*).

[22] See 'Free Speech in Parliament is Precious, says Lord Chief Justice' *The Guardian*, 20 October 2009 on the possible dangers of an over-subservient judicial approach to the scope of the privilege attaching to parliamentary proceedings.

(Acts of Parliament and delegated legislation[23]), whether they were made before the present Constitution or come into force after the Constitution. Interpreting both the Constitution and laws must be purposive, that is to say that the strict language used is not the be all and end all of what is meant.

What matters is the spirit of the Constitution and the rights and interests that it is designed to protect. Purposive interpretation is increasingly used in this country as a result of the Human Rights Act 1998 (HRA) and it has been used by the European Courts (especially in human rights and EU law cases) for many years. As explained later, the HRA respects parliamentary sovereignty so that if an Act of Parliament breaches human rights then such Act still continues in force. That quite unjust state of affairs is remedied in this Constitution, which makes it clear (see Articles 5 and 7) that most laws which are incompatible with the Constitution are liable to be held to be unconstitutional by the Supreme Court with the consequence that they are invalid (see further discussion in the Notes to Part 8). By definition, no *constitutional* provision can be invalid and so (see Article 6) the Constitution must be interpreted in a way that is compatible with the rights and interests that it protects.

Importantly, the Constitution is a living instrument. Article 6 makes it clear amongst other things that developments since the original Constitution was drafted are to be taken into account in interpreting it. This is intended to avoid the originalist controversy that has dogged constitutional interpretation in the USA where some judges, most notably Justices Antonin Scalia, Clarence Thomas and Robert Bork, have propounded the idea that the meaning of the US Constitution was fixed at the time that it was drafted so that any developments since then must be the subject of constitutional amendment if they are to become law.

Finally, a key idea underpinning the whole Constitution is that of *representative* democracy. Direct democracy involves direct participation by all citizens in political decision-making. Such a concept is often said to have been practised in ancient Athens.[24] On any view, direct democracy of that kind is not feasible in a modern, pluralistic state and there is obviously a need for representative institutions. But the institutions should, it is argued, be truly representative and, for reasons developed more fully in *Setting the Scene*, our present political system is not truly representative. Many Constitutions use the language of democracy without even mentioning the concept of representation that it necessarily imports. But Articles 2 and 6 expressly refer to the notion of representation and Article 6(i) makes it clear that the needs of a representative democracy constitute a principle of interpretation which informs the whole Constitution.

---

[23] Delegated legislation (often called secondary or subordinate legislation) is a law (often in the form of regulations) made under the authority of an Act of Parliament and containing details necessary to carry out specific matters relating to the Act.

[24] Whether this is in fact so has not always been accepted. See John Keane, *The Life and Death of Democracy* (London, Simon and Schuster, 2009) esp 42–44.

PART 2
LAWMAKING

PARLIAMENTARY PRIMARY LEGISLATION (ACTS OF THE WESTMINSTER PARLIAMENT)

10. There shall be a Parliament sitting at Westminster consisting of the Head of State, the House of Representatives (previously known as the House of Commons) and the Senate (previously known as the House of Lords). The number of members of the House of Representatives shall if possible be the same as (and if possible not more than) the number of members of the Senate. The House of Representatives and the Senate are to be known collectively as the Houses of the Parliament and, save as set out in this Constitution and subject to this Constitution or by separate law consistent with this Constitution, the internal parliamentary procedures previously obtaining for the conduct of enacting parliamentary primary legislation shall be unaltered but may themselves be subject to change as determined by either or both of the Houses of the Parliament in accordance with this Constitution.

11. The power to make Parliamentary primary legislation[25] under Part 2 vests, subject to the other provisions of this Constitution, in the Houses of the Parliament. Subject to this Constitution, the power to make such primary legislation is exercised through the enactment of Bills passed by both Houses of the Parliament and assented to by the Head of State under this Constitution whereupon they become Acts of Parliament.

12. The Head of State is not empowered to refuse to assent to a Bill duly presented for his or her assent save where the Supreme Court has, before assent, declared the Bill to be incompatible with this Constitution. In such a case the Head of State must refuse to assent to the Bill so presented unless the Supreme Court certifies that despite otherwise being in breach of this Constitution, assent is required to give effect to a requirement of European Union law.

13. The House of Representatives is to be elected under free, fair and equal elections based on the principle of universal suffrage for a fixed term of four years in accordance with the election procedure set out for the House of Representatives in Part 3 but subject to those laws to which Part 3 refers. The House of Representatives may only be dissolved before the end of that fixed term but must then immediately be dissolved by the Head of State and a general election called if—

---

[25] This term is defined in Part 14.

(i)   the government is defeated on the floor of the House of Representatives on a vote of no confidence and the Prime Minister (as he is then required to) resigns; and

(ii)   in such circumstances the Head of State having received the resignation of the Prime Minister is unable, after appropriate consultation, either to find a person best able in the opinion of the Head of State to form a new government or such a person has been found and has been appointed interim Prime Minister by the Head of State but cannot secure approval from the House of Representatives for that government within three weeks of the resignation of the Prime Minister.

14.   The Senate is as to seventy per cent of its composition to be elected under free, fair and equal elections based on the principle of universal suffrage at the same time as elections for the House of Representatives for a fixed term of four years in accordance with the voting procedure set out for the Senate in Part 4 of this Constitution. The elected part of the Senate is to be known as the elected body of the Senate.

15.   The Senate is as to thirty per cent of its composition to be appointed by an elected Senate Appointments Commission in accordance with the appointments procedure set out for the Senate in Part 4 of this Constitution. The appointed part of the Senate is to be known as the appointed body of the Senate and the term of office of an appointed member is to be in accordance with Part 4 of this Constitution.

16.   The rules relating to dissolution of the House of Representatives under Article 13 shall, once applicable, also require dissolution of the Senate.

17.   Bills other than Private Member's Bills and Money Bills (which originate in the House of Representatives) may originate in either the House of Representatives or the Senate and do not require either Crown consent or the consent of the government before they may be proceeded with.[26]

18.   Following passage of a Bill in either House, the Bill is sent to the other House.

19.   Either House may pass a Bill that has been sent to it or may amend or reject it.

20.   Where a Bill originates in the Senate and is then brought from the Senate to the House of Representatives the decision of the House of Representatives as to whether the Bill shall be passed or amended or rejected shall be final.

---

[26] Crown consent is currently required if a Bill affects Crown prerogative or the interests of the Crown, the Duchy of Lancaster or the Duchy of Cornwall. The primary rationale for this requirement logically falls away under the Constitution given the transfer of effective prerogative power to the executive (see Part 5).

21. Where a Bill that has originated in the House of Representatives is brought to the Senate and is amended by the Senate, the House of Representatives may agree to the amendment, reject it or agree to it in an amended form.

22. If the House of Representatives does not accept the amendment made by the Senate or if the Bill has been rejected by the Senate, the Bill is returned to the Senate in the form in which it has again been passed by the House of Representatives.

23. If the House of Representatives passes a Bill (other than a Money Bill) in two successive sessions and an interval of at least six months elapses between its passage on each occasion and on each occasion the Senate rejects it or amends it in a manner not agreed to by the House of Representatives, then the Bill may be presented to the Head of State for assent. Money Bills certified by the Speaker of the House of Representatives as such which are not passed by the Senate without amendment within one month after they are received may be presented for assent to the Head of State.

LEGISLATION OTHER THAN PARLIAMENTARY PRIMARY LEGISLATION OF THE WESTMINSTER PARLIAMENT

24. Instruments previously made by Order in Council and which are legislative in character shall henceforth be brought in as Bills.[27]

25. Otherwise, nothing in the arrangements set out in this Constitution for the enactment of primary legislation under Part 2 shall affect arrangements for the passing of secondary legislation.[28]

26. Similarly, nothing in the arrangements set out in this Constitution for the enactment of primary legislation by the Westminster Parliament shall affect the arrangements for the passing of secondary legislation or for the passing of legislation (whether primary or secondary as the case may be) by the devolved governments of Scotland, Wales and Northern Ireland.

OBSERVATIONS AND EXPLANATORY NOTES

Overview   This cluster of Articles addresses the subject of lawmaking under the Constitution. There are a number of traps that might surprise the unwary when seeking to formulate an acceptable structure setting out how laws are passed in the UK.

Primary and delegated legislation   There is the initial difficulty that laws come in different shapes and sizes. The most basic division is that between primary and secondary legislation. Parliamentary primary legislation in the sense used

---

[27] Orders in Council are formally made in the name of the Crown by the Privy Council.
[28] This term is defined in Part 14.

in Part 2 consists of Acts of Parliament made by the Westminster Parliament. Secondary (or delegated) legislation consists of laws that are passed otherwise than by such Act of Parliament but under authority conferred by an enabling Act. Secondary legislation may take a variety of forms. The main form of secondary legislation used in England is the statutory instrument, which is subject to certain controls by the Westminster Parliament. Secondary legislation may also be made by the Scottish Parliament, the Northern Ireland Assembly and the Welsh Assembly.

Devolution   Importantly, too, tiers of lawmaking institutions under the Constitution must take account of the significant political changes that have occurred in Scotland, Wales and Northern Ireland under devolution reforms since 1998. Devolution is intended to address the specific, and different, needs of the three nations (other than England) that currently comprise the UK. In Scotland there is a Scottish Parliament which may make primary legislation in relation to domestic matters, although the Westminster Parliament has retained legislative control in respect of other *reserved matters*. Similarly, in Northern Ireland, the Northern Ireland Assembly (albeit under special conditions that reflect the interests of the two communities) may also pass primary legislation in limited areas. By contrast, in Wales, the National Assembly of Wales (often called the Welsh Assembly) may not pass primary legislation.[29] As a matter of practical politics, a written Constitution might require sensitive drafting in terms of some of its detailed content in order to ensure that the concerns of those legislatures as to the nature of control from Westminster have been properly addressed.

Constitutional focus on Parliament as primary legislator   Although the position is quite complicated and, in respect of the devolved institutions, quite likely to change further,[30] the approach taken in the Constitution is to focus on the Westminster Parliament in its capacity as a primary legislator.[31] Arrangements in respect of secondary legislation and in relation to legislation passed by the three devolved bodies have (see Article 26) not been included in the Constitution.

This approach has been taken for several reasons. First, the Westminster Parliament may make laws that affect the whole of the UK in respect of non-devolved matters and has the ultimate power (unlikely to be exercised) to reverse the changes wrought by devolution. Thus, constitutionally, central power remains with the Westminster Parliament.

---

[29] The devolution reforms, though important, do not paint a complete picture. The UK is an historical creation. Wales has lacked a separate constitutional identity since (at least) the sixteenth century. Great Britain came about with the union of England and Scotland in 1707 (Act of Union). In 1801 the Kingdoms of Great Britain and Ireland merged to form the United Kingdom of Great Britain. The Irish Free State was created in 1922. The more recent constitutional devolution reforms are thus a stage, albeit an important stage, in an historical process that may yet be incomplete and should be capable of being accommodated in a written Constitution.

[30] See eg the recent Calman Report entitled *Serving Scotland Better: Scotland and the United Kingdom in the 21st Century*, which was published on 15 June 2009 and makes a number of detailed recommendations for legislative change in the context of Scottish devolution.

[31] The current arrangements for devolution present specific challenges for the establishment of a Bill of Rights and this is discussed further in the Notes to Part 9.

Secondly, the different powers accorded to the devolved institutions will, as mentioned earlier, be liable to change. There is indeed at least the possibility of more radical change with the likely prospect of a Bill for a referendum on Scottish independence some time in 2010. Whilst such changes raise potentially profound constitutional questions and a mechanism to cater for these kinds of changes is implicitly included in this Constitution as part of the amendment/referendum provisions in Part 13, the detail of the current devolution arrangements raises, in the main, no obvious constitutional issues of the type with which the present Constitution is principally concerned.[32] This is perhaps without prejudice to the intermittently bubbling but ultimately peripheral so-called *West Lothian question* (not sought to be addressed in this Constitution) which is, put simply, the supposed anomaly of Scottish MPs being able to vote at Westminster on domestic laws affecting only England but without English MPs having an equivalent say in domestic laws affecting only Scotland.[33]

Thirdly, turning to secondary legislation, whilst there may be a case for making the processes by which is is created more uniform and ensuring greater parliamentary protection (at least in England) for the scrutiny of such legislation, this is a matter which would necessitate consideration of the separate secondary legislative procedures throughout the UK, a comparison of those methods and a decision as to whether there is a need for unity of procedure. That itself might entail altering the powers of the different devolved authorities. It is a step too far for a first written Constitution.

Terminology   In creating a structure for the primary lawmaking powers of the Westminster Parliament, terminology is of some importance. In choosing the names of the institutions that currently comprise the Westminster Parliament a deliberate change was thought to be needed. If, as is argued, class distinction and feudal privilege have played a major part in a top-down allocation of authority, nowhere is this more evident than in the names we currently give to our lawmaking institutions. 'House of Commons' and 'House of Lords' perpetuate a 'gentleman versus player' kind of mentality that has no place in the modern world.

The term 'House of Representatives' gives emphasis to the underlying idea of democratic representation that is intended to be embodied in both Houses of the Parliament. The term 'Senate' is one that is usually used in a bicameral parliamentary system to denote the upper house. There is, of course, no magic in

---

[32] As a drafting alternative, it would be perfectly possible to include in a written Constitution a statement setting out the current devolution arrangements with express reference to the Scottish Parliament, the Northern Ireland Assembly and the National Assembly for Wales. The danger is that the level of detail needed to make the references meaningful could be considerable. However, as explained above, accommodation may have to be made in practice in the final provisions of a written Constitution for the legislative competence that has, in consequence of devolution, been accorded to the legislative bodies of Scotland, Wales and Northern Ireland.

[33] No attempt is made to resolve this issue here. It is probably the case that removing what some see as an anomaly would be of some political advantage to the Conservative Party, which has little presence in Scotland. However, matters of party politics are outside the scope of an attempt to draft a neutral Constitution.

these names and it is possible that more creative imaginations may come up with something a little more exciting.

Relationship between the House of Representatives and the Senate (Articles 10–23)   These Articles set out the framework for the legislative relationship between the House of Representatives and the Senate.

There have been many criticisms of the way in which parliamentary legislative business has been conducted, especially in relation to the lack of genuine scope for debate. This is grappled with more fully in Part 5. Article 10 is essentially neutral and simply makes it clear that unless the Constitution provides otherwise, Parliament is free to conduct its own procedures.

The current relationship between the House of Commons and the House of Lords is a delicate one. The Commons is an elected body whereas the House of Lords is not. Reform of the House of Lords has begun but is as yet incomplete. It is thought by many that if the House of Lords were to become a wholly elected body, it would claim equal legitimacy with the Commons and that this could cause constitutional difficulty. On the other hand, an appointed second chamber appears to lack all democratic legitimacy.

The solution adopted in this Constitution is to make the Senate part elected and part appointed. Considerations of legitimacy play a primary part in this since the House of Representatives can still, under the proposals here, lay the greater claim to being truly representative. As will be seen, however, the purpose of the part elected, part appointed proposal is also in part to ensure better scrutiny of proposed legislation and to ensure balance and lack of domination by the governing party as well as to prevent the second chamber from becoming too narrowly 'political'. However, in order to avoid assertions that such a system remains undemocratic because it remains the case that one third are appointed rather than elected members, the proposal as to composition (see Part 4) is to ensure that appointments to the Senate are made by a democratically elected Senate Appointments Commission.

It is hoped that a balance of this type will enable the House of Representatives still to claim primary legitimacy, and the constitutional relationship between that House and the Senate is predicated on that basis. With a few small changes, the Constitution preserves the essential dominance of the Commons (see Articles 17–23) and the essential structure of removal of the House of Lords' absolute legislative veto by the Parliament Acts of 1911 and 1949.

Role of the monarchy (Article 12)   One consequence of having a constitutional monarchy (using that term in its strictest sense) is that the monarch is subject to the terms of the Constitution. This is reflected in Article 12, which stipulates the circumstances in which the Head of State is required to grant assent to a parliamentary Bill. As a matter of constitutional theory the monarch (currently) has the power to withhold assent, and this was once exercised frequently. Nonetheless, as a matter of constitutional convention, the monarch is bound to accept the advice of the Prime Minister and now Royal Assent to a Bill is a formality.

Article 12 also stipulates one circumstance in which the monarch must *refuse* assent. This is where the Supreme Court has declared a Bill to be incompatible with the Constitution (and has not certified that enactment is required to give effect to a requirement of EU law). This is entirely new because the doctrine of parliamentary sovereignty formerly immunised parliamentary Bills and (save in human rights or EU cases) Acts of Parliament against the jurisdiction of the courts. What is proposed here is that a new power be given to the Supreme Court to declare proposed statutes (as well as actual statutes) to be in breach of the Constitution before enactment. This power is discussed more fully in the section on judges in Part 8.

Fixed term Parliament (Article 13)   An idea which is supported by many—that of a fixed term Parliament (of four years)—is included in Article 13. We already have fixed terms for the devolved bodies, local councils and Europe and, subject to carefully specified exceptions (also included in Article 13), there seems to be no sensible reason for leaving the calling of a general election to the strategic wiles of the incumbent Prime Minister.

There is also a case to be made for adopting the US practice whereby an incumbent government is eased in over a transitional period, although this is not included here as a constitutional requirement.

Dissolution matters (Article 16)   With a part-elected Senate (see below) dissolution of both the House of Representatives and the elected part of the Senate happens at the same time. The present proposal avoids the impasse created by the US system of electing a President separately from Congress[34] (and with Congressional elections themselves occurring at different times as between the House of Representatives and the Senate) with the consequent polarisation of interests that can occur as a result of altered electoral views.

PART 3
THE HOUSE OF REPRESENTATIVES

COMPOSITION

27.   In order to be elected to the House of Representatives, a person must be a citizen of one of the nations that comprise the United Kingdom, enjoy civil and political rights, have attained the age of eighteen, be legally resident in the United Kingdom and not be disqualified from occupying a seat in the House of Representatives by reason of one or more of the matters set out in Article 39 of this Constitution which are, where relevant, applied by this Article to the period preceding election or the taking up of office as they are by Article 39

---

[34] The US Congress is the analogue to the UK Parliament. It is the bicameral legislature of the federal government of the USA and consists of the Senate and the House of Representatives.

to the period following election or the taking up of office. There are no disqualifications from election or from continued membership of the House of
Representatives save as set out in or incorporated into this Constitution.

28.   A member of the House of Representatives may not be a member of the Senate, the Scottish Parliament, the Welsh Assembly, the Northern Ireland
Assembly or the European Parliament at the same time.

29.   The House of Representatives shall initially consist of the same members of
those constituencies as comprised the House of Commons immediately before the coming into force of this Constitution.[35]

30.   Following all elections (including by-elections but only by-elections after the
first general election) after the coming into force of this Constitution, and in
accordance with the procedure by which those elections take place as provided for in this Constitution, one half of the House of Representatives shall,
provided that there are sufficient eligible candidates, be women and one half
shall be men.

31.   The boundaries of the constituencies for election to the House of Representatives shall be determined by regular reviews of the appropriate Boundary
Commission in accordance with law.[36] Priority shall be given to the objective
of ensuring that the constituencies are compatible with the electoral system
chosen for such election and to reducing the number of directly elected two-
member constituencies to one half of their number at the time of the coming
into force of this Constitution.[37]

ELECTIONS

32.   The House of Representatives shall, subject to Article 33, be elected by election of members to two-member constituencies, and may also consist of
elections to multi-member constituencies[38] so as to represent the United
Kingdom with regard being paid to the need to reflect more accurately than
with simple majority voting the number of votes cast for each party. The
method of election shall include a method of proportional representation

[35] There are currently 646 MPs in the House of Commons.
[36] See Part 14 for the definition of 'appropriate Boundary Commission'. Revised constituency
boundaries require the consent of Parliament before they may be implemented. At present there are
646 constituencies in Great Britain with each one represented by a single Member of Parliament.
[37] One could be more creative. Geographical constituencies assume a commonality of interest
among those living in a particular area. But perhaps nowadays we share membership of meta-groups.
On that basis (a model is the functional constituencies in Hong Kong) there could be constitutional provision for both geographical constituencies and interest group constituencies such as professional or age
groups. But there is a concealed danger that allowing votes in additional constituencies could be seen
as potentially anti-democratic if it gave extra votes to particular classes of the electorate.
[38] See Part 14 for the definitions of 'constituency', 'two-member constituency' and 'multi-member
constituency'.

(which for this purpose may also include the system known as the alternative vote and other electoral systems designed to reflect more accurately than is the case with simple majority voting the number of votes cast for each party) to be set out in laws to be made and to have effect at the same time as the coming into force of this Constitution.

33. Each two-member constituency shall, unless there are no eligible candidates for that constituency, return one man and one woman at a general election. In addition, there may be a number of multi-member constituencies in order to give effect to the electoral system chosen for election to the House of Representatives. There must be an equal number of men and women returned by any multi-member constituencies. By-elections must be held when the seat of a member of the House of Representatives becomes vacant and the constituency in which the by-election is held shall, subject to the existence of an eligible candidate, return a representative of the same sex as that of the seat vacated. No by-election is to be held where the seat becomes vacant less than six months before the date of the holding of a general election.

34. Subject to this Constitution, rules relating to the timing and conduct of general elections,[39] the prescribed date by which (other than in a case to which Article 13 applies) newly elected members shall replace the existing Members of the Houses of the Parliament (before which time Parliament shall continue in existence and shall not be dissolved)[40] and the procedure to be applied to the holding of general elections including eligibility to vote shall be set out in laws to be made and to have effect at the same time as the coming into force of this Constitution. However, laws may not stipulate the age at which a person is to be entitled to vote as being lower than 16 or as being older than 18.

35. Save for any registered persons aged under 18 at the time of a general election, every person registered as a voter whose right to registration has not ceased must, as prescribed by law, and subject to such exceptions as are laid down by law, vote in every election in the constituencies in respect of which he or she is enrolled. Provision may be made by law for revocation of the right to vote for a stipulated period for repeated breach of this obligation. No law shall make it a breach of this obligation to fail to vote provided that there is reasonable excuse for failing to do so.

---

[39] The present system with, for example, an Electoral Commission supervising elections would be encompassed in such laws.

[40] This provision is designed to ensure that Members of the Houses of the Parliament are ordinarily not replaced until a prescribed date. This is achieved by Parliament not being dissolved so that MPs simply continue to hold office until they are replaced by the newly elected MPs. The position is different in the situations set out in Article 13(i)–(ii) where Parliament must be dissolved.

CONDUCT AND VACATION OF PLACE AS MEMBER

36.   Members of the House of Representatives shall be remunerated from public funds. Such remuneration, including allowances and other expenses, shall be determined by an independent authority established by law.

37.   Laws shall make provision for the registration of interests and other benefits as members of the House of Representatives are permitted to hold as well as for the supervision of such register, and for the declaration of such interests and other benefits as members are not permitted to hold.

38.   Laws shall make further provision for the standards of conduct to be observed by members of the House of Representatives.

39.   The place of a member of the House of Representatives shall, subject to this Constitution, automatically become vacant and a by-election shall be held if that member ceases to be qualified to sit in the House of Representatives under Article 27 or—

   (i)   dies;

   (ii)   is removed from office by being recalled by the voters within his or her constituency under this Constitution;

   (iii)   is criminally convicted of an offence punishable by imprisonment;

   (iv)   is criminally convicted of an illegal election practice;

   (v)   resigns by giving the Speaker a signed resignation;

   (vi)   ceases to have a right to be registered as a voter in an election to the House of Representatives;

   (vii)   has any interest being an interest of a kind prescribed by law as an interest that must not be held by a member of the House of Representatives;

   (viii) holds or occupies any office, employment or position of a kind prescribed by this Constitution or by law[41] as one that must not be held by a member of the House of Representatives;

---

[41] Holders of a number of offices and other positions are currently prevented from becoming MPs under, amongst other provisions, the House of Commons (Disqualification) Act 1975 (see Schedule 1 to the Act). The list is quite detailed and subject to change. It includes full-time police officers, civil servants and members of the regular armed forces. Hereditary peers who are not elected to sit in the House of Lords may, however, be members of the House of Commons (see the House of Lords Act 1999).

(ix)   resigns from or otherwise ceases (save by unlawful expulsion) to be a member of the political party for which he or she was a candidate at the time he or she was last elected to the House of Representatives.[42]

40.   The law may not prescribe other circumstances in which the place of a member of the House of Representatives shall or may become vacant except that it may prescribe bankruptcy as an automatic disqualification or may prescribe conditions under which bankruptcy will result in disqualification.[43]

41.   A number of voters in a constituency representing at least twenty per cent of the registered voters may petition the Speaker of the House of Representatives for the calling of a referendum to recall the mandate of one or both of the elected representatives for that constituency.

42.   When a number of voters equal to or greater than the number of those who elected the member vote in favour of recall then, provided that this number of voters is equal to or greater than twenty-five per cent of the total number of registered voters who vote in the recall referendum, the mandate shall be deemed revoked and immediate action shall be taken to fill the permanent vacancy as provided for by this Constitution and by law.

BUSINESS

43.   All questions proposed for decision in the House of Representatives shall, subject to this Constitution, be decided by a majority vote.[44] There is no casting vote and the question concerned shall be deemed to be lost unless there is a majority vote. The House of Representatives may act despite a vacancy in its membership and the presence of or the participation in its proceedings of a person not entitled to be a member does not invalidate the proceedings.

44.   Subject to this Constitution the House of Representatives shall—

(i)   decide its procedure;

(ii)   elect its Speaker by such method as it shall decide (whether or not the method of election decided upon is by majority vote).

---

[42] This last category imports potential difficulties. As drafted it would catch those moving from a specific party allegiance to becoming an independent. It would catch those such as Dick Taverne, who moved from Labour to Democratic Labour (albeit after a by-election) and it would catch an emergent party such as the SDP, whose claim, at least initially, was that they were the true inheritors of the Labour tradition and that it was the Labour Party that had deviated. Despite these difficulties, there seems to be no principled reason for not requiring a by-election where the electorate has voted not necessarily merely for a candidate but also for the policy of the party to which that candidate belonged when elected to Parliament.

[43] The former law on bankruptcy, being automatic disqualification on being elected or sitting as an MP, was changed by the Enterprise Act 2002 and is now qualified in a number of respects.

[44] See Part 14 for a definition of the term 'majority vote'.

POWERS OF THE HOUSE OF REPRESENTATIVES

45.   The powers of the House of Representatives are derived from this Constitution.

46.   Apart from its other powers conferred by this Constitution and subject to this Constitution, the House of Representative shall have power to do those things which are calculated to facilitate or are conducive or incidental to the discharge of its functions under this Constitution.

OBSERVATIONS AND EXPLANATORY NOTES

Composition of the House of Representatives (Articles 27–28)   Although the age requirement for eligibility to sit as an MP is still 18 (see Article 27; it was reduced from 21 in 2006), more stringent requirements are laid down, in terms of MPs' conduct, as to their continued eligibility to sit in Parliament (see further Notes to Article 36 et seq below). The opportunity has also been taken to make it clear that a Westminster MP may no longer sit simultaneously in a devolved legislature (Article 28). This was one of the recommendations set out in the Kelly Report,[45] which has not, at the time of writing, been implemented.

More women in Parliament (Articles 29–31, 33)   Important changes are proposed in these Articles. There is a new requirement, consistent with Article 8 of the Constitution, that each constituency elect a man and a woman (or an equal number of men and women in multi-member constituencies: see below) provided that there are eligible candidates (see Article 33). The effect of this is that following the first general election the House of Representatives will consist, so far as possible, of an equal number of men and women (see Article 30).

The number of women in the House of Commons is currently very small. As at 27 July 2009 there were only 126 female MPs and 519 males. A survey undertaken by the Fawcett Society some years ago suggested that at the then current rate of progress it would take the Labour Party 50 years to secure an equal number of men and women, the Liberal Democrats about 40 years and the Conservative Party 400 years.

While some of these estimates may have changed with subsequent developments, including the new-found appreciation of the need for wider constitutional reform in the aftermath of the expenses scandal, it seems clear that, short of a fundamental overhaul of the system, little will change in respect of the relative proportion of men and women in Parliament. A possible alternative to mandatory equal representation would be to permit constituencies to make women-only selections. This was adopted by Labour in some constituencies for the 1997 general election and it produced 18.2 per cent female representation in 1997 as compared with only 9.2 per cent in 1992. Due to concerns about the legality of such quotas, all-women shortlists were legalised under the Sex Discrimination (Election Candidates) Act 2002. They will remain

---

[45] *MPs' Expenses and Allowances—Supporting Parliament, Safeguarding the Taxpayer* (November 2009) Recommendation 40.

lawful until 2015. However, only the Labour Party currently uses such lists. Both the Liberal Democrats and the Conservatives have opposed them in principle, although the Conservative Party has recently announced its intention to impose all-women shortlists on at least some local associations from 2010. Under the current version of the new Equality Bill the period within which women-only shortlists could be used would be extendable until 2030.

A temporary experiment such as women-only shortlists, currently only used by one political party, is far from ideal and there is still a risk that such a practice will be held unlawful under either EU law or under the European Convention on Human Rights (ECHR) should the issue be tested before the European Courts. It is strongly arguable that there is a need for wholesale reform. It is likely that a constitutional principle of affirmative action to ensure greater gender equality in Parliament would arouse some hostility. There will be those who say that merit will always win out and those who contend that if there is to be affirmative action in respect of gender then why not for all other forms of discrimination? One response to this is that decades of failure to act have produced the present situation, which remains one of unjustified inequality as between the sexes in Parliament. Another response is that it is necessary to start somewhere and that if the present experiment works it could be replicated in other contexts. Nonetheless, the arguments will rage and it is right that they should do so.

But, in any event, an undoubted difficulty with a reform of this nature is that it could in the immediate term more than double the number of MPs under the proposals set out. The proposal involves the creation of two-member constituencies and probably—depending on the form of electoral system adopted (for which see below)—multi-member constituencies. This is by no means a new idea in UK politics. Multi-member constituencies (usually, in fact, two-member constituencies) were common in the nineteenth century and the last one was abolished in 1950. It would, however, drain significant resources (including taking up already limited space) at a time when there is controversy as to whether we already have too many MPs. Nick Clegg, leader of the Liberal Democrats, has proposed a reduction to 150 MPs with correspondingly larger constituencies to be drawn up by the Boundary Commissions. However, the longer-term result of the proposals set out in this Constitution (see Article 30) is that the number of sitting members will probably not be much greater than their present number; the substantive difference is that the sexes will be equally (or almost equally) represented.

Proportional representation (Article 32)   A second major constitutional reform is that proposed for the system of electing members of the Houses of the Parliament. This is quite a complicated and somewhat technical topic and is made more complicated if one opts for gender equality. The Constitution puts in place a first stage of electoral reform, namely the structural transition from a first-past-the-post (FPTP) system to one of fairer representation, if not necessarily proportional representation in the strictest sense. It is, however, a requirement of the Constitution (see Article 32) that the detail of which electoral system, including proportional representation (as defined), is to be chosen is to be set out in a law that comes into force at the same time as the Constitution. The detail will need to be very carefully considered and is likely to require much empirical including comparative research, especially if gender equality for elections to Parliament is accepted as a basic principle to be adopted.

Proportional representation, or PR (in the extended sense used here, which includes the alternative vote (AV) and comparable electoral systems: see below) is to be contrasted with the FPTP system currently in operation for election to the House of Commons. FPTP is a winner-takes-all system for single-member constituencies in which victory by a single vote is all that is required to secure a parliamentary seat.

The random unfairness of this electoral system has been extensively documented. Although FPTP is often said to produce strong government,[46] the reality is that it produces arbitrary government in that the party with the highest number of constituencies wins, whatever its share of the national vote. Since the Second World War every election has produced a winning party with less than 50 per cent of the vote.

This can lead to serious injustices. For example, in the 2005 general election the Liberal Democrats secured 22 per cent of the national vote but gained only 10 per cent of the seats in the House of Commons. In the 1983 general election the combined vote share of the two major parties was 70 per cent, which enabled them to gain 93 per cent of the seats. On two occasions the majority party has even received fewer votes than its main rival (1951 and February 1974).

By contrast, PR in its strictest form aims to approximate the percentage of votes cast to the percentage of seats gained. It is the system used for elections in Scotland, Wales, Northern Ireland and London but has never been applied to Westminster elections.

There are many different types of PR, as well as particular voting systems which are arguably less unfair than FPTP but which are not strictly PR since they do not take account of the size of the vote.

The main non-PR system, AV[47], permits voters to cast votes for the various candidates in order of preference. The candidate who receives the most first preference votes (that is, more votes than the other candidates combined) is elected. If there is no such candidate then the second preference votes of the candidate finishing last are redistributed and this process is repeated until a candidate emerges who has received more first preference votes than the others combined. One advantage of AV is that it can easily be used in the single-member constituencies that we currently have. Another advantage is that it preserves a constituency link, thus ensuring that voters are casting their votes for specific candidates linked to the constituency.

---

[46] For a useful corrective to the perceived necessity for 'strong' government, see *Making Minority Government Work* (Institute for Government, 3 December 2009), which draws on experience from effective minority governments in New Zealand, Canada and Scotland.

[47] Another possible method entailing the notion of an absolute majority is the 'second ballot' method by which all candidates except the last candidates (usually two) go through to a second and final FPTP round. This would also be compatible with two-member constituencies with separate gender-lists.

AV could also be used as an electoral model for the proposed two-member constituencies that would result from gender equality (see above), since voters could cast their preferences for the candidates on each gender-list, and each list would be subject to application of the AV system. In his 2009 speech to the Labour Party Conference Gordon Brown offered a national referendum if Labour were to win the election on the question of whether elections to Westminster should continue to take place under FPTP or be replaced by AV.

However, AV might be even more out of line with the overall votes cast for each party than FPTP. This was the conclusion reached following research conducted by Democratic Audit in 1997. If that were likely to be the position, another form of PR would have to be devised which could either be adapted to two-member constituencies based on gender equality or might require the creation of multi-member constituencies (the latter being permitted though not required under the Constitution).[48]

Alternative vote plus (AV+) was the system of (quasi) PR invented and chosen by the Jenkins Commission, a body set up in 1997 to consider reform of the voting system following the general election that first voted New Labour into power. Under this system most MPs would be directly elected by AV (see above). There would then be a relatively small number (perhaps 15–20 per cent) of additional members elected from regional top-up lists. Whilst still retaining a considerable electoral advantage for the two main parties, AV+ introduces an element of PR which could produce a fairer electoral system than the present one. Thus, AV+ enjoys quite a wide measure of support because it is thought to combine the potential for strong government with greater equity as between all competing political parties.

AV+ contains some element of PR. However AV+ would probably involve some break to the constituency link (that is the link between a Member and his or her constituency) to accommodate the additional MPs that would be voted in from regional top-up lists.

As to PR in its fullest sense, one system is the *party list*. This is a system of PR by which the parties provide candidate lists which are then matched to the percentage of votes cast. Thus, if the Liberal Democrats obtain 30 per cent of the national vote, they are allocated 30 per cent of the seats. The list may be a closed list, where voters have no influence over the identity of the candidates on the party lists. Alternatively, the list may be open, meaning that voters have varying degrees of influence over the identity of the candidates that receive seats. A party list electoral model breaks the constituency link, although this can be mitigated by drawing up regional lists. It might, at least in part, be adapted to two-member constituencies of the kind proposed by this Constitution but would more probably require multi-member constituencies. It would appear to be capable of eliminating wasted votes altogether, but the break with the constituency link makes it difficult to reconcile with the two-member equal gender constituencies mandated in part by the Constitution.

---

[48] The exact method by which votes should be cast will depend on the form of PR (as defined) that is selected.

Another well-known variant of PR is the single transferable vote (STV) system, which is used in, amongst other countries, Australia and Ireland. It is suitable for multi-member constituencies. In STV the single votes cast may be transferred to different candidates (the number of candidates depending on the size of the constituency) but votes cast for candidates who are not successful (or which are not necessary to secure election) are then re-allocated to the other candidates according to voters' express preferences until all are eliminated but the most successful candidates.

One of the objections to STV in multi-member constituencies is that, like the party list, it breaks the constituency link. It is probably not suited to two-member constituencies based on equal gender representation unless the constituency link is to be abandoned. However, such a break is not envisaged in the proposals here.

Party list systems and STV would in fact give a considerable advantage to the Liberal Democrats, who have been underrepresented in Parliament for a great many years. However, for that reason amongst others, neither system of PR is likely to receive support from the two main political parties even if either of them could be accommodated within the electoral system proposed here which contemplates most constituencies being two-member constituencies with a strong constituency link.

The key choice to be made is between simple FPTP[49] and PR (including AV and similar systems) and this Constitution comes down firmly in favour of the latter, with the detail to be worked out in separate laws following a period of empirical research. This was the conclusion of the Power Inquiry, an inquiry established in 2004 under the chairmanship of Baroness Kennedy with the remit of exploring ways of increasing political participation in Britain. The Power Inquiry was concerned that FPTP compounded the problem of voter apathy because under FPTP so many votes were wasted, in the sense that they had no prospect of affecting the electoral outcome in particular constituencies.

Care needs to be taken in relation to the electoral system chosen because the nature of that system may have an effect on other aspects of the Constitution, such as by-elections and the recall of MPs.

Compulsory voting (Articles 34–35)   The third change proposed in this Part of the Constitution is the introduction of compulsory voting, although there are strong arguments for not stigmatising it by way of criminal or even civil penalty (see Article 35). The sanction proposed for not voting is loss of entitlement to vote for a stipulated period. However, if the voting age were reduced to 16 or 17 (see Article 34, which envisages that such a law could be introduced), there would be no duty to vote on those below the age of 18.

---

[49] A possible variant of simple FPTP would be second-past-the-post, namely the election of the first two candidates with the highest votes. It would be interesting to ascertain what changes in party representation at Westminster this might produce. However, the two-member constituencies that this would require would not (as proposed in the Constitution) be gender-dependent. Thus a second-past-the-post electoral model would not easily be compatible with the proposals in the present Constitution.

Compulsory voting has a respectable heritage, having been used in ancient Athens where red-stained ropes were used to herd recalcitrant voters into the assembly place and identify those who were trying to shirk their duty. Some countries, such as Australia and Belgium, now provide for compulsory voting. Some impose penalties for failing to vote; others do not enforce the requirement. The model adopted here is similar to that used in Belgium, where repeated failure to vote may result in disenfranchisement.

There are many good reasons to consider the imposition of compulsory voting for persons over 18 years of age. It reflects the idea that voting is a civic duty and, arguably, confers greater legitimacy on the party forming the government by the far higher turnout of voters that is likely to result. Although there are objections to imposing a requirement to do that which, it may be said, is an entitlement rather than a duty, the underlying justification behind proposing compulsory voting is the argument that, with other changes, it is likely to increase citizen engagement. Turnout in general elections since 1997 has plummeted. Whilst some have blamed this on voter apathy, Baroness Kennedy's recent inquiry into democracy concluded that voters are not alienated from politics as such but feel that they have no active influence under the present electoral and party political system. Compulsory voting, without more, is unlikely to produce real change. However, if the wider electoral changes and alterations to the current party political system proposed by this Constitution are adopted, voters will have more influence. Compulsory voting is a logical component of a representative democratic society. In such a society, citizens have a real influence in shaping decision-making and are expected, as part of their civic responsibilities, to exercise that influence. This is consistent with a developing concept of citizenship which, it seems to be common ground between the parties, should be encouraged.

MPs' interests and conduct (Articles 36–42)   Public anger over the expenses scandal in 2009 compelled legislative reform and this led to the inquiry by Sir Christopher Kelly[50] and the perhaps over-hasty passing of the Parliamentary Standards Act 2009, which is directed towards the House of Commons. That Act creates an Independent Parliamentary Standards Authority[51] (IPSA) and an officer known as the Commissioner for Parliamentary Investigations. The IPSA is responsible for drawing up schemes of members' allowances and for paying the salaries of MPs. In addition, it will prepare a Code of Conduct to be observed by MPs in relation to their financial interests. The 2009 Act provides that the Commissioner will investigate lapses in MPs' conduct, including breaches of that Code. The making of false claims by MPs is a criminal offence punishable by up to 12 months' imprisonment.

These are all worthy and much-needed reforms of a practice that was subject to widespread abuse. But it should not obscure the fact that much stronger and

---

[50] Sir Christopher Kelly's report *MPs' Expenses and Allowances* (n 45) was published on 4 November 2009.
[51] The first chairman of the IPSA is Sir Ian Kennedy.

entrenched reform will be needed to restore trust to the House of Commons and, as importantly, the House of Lords.

This Constitution therefore proposes entrenched provisions for independent control over MPs' expenses and allowances (Article 36), registration of permitted interests with declaration of non-permitted interests (Article 37), and standards of conduct (Article 38). These provisions build a little on the current legislation and, as importantly, place external constitutional restraints on MPs' interests and conduct which possess additional, symbolic force.

The blatant cynicism displayed by some MPs over expenses claims has engendered interest in the possibility of constituents being able to force them out of office. This option is supported by the Conservatives and the Liberal Democrats and is under consideration by Labour. The specific proposal reported as being supported by Nick Clegg for the Liberal Democrats is one that would trigger a recall mechanism if only 5 per cent of constituents signed a petition demanding a by-election.[52]

Some care needs to be given to these proposals. There is a real danger of electoral abuse if so small a proportion of the electorate can mandate a by-election merely because they are dissatisfied with their sitting MP. Stringent safeguards need to be built in so as to prevent such abuse. 5 per cent is a very small percentage to trigger a by-election which might well be opposed to the wishes of the majority of the electorate. The option envisaged in this Constitution (see Articles 41–42) is borrowed from the Venezuelan Constitution, which introduced a similarly worded provision in 1999 and used it in 2004 to decide whether President Chavaz should be recalled from office. In the event he was not recalled. The mechanism encompasses two stages. The first stage requires 20 per cent of the constituency electorate to trigger a recall referendum. The second stage leads to a by-election but only if a specified number and proportion of registered voters vote for recall in the referendum.

The positive outcome of a recall referendum is but one of a number of ways in which, under this Constitution, MPs are, or become, automatically disqualified from sitting in the House of Representatives (see Articles 27 and 39).

Article 39 lays down a number of eligibility requirements for continued membership of the House of Representatives beyond those of age and citizenship (for which see Article 27). New provisions[53] (other than recall) include (i) a criminal conviction of an offence punishable by imprisonment (the current disqualification under the Representation of the People Act 1981 only disqualifies MPs from sitting if they are detained for any offence for more than a year or detained indefinitely), (ii) the holding of an interest proscribed by law (there is no current automatic disqualification for interests held by MPs that may compromise or may reasonably be thought to compromise their independence when voting for particular proposals which might conflict with those interests), and (iii) ceasing to be a member of the political party on whose policy platform he or she was elected (currently, an MP may in exceptional circumstances be rejected by his or her party or may simply disagree with its policies and resign but still remain in office).[54]

Nothing in the Constitution diminishes the effect of the Parliamentary Standards Act 2009, but, as can be seen, the reforms suggested in the Constitution's provisions go rather further.

Other matters (Articles 43–46)   Articles 43–44 deal with the procedure of the House of Representatives. Finally, Part 3 of the Constitution ends (see Articles 45–46) with a reminder—implicit in the very existence of a written Constitution—that the lawmaking and other powers of the House of Representatives are derived from the Constitution (and, therefore, not from parliamentary sovereignty).

It should also be noted that new powers including a parliamentary veto over the exercise of former prerogative powers by both the House of Representatives and the Senate are contained in Part 5 of the Constitution (see Articles 91–92). Some of these controls go further than the present Government has indicated it wishes to go. In particular, anticipated measures currently enshrined in the 2009 Constitutional Reform and Governance Bill do not currently appear to envisage a parliamentary veto on any aspect of the exercise of executive powers.

PART 4

THE SENATE

COMPOSITION OF THE SENATE

47. The composition of the Senate shall initially consist of the same members as comprised the House of Lords immediately before the coming into force of this Constitution.[55]

---

[54] In the latter case, a by-election would be triggered and the MP in question could stand as an independent candidate.

[55] At present the House of Lords has 706 members. There are 588 life peers (appointed by the Crown on the advice of the Prime Minister but usually nominated by political parties); 92 hereditary peers (elected from within the overall number of hereditary peers) and 26 bishops.

COMPOSITION OF AND STANDARDS FOR THE ELECTED BODY OF THE SENATE

48.   The elected body of the Senate is to be established by elections to be held at the first general election following the coming into force of this Constitution and, except where a seat is vacated, members of the elected body will hold office for the same period as members of the House of Representatives.

49.   Only citizens, enjoying civil and political rights, of one of the nations that comprise the United Kingdom, who have attained the age of forty, are legally resident in the United Kingdom, and are not disqualified from occupying a seat in the Senate may be elected to the elected body of the Senate.

50.   The number of members of the elected body of the Senate shall be 70 per cent of the number of members of the Senate.

51.   The provisions of Articles 36–38 of this Constitution shall apply, with the necessary modifications, to members of the elected body of the Senate.

52.   The circumstances in which a seat in the elected body of the Senate shall automatically become vacant or, as the case may be and as applicable, shall not become available to be occupied by a person shall, with the necessary modifications, be the same as those applicable to the House of Representatives as specified in Articles 39 to 42 of this Constitution except that Article 39(vi) shall not apply,[56] and the references in those Articles to the House of Representatives shall be references to the elected body, and the references to constituency shall be references to the large, regional constituencies represented by members of the elected body (which shall be known as the larger regional constituencies)[57] and not to the constituencies represented by members of the House of Representatives. There are no disqualifications from election or from continued membership of the elected body save as expressly set out in this Constitution.

53.   A member of the elected body may not be a member of the House of Representatives, the Scottish Parliament, the Welsh Assembly, the Northern Ireland Assembly, the European Parliament or the appointed body of the Senate at the same time.

---

[56] Members of the House of Lords are not currently entitled to vote in a General Election and there are no proposals in this Constitution to enable members of the Senate to do so. It is for consideration whether or not, once the Senate becomes a largely elected body, Members of the House of Representatives (or of the Senate) should be entitled to vote in elections for the elected body of the Senate. These are probably matters to be left to the legislature to decide and would not appear to raise significant constitutional issues.

[57] See Part 14 for the definition of 'larger regional constituency'.

54. Following all elections (including by-elections) after the coming into force of this Constitution, and in accordance with the rules for those elections as set out in this Constitution and laws giving effect to this Constitution, one half of the elected body of the Senate shall, provided that there are sufficient eligible candidates, be women and one half shall be men.

55. The boundaries of the larger regional constituencies of the elected body shall be determined by the appropriate Boundary Commission[58] in accordance with law and, thereafter, monitored by regular reviews of the appropriate Boundary Commission, and their number shall reflect the eligible number of members of the elected body. Priority shall be given to the objective of ensuring as far as possible that the size of the larger regional constituencies taking into account the size of the elected body of the Senate and the appointed body of the Senate enables the number of Members of the Senate to be the same, so far as is possible, as that of the members of the House of Representatives.

ELECTIONS TO THE ELECTED BODY OF THE SENATE

56. Articles 32 to 35 of this Constitution shall, with the necessary modifications but subject to Article 57, apply to elections to the elected body of the Senate as they apply to elections to the House of Representatives except that the references in Articles 32 to 35 to the House of Representatives shall be references to the elected body, and references to constituencies shall be references only to the larger regional constituencies and not to the constituencies represented by members of the House of Representatives (whether two-member constituencies or multi-member constituencies). Larger regional constituencies may, subject to this Constitution, consist of two or more elected members.

57. The method of election to the elected body of the Senate shall give priority to the need for a fair balance in relation to the votes cast as between political parties seeking election of their members to the elected body.

THE APPOINTED BODY OF THE SENATE

58. The appointed body is to be established by appointments, following open competition, made by a body known as the Senate Appointments Commission after the coming into force of this Constitution and before the first general election after its coming into force. The appointments shall take effect at the same time as the date on which the members of the elected body of the Senate take up their seats in accordance with law.

[58] See Part 14 for the definition of 'appropriate Boundary Commission'.

59. Only citizens enjoying civil and political rights, of one of the nations that comprise the United Kingdom, who have attained the age of forty, are legally resident in the United Kingdom, and are not disqualified from occupying a seat in the Senate may be appointed to the appointed body of the Senate. There are no disqualifications from appointment or from continued membership of the appointed body of the Senate save as set out in or incorporated in this Constitution. A member of the appointed body of the Senate may not, however, be a member of the House of Representatives, the Scottish Parliament, the Welsh Assembly, the Northern Ireland Assembly, the European Parliament or the elected body of the Senate at the same time.

60. Subject to this Constitution, the number of members of the appointed body of the Senate shall be thirty per cent of the number of members of the Senate.

61. The provisions of Articles 36–38 of this Constitution shall apply, with the necessary modifications, to members of the appointed body of the Senate.

62. The term of office of a member of the appointed body of the Senate shall be the same as that of a member of the elected body of the Senate who is elected at a general election. Appointment to the appointed body is renewable at the discretion of the Senate Appointments Commission for the same period or periods, with the appointment taking effect at the same time as the date on which the members of the elected body are elected.

63. The circumstances in which a seat in the appointed body of the Senate shall automatically become vacant or, as the case may be and as applicable, shall not become available to be occupied by a person and shall render a person ineligible for appointment or continued appointment are if that person—

    (i)   dies;

    (ii)   is criminally convicted of an offence punishable by imprisonment;

    (iii) resigns by giving the Lord Speaker[59] a signed letter of resignation;

    (iv)   has any interest being an interest of a kind prescribed by law as an interest that must not be held by a member of the appointed body;

    (v)   holds or occupies any office, employment or position of a kind prescribed by this Constitution or by law as one that must not be held by a member of the Senate.

64. The law may not prescribe other circumstances in which the seat of a member of the appointed body of the Senate shall or may become vacant except that

---

[59] In the House of Lords the equivalent of the Speaker in the House of Commons is known as the Lord Speaker.

it may prescribe bankruptcy as an automatic disqualification or may prescribe conditions under which bankruptcy will result in disqualification.

65.   Where a seat on the appointed body of the Senate becomes vacant there shall be a competition for appointment. However, no competition for appointment is to be held where the seat becomes vacant less than six months before the date of the holding of a general election until the whole of the appointed body becomes eligible for reappointment on the holding of the general election.

66.   In appointing the initial candidates to the appointed body of the Senate, the Senate Appointments Commission shall, subject to this Constitution, have regard amongst other factors to the importance of some continuity of appointment of existing members of the Senate at the time of coming into force of this Constitution, to the need for ensuring an overall balance in terms of independence, representation of men and women, as well as regional representation, to the extent to which candidates have contributed towards society and the likelihood of their contribution to public service in the Senate, and to the need for outstanding personal qualities including integrity and independence, as well as to the overall representation of national interests consistent with this Constitution that will be served by the election of individual candidates and by the list of appointed candidates as a whole.

67.   In deciding whether to renew appointments to the appointed body of the Senate the Senate Appointments Commission shall, subject to this Constitution, have particular regard to the record of attendance and quality of attendance of the candidate seeking renewal of his or her appointment as well as, amongst other things, to the matters set out in Article 66.

THE SENATE APPOINTMENTS COMMISSION

68.   There shall be a body corporate called the Senate Appointments Commission which shall be an elected body responsible for making all appointments to the appointed body of the Senate. Laws shall be made which provide separately for matters relating to the election of the Senate Appointments Commission ensuring, amongst other things, that the electorate is informed as to the merits of the eligible candidates for election to the Commission, for the funding of elections, for the spending limits (if any spending is to be allowed) to be applied to such elections, and for the remuneration of those elected to the Commission. Laws may also make separate further provision relating to the work of the Senate Appointments Commission.

69.   The Commission shall consist of a Chairman and fourteen other Commissioners. Those standing for election as Chairman and Commissioners must fulfil the eligibility qualifications as set out in Article 59.

70.   The Commissioners shall be elected by a postal vote of registered electors throughout the United Kingdom from a list of eligible candidates to be drawn up by an independent statutory body. The first such list, which shall contain not less than thirty and not more than fifty names, shall be drawn up by the current members of the Judicial Appointments Commission. The list of eligible candidates shall comprise only citizens who enjoy or have had a distinguished career in any aspect of national or international life whether in the public or private sector.

71.   Subject to this Constitution, subsequent lists shall be drawn up from time to time by other independent bodies as determined by law.

72.   Those candidates receiving the highest number of votes in the election shall be selected as Commissioners and the candidate receiving the highest number of votes shall be selected as Chairman. If a vacancy arises for the office of Commissioner the candidate receiving the next highest vote in the original postal ballot shall be eligible for office. Where the office of Chairman becomes vacant the Commissioner receiving the next highest vote in the original postal ballot shall be eligible for office.

73.   Commissioners shall serve for the same term as that of the appointed body of the Senate but are not eligible for re-election. Commissioners are automatically disqualified from office if they are convicted of an offence punishable by imprisonment.

BUSINESS

74.   All questions proposed for decision in the Senate shall, subject to this Constitution, be decided by a majority vote. There is no casting vote and the question concerned shall be deemed to be lost unless there is a majority vote.

75.   The Senate may act despite a vacancy in its membership and the presence of or participation in its proceedings of a person not entitled to be a member does not invalidate the proceedings.

76.   Subject to this Constitution the Senate shall—

   (i)   decide its procedure;

   (ii)   elect its Lord Speaker by such method as it shall decide (whether or not the method of election decided upon is by majority vote).

POWERS OF THE SENATE

77.   The powers of the Senate are derived from this Constitution.

78.   The Senate shall have power to do those things which are calculated to facilitate or which are conducive or incidental to the discharge of its functions under this Constitution.

OBSERVATIONS AND EXPLANATORY NOTES

Background to House of Lords reform   The idea of reforming the House of Lords has probably caused more recent and heated debate than any other aspect of constitutional reform. This is largely because of the strength of the competing arguments.

The 1997 Labour manifesto contained the following promise: 'The House of Lords must be reformed. As an initial self-contained reform, not dependent on further reform in the future, the right of hereditary Peers to sit and vote in the House of Lords will be ended by statute.' This was partially achieved by the House of Lords Act 1999 which left a rump of 92 hereditary peers pending further reform. But further reform has not yet happened. More than a decade ago, a respected peer observed: 'to seek to reform the House by first abolishing the hereditary peers without deciding the final constitution and form of the second chamber seems to me dangerous and irresponsible folly.'[60] Thus far at least, it might be thought that Baroness James has been proved right.

Unsurprisingly, there has not been a consensus as to how to achieve reform. As long ago as the Parliament Act 1911 the need to modernise the House of Lords was apparent. The entitlement of hereditary peers to participate in government merely by virtue of their birthright had long been seen as indefensible, but lassitude followed because of the obstacles to comprehensive reform that were perceived to exist. The Preamble to the 1911 Act stated prophetically: '... it is intended to substitute for the House of Lords as it at present exists a Second Chamber constituted on a popular instead of hereditary basis, but such substitution cannot be immediately brought into operation.'

There are powerful arguments for retaining the status quo, at least in the form of a wholly *appointed* (as opposed to *elected*) second chamber. The danger of a predominantly elected second chamber is that it will largely be composed of professional, full-time career politicians. There is much to be said for the current arrangement or something similar in which men and women with experience and expertise in diverse fields come together to make specialised contributions as the need arises.

True it is that the House of Lords, as currently constituted, is something of an anomaly. In a literal sense it can hardly be said to be a representative (and hence democratic) institution. On the other hand the system works and the House of Lords has often proved to be a more independent body than the House of Commons, especially where executive-driven legislation is being forced through Parliament. The composition of the current House of Lords in which as a matter of deliberate policy no party has an overall majority also provides a counterbal-

[60] PD James, *Time to be in Earnest—A Fragment of Autobiography* (London, Faber and Faber, 1999) 129.

ance to the House of Commons in an electoral FPTP system in which the governing party now almost invariably has much less than 50 per cent of the popular vote. It may also be said that an elected second chamber has the demerit of giving that chamber added legitimacy, thereby creating tension with the House of Commons which is, in reality, the chamber designed to wield final legislative authority.

There are equally compelling arguments for an elected second chamber. The 'added legitimacy' argument is, properly analysed, a reason for having a mainly elected House. Whatever reforms are undertaken, it can always be made clear (and is made clear in this Constitution) that the first chamber (the House of Representatives) wields the superior legislative authority. In the present climate of distrust, what is arguably needed is a *more* rather than *less* legitimate second chamber in which the executive is made more accountable to parliamentary scrutiny and in which the public have confidence. This is more likely to be achieved in an elected rather than an appointed second chamber.

The history of House of Lords 'reform' has for the most part consisted of the struggle for primacy of the Commons over the Lords and the removal of the historical power of the latter to veto any legislation. This resulted in the Parliament Acts of 1911 and 1949. The power of the Lords to veto legislation was curtailed in the 1911 Act by removing their power to veto money bills and by giving the Commons power to trump the Lords' veto over other legislation after three parliamentary sessions. The 1949 Act allowed the Commons to overrule the Lords' veto after only two parliamentary sessions.

Another important restriction on the former powers of the House of Lords came in the form of a constitutional convention (conventions are addressed separately in Part 12 of the Constitution) called the Salisbury Convention. This convention, which developed during the twentieth century, was introduced by Lord Salisbury and operates to prevent the House of Lords from opposing (in the second or third readings) any government legislation that has been advanced in its election manifesto.

There were also piecemeal reforms to the system of hereditary peerages in the sense that life peerages were introduced by the Life Peerages Act 1958. Virtually all peerages created since then have been life peerages rather than hereditary peerages. The system of hereditary peerages was further weakened by the Peerage Act 1963, which allowed hereditary peers to disclaim their peerage and (if so minded) stand for election in the Commons.

There matters stood until Labour took office in 1997. A Royal Commission set up to examine reform issues in 1999 (under the chairmanship of Lord Wakeham) recommended a largely appointed House of Lords but with approximately one fifth or one third of members being elected. The concern was to modernise the second chamber (for example, peerage would no longer be a requirement of membership) but, at the same time, to avoid it being filled with professional politicians.

The government accepted the Commission's recommendations and even went so far as to announce the members of a non-statutory appointments commission. However, cross-party discussions failed. It became increasingly clear that the media and public response to reform was that there was a need for many more elected members. After further protracted and inconclusive debate a 2003 vote in the Commons and the Lords resulted in the Commons failing to vote for any single reform proposal, while the Lords voted strongly in favour of an all-appointed House.

However, the tide is now turning strongly in favour of a largely elected second chamber. A 2007 White Paper proposed a 50/50 elected/appointed House. But a vote in the Commons later in 2007 on the proposals in that White Paper resulted in a strong majority for an 80 per cent or all-elected upper House (with the Lords, perhaps predictably, still voting for an all-appointed House). This led to the publication of a 2008 White Paper[61] setting out proposals based on the result of the Commons' vote (and proposed abolition of the remaining hereditary peers) as well as proposals addressing the options for electoral systems for an elected House.

This Constitution contains proposals for a largely elected second chamber but resists following the current White Paper proposals for an exclusively elected House or even for an 80 per cent electoral model; instead it suggests a 70 per cent elected and 30 per cent appointed House (see Articles 50 and 60). In this particular respect it is in accord with both the recommendations of the recent Power Inquiry and a reform package drawn up in 2005 by a cross-bench party group of senior MPs under the auspices of the Constitution Unit at University College London.

Composition of the Senate (Article 47)   It will take time to introduce changes which transform the House of Lords from a wholly appointed body to a 70 per cent elected, 30 per cent appointed body (or any comparable change). It is therefore proposed that when the Constitution comes into force the membership of the House of Lords remains the same so that the changes can be synchronised as between what will be new and different parts of the Upper Chamber.

Composition of, and standards for, the elected body of the Senate (Articles 48–55)   There is some danger of the party political machine taking over an elected second chamber, and the proposals in this Constitution are designed to reduce that risk. One such proposal (also adopted by the Power Inquiry) is to place an age-related eligibility requirement of 40 on membership of the Senate (Article 49; see also Article 59).

As the Power Inquiry observes, such a requirement makes it less likely that career politicians will seek membership, since their trajectory commonly involves a seamless transition from politics student to researcher for an MP to policy adviser, before entering Parliament at a young age. Moreover, an age-related requirement of this kind is likely to encourage women to seek membership (whether by election or by appointment); by 40 they may have had their chil-

---

[61] *An Elected Second Chamber: Further Reform of the House of Lords*, Cm 7438.

dren and be ready to seek new challenges. Despite this, it may be argued that a difference in age-eligibility will not produce significantly different types of persons running for election to the two Houses and that a much longer—possibly even non-renewable—term of office for elected senators is what is needed so that they become very much more independent of party (see, however, immediately below).

Consistent with the aim of achieving simplicity where possible, this Constitution does not in fact propose (as does the 2008 White Paper, the Power Inquiry and the 2005 cross-bench reform package) three finite and non-extendable parliamentary terms (currently between 12 and 15 years) for elected members of the Senate or (as the 2008 White Paper suggests) three similar electoral cycles for appointed members.[62] What is proposed instead is the same electoral and appointed terms of office in the Senate as in the House of Representatives (Article 48; see also Article 62). In the case of elected members, they may seek re-election (subject to other provisions of this Constitution relating to political parties), and appointed members may seek reappointment (though they will not be automatically entitled to reappointment). A key principle of the 2008 White Paper is that members of the Senate should serve a long term of office. However, this Constitution suggests a less rigid approach, namely that members of the Senate *may* serve a long term of office but there is no necessity that they should do so.

It is also proposed that the total number of members of the Senate should (if the arithmetic allows) match that of the House of Representatives (Article 55). The constituencies for the elected body of the Senate are likely to be somewhat larger than those of the House of Representatives and they are here called larger regional constituencies (Article 52). Larger regional constituencies for elected members of the Senate are consistent with the aims of the 2008 White Paper.

The provisions relating to conduct standards and registration of relevant interests that apply to the House of Representatives also apply, by Article 51, to the elected body of the Senate.

Elections to the elected body of the Senate (Articles 56–57)   Many of the other provisions relating to elected members of the Senate (and more generally relating to Business and Powers of the Senate) are parallel provisions (with minor consequential changes) to those relating to members of the House of Representatives, and reference should be made to those provisions in the Notes to Part 3 on the House of Representatives.

However, a slightly different provision is that in choosing the method of PR for elections to the elected body of the Senate, priority be given to the need for balance in relation to votes cast as between parties (see Article 57). The purpose of this is to make it easier to break the constituency link in elections to the elected body of the Senate where a relationship between an MP and constituents does not have the significance than it has in elections to the House of

---

[62] There is an argument that having electoral cycles injects more variety into the Upper House. However, the eligibility requirements and appointment procedures have been designed to maintain an eclectic mix.

Representatives. The detail of which form of voting system (see also Notes to Part 3 of the Constitution) is the most appropriate for an elected second chamber may require more consideration. What is needed is a system that will facilitate the best balance amongst the political parties in the Senate.

STV may well be the best method of PR for the reasons set out in the 2008 White Paper, which, whilst suggesting a variety of possible voting methods, observed of STV that (in common with a list system) it would help to produce a greater balance between parties in the second chamber than other form of voting. While STV is, as the White Paper points out, more complicated than a list system (and would require particular scrutiny in the context of equal gender representation in terms of how votes should be cast and how many party candidates should be available for election), it would seem that in principle any form of list system would be likely to weaken the prospects of independent candidacies and candidates who were not from the main parties. For that reason, STV may well be preferred as the method of PR for electing the elected body of the Senate.

Provisions relating to the appointed body of the Senate (Articles 58–67) Appointments to the appointed body are to be made by a body known as the Senate Appointments Commission (Article 58; see also Notes on the Senate Appointments Commission below). The provisions dealing with standards of conduct and interests to be registered, composition of the appointed body of the Senate and vacation of office for misconduct etc mirror, with necessary modifications, the parallel provisions relating to the elected body (see Notes on the elected body of the Senate above).

It is necessarily implicit in the qualification requirements for appointment (or indeed election) to the Senate (see Article 59) that holding a peerage is not a requirement. There are no proposals in this Constitution to abolish either hereditary or life peerages. This is a matter of government policy, and in fact the present Government has signalled in its Constitutional Reform and Governance Bill an intention to remove hereditary peers from the House of Lords by not replacing current peers with their heirs when they die.

With reference to making appointments to the Senate some general criteria are set out (see Articles 59 and 66). For the most part they include those suggested in the 2008 White Paper; they also refer to the need to exercise quality control over the list of appointed candidates as a whole so that the list is truly representative. In this fashion, it is likely that many existing members of the House of Lords would be appointed under the new system. Since the process for selecting members of the Senate Appointments Commission (see Notes on the Senate Appointments Commission below) is itself designed to elicit the highest possible quality of Commissioners making appointments to the Senate, the criteria in Article 66 are not overly prescriptive and are couched in general terms. No specific bar has been imposed on past politicians or past office-holders being appointed. It may be counter-productive to do so if they satisfy the test of merit. However, by imposing criteria which compel consideration of an overall balance in terms of, amongst other things, independence, the aim is that the danger of partisanship is reduced.

An important concluding provision in respect of Senate appointees is Article 67. Under this Article it is clear that appointments may be renewed, but the Commission is required, when considering renewal, to examine the attendance record and quality of attendance of the appointee in question. Because of this requirement it is neither possible nor desirable to guarantee an equal number of men and women, though the general criteria for selection include the need to have regard to the overall balance in terms of the representation of men and women (see Article 66).

Senate Appointments Commission (Articles 68–73)   These provisions deal with the mechanism for making appointments to the Senate. An *elected* Senate Appointments Commission is envisaged in order to enhance the legitimacy of appointments made by the Commission. This is significant in circumstances in which the persons appointed to the Senate are being appointed to be completely independent. Articles 68–72 set out a scheme of election to the Commission which involves a list being drawn up from an independent appointed body (which will differ from general election to general election) by reference to identified characteristics. It is proposed (Article 73) that Commissioners should serve only once and for the term of the Parliament.

Other matters (Articles 74–78)   These provisions, which concern procedure in, and the residual powers of, the Senate are mirrored in Articles 43–46 relating to the House of Representatives, and reference should be made to the Notes on those provisions.

PART 5
EXECUTIVE GOVERNMENT[63]

APPOINTMENT AND RESPONSIBILITIES OF MINISTERS AND ADVISERS

79.   The Head of State symbolises the unity of the State and, in that capacity, possesses executive authority. However, the Head of State has no power outside this Constitution and, except as provided for under this Constitution, must act where there is power to act only on the advice of the Prime Minister acting through Cabinet as provided for by this Constitution.

80.   There shall be a Prime Minister who shall be appointed by the Head of State. The Prime Minister shall be a member of the House of Representatives who, in the Head of State's opinion,[64] will be able to form a government that has

---

[63] This section poses particularly difficult questions of definition. *Towards a Codified Constitution* (the draft paper referred to in the Notes to the Preamble) identifies no fewer than 21 institutions and a number of terms such as 'the executive' which could be given constitutional status or definition.

[64] If the Head of State acted in bad faith or otherwise unlawfully in forming a judgement, this would be a breach of Articles 4 and 80 and would be enforceable in the courts (see Article 176).

the confidence of a majority of the House of Representatives. The Prime Minister shall have power to appoint and dismiss members of the Cabinet.[65]

81.　Subject to this Constitution, executive power shall be vested in the Prime Minister, acting through Cabinet. However, nothing in the conferment of that power limits provisions in this Constitution, or laws compatible with this Constitution, from conferring on specified persons or bodies specific executive or other functions or power including freedom from direction or control by any person or authority in relation to the performance of their functions or exercise of their power.

82.　All Cabinet ministerial appointments, other than that of Prime Minister, shall be made by the Prime Minister, who shall also have the power to dismiss Cabinet Ministers. The Prime Minister shall, so long as the number of Cabinet Ministers permitted under this Constitution is not exceeded,[66] determine the offices of State comprising the Cabinet.

83.　To be eligible for appointment to the Cabinet, a Minister must be a member of the House of Representatives or of the elected body of the Senate.

84.　The Cabinet is collectively responsible to the Houses of the Parliament for the governance of the State.

85.　Subject to this Constitution the Prime Minister may make Ministerial appointments outside the Cabinet and may also appoint persons to advise the Cabinet who are not members of the House of Representatives or of the elected body of the Senate. However, except where the holder of such appointment is a member of the House of Representatives or of the elected body of the Senate, their appointment must be confirmed by the House of Representatives by a process to be determined by the House of Representatives and such persons must be accountable to the House of Representatives through select committees as provided for in this Constitution. The Prime Minister may dismiss any Minister or adviser whom he or she has appointed.

86.　All Ministers are also individually responsible to the Houses of the Parliament for all acts done by or under the authority of the Minister in the execution of his or her office. They shall have such individual responsibilities as the Prime Minister shall determine from time to time according to law. The Prime Minister shall also have individual responsibility to the Houses of the Parliament for any part of the business of the Government not assigned by him to a Minister or Ministers.

---

[65] See Part 14 for a definition of 'the Cabinet'.

[66] The maximum number is 22 Ministers other than the Prime Minister (see Part 14). The current Cabinet consists of this number and an increase in that number is probably undesirable. However, removing such a limitation is not crucial.

87.   Before taking office the Prime Minister, Cabinet Ministers, other Ministers and advisers must swear an oath of allegiance to this Constitution as set out in Schedule [ ][67] and in the manner there prescribed.

88.   Apart from dismissal where applicable, but subject to this Constitution, the appointment of a Minister (including the Prime Minister) or adviser terminates if he or she resigns, if the Prime Minister resigns or, where membership of the House of Representatives or of the Senate is a precondition of that appointment (or was the basis on which that appointment was made), if the Minister or adviser ceases to be a member of the House of Representatives or Senate as the case may be.

89.   If a Minister's appointment (including that of the Prime Minister) ceases by virtue of the expiry or dissolution of the House of Representatives he or she shall continue in office until the appointment of a new Minister or Prime Minister. The appointment of a new Prime Minister shall have the effect of terminating all other appointments of Ministers and advisers.

THE EXECUTIVE POWERS OF MINISTERS

90.   Laws may confer specific executive and other powers on Ministers. In particular, the raising by the Government of revenue or moneys, whether through the imposition of taxation or otherwise, must be authorised by or under the enactment of a Bill passed by the Houses of the Parliament under Article 11.

91.   Except as otherwise provided by this Constitution, but subject to this Constitution, the powers formerly exercised under Crown prerogative shall be abolished but shall become constitutional powers exercisable by the Prime Minister acting through Cabinet. However, the express powers set out in Article 92(i)–(viii) shall not be exercised without the prior approval of Parliament sitting as a single Assembly and exercised by majority vote.

92.   The exercise of such powers of the Prime Minister acting through Cabinet shall include power—

(i)   to direct the disposition of the armed forces in the United Kingdom;

(ii)   to issue and withdraw UK passports;

(iii) to make treaties;

(iv)   to commission officers in the armed forces;

(v)   to declare war;

[67] A form of oath is not included here or elsewhere in the Constitution.

    (vi)   to make peace;

    (vii) to deploy the armed forces on operations overseas;

    (viii) to accredit and receive diplomats;

    (ix)   to exercise other executive powers not conferred by statute and not otherwise conferred by this Constitution on the Head of State or other person or body.[68]

THE HEAD OF STATE

93.   The Head of State derives his or her authority and powers from this Constitution.

94.   The Sovereign reigning at the time of the coming into force of this Constitution shall, provided that they swear an oath of allegiance to this Constitution as set out in Schedule [ ] and in the manner there prescribed, become Head of State. The civil list[69] shall be established by law.

95.   The Sovereign and his or her successors shall no longer be Head of the Church of England and that Church shall henceforth be disestablished. The former powers of the Crown over the Church of England and any other powers exercised over that Church by Parliament or by third parties are transferred to the General Synod of the Church of England and shall be exercised in accordance with any rules laid down by that body.

96.   The rules determining the line of succession to the throne, including rules for the appointment of a Regent in case of the Sovereign's incapacity or minority, shall be determined by a law which shall come into effect at the time of coming into force of this Constitution but which shall be subject to this Constitution.

97.   In determining the line of succession to the throne and any rights, privileges and dignities belonging thereto as provided for in this Constitution or by law no account shall be taken of gender or religion notwithstanding any previous custom or rule of law to the contrary. Nor shall royal consent be required for any marriage. Nor shall the Sovereign be required to be a Protestant, nor to declare allegiance to the Protestant faith. The Royal Marriages Act 1772 shall have no continuing legal effect and the other Royal Acts[70] shall, to the extent that they are inconsistent with this Constitution, have no continuing legal effect.

---

[68] Such as recognising foreign jurisdictions.

[69] The term 'civil list' is defined in Part 14.

[70] The term 'Royal Acts' is defined in Part 14.

98.   The new Sovereign may accede to the throne and become Head of State only after swearing an oath of allegiance to this Constitution as set out in Schedule [ ] and in the manner there prescribed.

99.   The Head of State has the right to be informed by the Prime Minister on all matters relating to the governance of the United Kingdom.

100.   The former powers exercised under Crown prerogative shall no longer be exercisable by the Head of State. The Head of State shall have the powers and duties conferred or imposed elsewhere in this Constitution subject in all cases to the constraints imposed by this Constitution. Subject to these constraints the Head of State shall also have power—

(i)   to summon, prorogue and dissolve Parliament;[71]

(ii)   to exercise the prerogative of mercy;

(iii)   to grant honours;

(iv)   to create corporations by Charter;

(v)   to receive diplomats.

ROLE OF THE ATTORNEY-GENERAL

101.   The Attorney-General shall be the chief legal adviser to the Government but shall not henceforth be entitled to exercise any functions of a political nature whether for and on behalf of the Government or otherwise.

102.   A person shall not be eligible to be appointed as Attorney-General unless he or she is qualified to practise as a barrister or solicitor in the United Kingdom and has been so qualified for at least ten years.

103.   The Attorney-General shall not be eligible for appointment as a Minister or for membership of the House of Representatives or of the Senate and must resign any such membership as a condition of holding office as Attorney-General.

104.   The Attorney-General may exercise any other function as provided for by law provided that it is compatible with, and subject to, this Constitution.

---

[71] The effect of Articles 34 and 56 is to require laws that specify the time at which the newly elected Members of the Houses of the Parliament assume their office. Such laws will generally constrain the theoretical ability of the Head of State to summon and dissolve Parliament, making it, in that respect, a purely symbolic activity.

RELATIONSHIP BETWEEN THE EXECUTIVE AND PARLIAMENT

105. The exercise of executive power shall, except where it is otherwise necessary to exercise emergency executive power in accordance with this Constitution, be accountable to the Houses of the Parliament as provided for in this Constitution and as provided for by laws made for that purpose pursuant to this Constitution.

106. Select committees of the House of Representatives and the Senate and of Joint Committees of the Houses of the Parliament shall be composed of members of each of the Houses of the Parliament chosen from time to time by means of a free and independent secret voting system in a manner determined by each House.[72]

107. There shall also be established by means of such independent voting system a new select committee of the House of Representatives which shall have the remit of scrutinising the activities of the executive in supranational bodies and multinational negotiations.

108. Select committees of the House of Representatives and of the Senate shall have the power to subpoena and examine witnesses in proceedings before such committees and to compel the disclosure of documents including from departments of Government.

109. Select committees of the House of Representatives and of the Senate shall have the power to co-opt members with specialist expertise (whether or not a member of either House) to assist them in their deliberations if it is considered expedient to do so.

110. A select committee of the House of Representatives shall have the power to require such persons as have been appointed by the Prime Minister under this Constitution (whether Ministers or special advisers) but who are not members of the House of Representatives or of the elected body of the Senate and whose appointment has been confirmed by the House of Representatives to provide a report from time to time of the manner in which they have exercised their functions and to appear at such times before that select committee as the committee shall, in its discretion, determine to account for the manner in which the relevant functions have been exercised.

111. The House of Representatives and the Senate shall have such power to initiate legislation and public inquiries in certain circumstances as may be provided for by law.

---

[72] A number of detailed recommendations, including recommendations for strengthening the work of the select committees, were made by the Reform of the House of Commons Committee under the chairmanship of Tony Wright MP in its first report, *Rebuilding the House* (24 November 2009). These recommendations, if implemented, should be read alongside the proposals contained in this draft Constitution. At the time of writing, none of the recommendations have been implemented.

OBSERVATIONS AND EXPLANATORY NOTES

Executive power and executive authority   In this Constitution, executive power and the executive authority of the state are distinguished. Executive *power* refers to the governmental authority and responsibility that, in the UK, is exercised by the Prime Minister through the system of Cabinet government. The executive *authority* of the state has traditionally been vested in the monarch. Executive authority is now largely symbolic, but executive power—unless carefully supervised—can quickly spiral into dictatorship. An example of this was the rise of Nazism in Germany from 1933. Nazism's original source of authority was democratic but Hitler used the institutions of the state to make laws which were the very antithesis of democracy.

Questions raised by the need to control executive power   The exercise of executive power and the means of regulating and controlling it give rise to a number of constitutional issues that, in any democratic constitution, need to be carefully addressed.

Two questions are of particular importance and resonance in modern Britain. First is the question of how best practical effect is to be given to the doctrine of separation of powers in order to guard against the dangers to democracy of an over-mighty executive (or judiciary). Secondly, how best in a representative democracy can the institutions of government be made directly accountable to the voters? Resolving these questions should be the leitmotif of any modern Constitution for the UK and they are closely related.

Fusion not separation of powers   The traditional constitutional doctrine of separation of powers is that in a democracy, power that is exercised by the executive, the legislature and the judiciary should be separated so that each provides a check on the other. One of the main complaints about the British system of government is that separation of powers is not really working. Parliament (the legislature) has, it is argued, become the tool of the executive, so that in reality Parliament is not exercising proper legislative scrutiny over the wielding of executive power. In a different and potentially contradictory sense it is also often contended (especially in the field of human rights) that the judges are interfering with laws in such a way as to reduce the effectiveness of Parliament's (in reality executive government's) intentions when passing the law in question.

In Britain we do not, strictly, have separation of powers between the executive and Parliament. Nor until the creation of the Supreme Court from October 2009 did we enjoy separation of powers as between the legislature and the judiciary, because judges at the then highest level of court—the House of Lords—were also members of that House and entitled to vote on legislation. This was an historical anomaly in an age when, for example, EU law could require House of Lords judges to hear challenges to legislation which they may have voted on as members of the House of Lords.

In this respect, what we have in Britain is not so much a *separation* of powers as a *fusion* of powers. Government ministers must by convention be selected from Parliament, and the Prime Minister and Chancellor of the Exchequer must be selected from the House of Commons. Separation of powers would operate to *prevent* a minister from being a member of either House. Indeed, under the Act of Settlement of 1701 there was a clause (clause III) that included a stipulation that 'no person who has an Office or Place of Profit under the King ... shall be capable of serving as a Member of the House of Commons'. In the eighteenth century a person having an office or place of profit under the King was the equivalent of a minister today. Had this clause survived (it was repealed in 1705) it would have set Britain on a somewhat different constitutional course, leading, perhaps, to a true separation of powers.[73]

Danger of an over-mighty executive   The significance of having a fusion of powers is that it makes the relationship between the executive and Parliament a delicate one, in relation to which great care is needed to ensure that the executive is not given unfettered influence to pass whatever laws it wishes.[74] The growth of the modern two-party system has rendered this danger all the more acute in that, coupled with an FPTP winner-takes-all electoral system, the party achieving an electoral majority is usually able to dominate the House of Commons and in practice (because of the legislative primacy of the House of Commons) the second chamber as well.

It should also be borne in mind that the dangers of unchecked executive power are reinforced by the government whips, who wield considerable power. The Chief Whip (who has a seat in Cabinet) of the governing party in the House of Commons is in overall charge of the whipping system by which members of the party, on pain of sanction, are compelled to attend the House and vote as the government dictates. Such a system has the effect of creating a career hierarchy in which pleasing the whips can take priority over independent judgement.

With all its interlocking dynamics heavily favouring the executive branch of government, the risk of an over-powerful executive is mitigated only (it cannot be avoided altogether) by making significant constitutional changes.

Indeed, more profound changes are probably needed due to the tendency in recent times for Prime Ministers to appoint special advisers who have no connection with either House of Parliament yet who hold power that can, at least in some cases, rival that of Cabinet Ministers. This trend, started by Margaret Thatcher (1979–90), resulted in several influential appointments being made under Tony Blair (1997–2007) (most notably that of Alistair Campbell (1997–2003)) and has continued under Gordon Brown (2007–). The latter has also made several Cabinet appointments from the House of Lords, which, as currently constituted, is a wholly unelected body.

---

[73] For a large part of the last century, an MP who was made a Minister had to stand for re-election.

[74] Bagehot considered that a fusion of powers was superior to a separation of powers and that there was a distinction to be drawn between *efficient* and *dignified* parts of the constitution—the latter being typically exemplified by the Crown. This may have been true in the nineteenth century, when the UK constitution was more balanced with a strong House of Lords. But the constitution has become less balanced with the weakening of the House of Lords in the Parliament Acts of 1911 and 1949 and the growth of the modern party system. These points are well made in The Hon Mr Justice Beatson's 'Reforming an Unwritten Constitution', 31st Blackstone Lecture (2010) 126 *Law Quarterly Review* 48.

It is probably unrealistic to consider a change from fused to separated powers. That being so, what is needed are changes to the electoral system (by reducing the dominance of the two-party system through PR) and to the party system (by reducing the influence of the whips), by increasing the legitimacy and powers of the House of Lords (where no party has a clear majority but where the House of Lords is wholly unelected) and (the key area for reform) by increasing the independence of Parliament (but especially the House of Commons) vis-a-vis the executive.

Who wields executive power? (Article 79)   The starting point for regulating executive power more effectively is to identify who wields it and then to circumscribe the nature of the powers that may be exercised.

Britain does not have a constitutional monarchy in the strictest sense. As a matter of constitutional theory, the British monarch becomes entitled to exercise prerogative power on a hereditary basis. In strict theory, the monarch may exercise largely unchecked prerogative power. The fact that as a matter of constitutional convention the advice of the Prime Minister, which the Queen must accept, determines how prerogative power is exercised does not alter the theoretical constitutional position of the monarch. But that is not constitutional reality.

This Constitution recognises the constitutional reality that the Queen exercises no effective power but nonetheless has an important symbolic role to play in society. It therefore identifies her role as being holder of executive authority as opposed to executive power (see Article 79).

The exercise of executive power (Articles 80–92)   Articles 80–92 set out the *main* ways in which executive power may be exercised under the Constitution. There are, broadly, three proposed categories: (i) the power of the Prime Minister to appoint ministers and special advisers (see Articles 82 and 85); (ii) the conferment of executive functions by law (see Articles 81 and 90); and (iii) the executive power of the Prime Minister acting through Cabinet in respect of prerogative power not currently controlled by laws (see Articles 91–92).

As to appointments, under the Constitution ministerial appointments remain for the most part under the effective control of the Prime Minister (other than his/her own appointment, which continues to be made by the Head of State). Some have proposed that Parliament should have the power to veto key appointments, but confirmation hearings (such as those that take place in the USA where hearings are held by the US Senate to gather information in order to decide whether to approve or reject candidates for high federal office who are nominated by the President) would slow the process of appointing ministers and would, it is suggested, unnecessarily and detrimentally hamper the process of executive government.

However, this should not be at the expense of accountability. Ministers appointed from the House of Commons or from the (elected body of the) Senate will, by definition, have to account to the electorate. They will also in practice be accountable to their respective elected House.

This does not apply to special advisers, who are almost invariably not members of either House and have never been elected. In addition, there is some merit in appointing ministers who have special expertise despite the fact that they have not been elected and are not members of either House. In practice, this is not currently permitted. The risk of allowing such persons to be appointed to influential posts with the prospect of exercising, or affecting the exercise of, governmental powers is that of lack of accountability. The risk of not doing so is the consequent loss of talent and expertise.

There are, no doubt, many ways in which these difficulties could be tackled. However, if it is accepted that some appointments of such persons outside Parliament are in principle justified, there seems little merit in banning special advisers or retaining the convention that requires all ministers to belong to one or other of the two Houses (especially when the House of Lords is currently non-elected).

The Constitution envisages that the appointment of special advisers should continue and that the convention whereby ministers must belong to one of the two Houses will cease except at Cabinet level. But the appointment of special advisers and ministers who are not members of a relevant elected body must be endorsed by the House of Representatives (see Article 85) and such appointees are required to provide regular progress reports to a special committee of that House (see Article 110).

These constitutional reforms in respect of special advisers do not affect the new reforms contained in the Constitutional Reform and Governance Bill 2009 (referred to in Notes to Part 11), which will run in parallel.

As to conferring executive functions by law, this is the most common source of such functions, and it is in substance the statutory source of power that renders the exercise of executive power subject to judicial review. Articles 81 and 90 make it clear that nothing in the Constitution is designed to change that state of affairs. However, any laws that are enacted which confer such functions must (see Article 5) be compatible with the Constitution.

The third method of exercising executive power permitted by the Constitution is through the transfer of prerogative power to executive government under Articles 91–92. This is considered immediately below.

Transferring prerogative power (Articles 91–92)   The transfer of most prerogative power from the Queen under Articles 91–92 forms part of a scheme of profound constitutional change as regards the Crown. Other significant proposed changes to the Crown are addressed below in the Notes on Articles 93–100.

In practice, and as a matter of constitutional convention, prerogative powers are exercised by the Prime Minister on (theoretical) behalf of the Queen. Many former prerogative powers were qualified during the Commonwealth and in the so-called Glorious Revolution of 1688. Others have over the centuries been restricted by statute. But some important powers remain. Of these, there are powers which are (in the words of the House of Commons Public Administration Select Committee) 'sweeping, but little-understood'. They allow governments to (amongst other things) ratify international treaties, go to war, regulate the civil service, issue passports and grant honours. However, none of them requires parliamentary approval and not all of them are even reviewable in the courts.

Gordon Brown had promised to reform the use of prerogative powers, and various proposals in the 2009 Constitutional Reform and Governance Bill currently before Parliament suggest such a change. However, by no means all prerogative power will be subject to fundamental change. In particular, neither a decision to go to war nor treaty ratifications will be subject to absolute parliamentary veto. The new Bill retains executive discretion to bypass parliamentary scrutiny in making treaties and there is only a governmental assurance that Parliament would, in practice, be consulted before a decision was made to go to war. Nothing in terms of a parliamentary veto is proposed to be enshrined in legislation. The most significant reform of the prerogative relates to management of the civil service, which is addressed separately in Part 11 of this Constitution.

The Constitution seeks to entrench this category of executive power by abolishing Crown prerogative altogether and making all pre-existing prerogative powers constitutional in nature (and so accountable to the courts) rather than allow it to become subject to the vagaries of intermittent and changing legislation. Thus, a number of prerogative powers currently exercised by the Crown (though in reality always exercised consistently with advice tendered by the Prime Minister) are formally transferred to the Prime Minister acting through Cabinet (see Article 92) but subject to the control of the Constitution.

Whether exercised by the Crown or the Prime Minister, it is strongly arguable that there should be tighter, not fewer, controls on the exercise of such powers and that immense powers of this kind should be subject to parliamentary veto. Controversial treaties have been (the Treaty of Accession to the Common Market) or could have been (the Treaty of Maastricht) ratified under the royal prerogative without Parliament being involved. In more recent times the Iraq war, declared in the face of strong public opposition, could have been embarked upon without the need for parliamentary endorsement. Likewise, the unjust extradition treaty negotiated between the UK and USA, which allows extradition to the USA without even a prima facie case having to be shown and with no reciprocity offered by the USA, did not need parliamentary endorsement.[75] The Constitution provides, at least in most cases, for a parliamentary veto by majority vote in such cases by the two Houses sitting as a single Assembly (see Article 91).[76]

---

[75] The Treaty has led to very controversial decisions such as that affecting the computer hacker Gary McKinnon, who, if extradition is confirmed, will it is claimed commit suicide. A further judicial review hearing of the decision of the Home Secretary not to prevent Mr McKinnon's extradition is scheduled for April or May 2010.

[76] It is for consideration whether the existence of parliamentary controls of this kind should prevail in true situations of emergency. The difficulties posed by emergency powers are considered in Part 6 and the Notes thereto. However, it is proposed that Parliament should always have a veto over certain executive powers. It is considered that, for example, a declaration of war would in reality be preceded by a period in which Parliament could be convened.

The monarchy (Articles 93–100) The issues surrounding changes to the constitutional position of the monarchy are likely to be controversial and will warrant the most careful consideration.

Abolition of the monarchy has often been proposed by a minority. But the break with centuries-old tradition that this would entail is not considered to be in the national interest (see also *Setting the Scene,* where the considerable virtues of the monarchy are discussed). One of the difficulties with half-way House of Lords reform is that tradition has been violated without any corresponding improvement in the vices that bedevil a wholly unelected body. Indeed, one of the many curiosities of the current House of Lords is that it is solely the hereditary peers who elect which of their dwindling number outside the Lords will replace those current members who die. Even where breaking with tradition is necessary it does not follow that the symbolic nature of that tradition should be destroyed.

However, a hereditary system of monarchy can only sensibly be defended if the monarch's authority is purely symbolic. That is precisely what is envisaged in Articles 93–100 (and Article 79, considered above). These provisions accept the principle of a hereditary monarch but set out procedures to be followed before the successor to the throne can become Head of State.

The change of substance is that the Head of State (whether monarch or President) is subservient to the Constitution. This is the position in nearly all democracies with a written Constitution and it would be the position if we had a truly constitutional monarchy. That is why Articles 94 and 98 mandate (as does the Belgian Constitution) the monarch's taking of an oath of allegiance to the Constitution before constitutional powers may be assumed.

Retaining the monarch as Head of State with essentially symbolic authority does not necessarily entail disestablishing the Church of England (of which the Queen is the supreme head). However, separating Church from State is a necessary precondition of a modern, secular constitution in which multiculturalism is an important foundation (see the Preamble and Notes thereto). Moreover, adherence to a hereditary monarchy and State Church has impeded reform of the House of Lords. Both the hereditary principle and the asserted need for bishops and archbishops in the House of Lords are said to be important. If they were replaced by an elected House, they would, it has been argued, be a threat to the continuation of the monarchy itself. The Constitution envisages that, amongst other things, the Church of England will be disestablished (see Article 95) and that inconsistent statutes (Article 97) will no longer have legal effect.

The powers retained by the Head of State are contained principally in Articles 12, 13, 79, 80 and 100. First, (Article 12) the Head of State must assent to all Bills presented save where the Supreme Court has, under new powers (see below), held that such legislation would be incompatible with the Constitution. Secondly, (Articles 79 and 93) the Head of State derives all power from the Constitution and any powers conferred are subject to the constraints imposed by the Constitution. Thirdly, (Article 79) the Head of State wields executive authority which symbolises the unity of the State. Fourthly, (Articles 13 and 80) the Head

of State appoints the Prime Minister but is constrained by the constitutional requirement that this must be the person best able to enjoy the confidence of
Parliament. This essentially replicates the present position where, in substance,
the Prime Minister is the head of the political party in power. As explained later,
all breaches of the Constitution are potentially actionable in the courts and it
follows that the Sovereign as Head of State (who according to current constitutional theory can do no wrong) could be subject to judicial review if the
constitutional power to appoint the Prime Minister were abused. Finally, the
Head of State has the express powers referred to in Article 100, which are more
symbolic than substantive in nature.

The changes envisaged here have the benefit of both retaining and modernising
the Crown as an institution. Modernisation is achieved by repealing the Royal
Marriages Act 1772 and those parts of other statutes (the Bill of Rights 1688,
Coronation Oath Act 1688, Act of Settlement 1700 and the Acts of Union) the
combined effect of which has primarily been to require the monarch to be a
Protestant and to declare allegiance to Protestantism, to prevent the monarch
from becoming or marrying a Roman Catholic, and to seek to ensure succession
through the male line. Some of these reforms (the religious requirement applying to a monarch's spouse and the preference for men in the line of succession)
were the subject of a Private Members' Bill in 2008–09—the Royal Marriages
and Succession to the Crown (Prevention of Discrimination) Bill—which was
adjourned due to lack of parliamentary time and was not, thereafter, proceeded
with.[77] Some of the language in Article 97 is taken from clause 1 of the abortive
Bill.

The Attorney-General (Articles 101–04)   The Attorney-General (A-G) is the
chief law officer of the Crown in England and Wales and provides legal advice
and, where appropriate, legal representation in court (often in sensitive criminal
prosecutions) on behalf of the Crown and departments of state. Yet, the A-G is
also supposed to serve as a key government minister. There is a clear conflict
of interest here, as was evidenced by the embarrassment over Lord Goldsmith,
as A-G, having to advise objectively on the legality of the Iraq war yet also having to defend the war as a government minister.[78] Similarly, the criminal probe
undertaken by the Serious Fraud Office into allegations of unlawful arms deals
between BAE Systems and Saudi Arabia was dropped after Tony Blair wrote to
the A-G pointing out that prosecutions could endanger national security.[79]

Difficulties of this kind would not arise if the A-G's role were confined to law
rather than embracing both law and politics. The Government originally proposed reforms to the office of A-G in the Green Paper leading up to the

---

[77] There have been suggestions that constitutional changes of this kind might require the consent
of the Commonwealth under the Statute of Westminster 1931. However, this is not considered by many
commentators to be an obstacle in practice and the effect of a written Constitution would be that the
former Royal statutes would no longer have legal effect (see Article 97).

[78] There is a growing view that the Iraq war was in fact illegal. See Johan Steyn, 'Not Just a Disaster:
Invading Iraq was Illegal' *Financial Times*, 1 December 2009. The open sessions of the Iraq Inquiry
began on 24 November 2009 and are continuing at the time of writing (January 2010).

[79] See Tom Clark, 'A New Politics: One Law for All' *The Guardian*, 20 May 2009.

introduction of what became the Constitutional Reform and Governance Bill 2009. However, these proposals have been dropped and are now unlikely to be proceeded with.

An argument often used against reform is that the A-G's dual role gives him a necessary wide perspective when providing legal advice and representation. However, such an argument could be said to be just as relevant to judicial membership of the House of Lords, which, it is now accepted, is a violation of the principle of separation of powers (see Notes on the Supreme Court below). This Constitution (see Articles 101, 103) does not allow the A-G to exercise functions of a political nature or to be a member of either House of Parliament, and requires the holder of such an office to resign membership of the Houses of the Parliament as a condition of appointment.

The executive and Parliament (Articles 105–11) Alongside the significant strengthening of parliamentary control over former prerogative powers (see above) there is a widely recognised need to strengthen the power of Parliament against the executive more generally. This is largely sought to be achieved by enhancing the select committee system that is currently increasingly relied upon in both the House of Commons and the House of Lords.

Select committees are committees that deal with specific fields or issues. They comprise a small number of members of the relevant House, chosen ostensibly for their expertise in those areas rather than for any party adherence. This gives them a degree of legitimacy and authority. Select committees of the House of Commons generally mirror the work of government departments and agencies, whereas those in the House of Lords are concerned with wider issues such as constitutional reform. Some select committees are joint committees of both Houses, such as the Joint Committee on Human Rights, which currently consists of six Members of Parliament and six members of the House of Lords.

There are, however, two significant practical difficulties which reduce the effectiveness of the committee system. First, it is the party managers (the whips) who are responsible—in practice—for choosing the membership, including the committee chairman. Secondly, the select committees have no real power. The result is that the committee system replicates in miniature parliamentary dynamics as a whole, which, as explained above, are heavily in favour of a strong executive and weak Parliament.

The reforms suggested in this Constitution greatly strengthen the select committees and emasculate the party whips (see Articles 106–11). What is first proposed is that the method of selecting members must change. The power to select members should be taken away from the party whips; the process should be undertaken instead by a secret and independent voting system to be decided by the House concerned (see Article 106). Secondly, the powers of the relevant committees should be enhanced in a number of ways, including conferring the power (currently lacking) to subpoena and examine witnesses (Article 108), to co-opt members with specialist expertise (Article 109), and—in the case of a relevant select committee of the House of Representatives—to ensure the parliamentary accountability of certain Prime Ministerial appointments of unelected persons (Article 110). A recommendation of the Power Inquiry (adopted in Article 107) was that an overarching select committee should be established, which would scrutinise how the executive acts on the international level.

Article 111 provides that both Houses of the Parliament have power to initiate legislation and public inquiries as provided for by law. The need for consideration of such a power by the relevant select committee with expertise in this area was recommended by the Power Inquiry, which was chaired by Baroness Kennedy. At present Parliament has no such power. If Parliament had such a power it would, in conjunction with stronger select committees, go some way to weakening the executive's control over what legislation is introduced. It would also make it more difficult for the executive to resist exposure in areas that central government would rather not and be subjected to public scrutiny. But the conditions of the exercise of such power require careful consideration.

PART 6
EMERGENCY POWERS

112. Emergency laws enacted by Parliament shall be subject to the provisions of, and effects provided for by, this Part of the Constitution and they may only be made in accordance with this Part of the Constitution. No emergency law may derogate from a fundamental provision of this Constitution as defined in Part 14 and any person or body having a sufficient interest in the matter may bring legal proceedings in the appropriate court or tribunal concerning such alleged breach by an emergency law or any other alleged breach of an emergency law under this part of the Constitution to the extent permitted by (as the case may be) Articles 113, 176 and 179.

113. Subject to Articles 112 and 180, no provision of this Constitution may be invoked, interpreted or applied so as to invalidate or seek to invalidate any law enacted by Parliament which is enacted in time of war or armed rebellion and which is expressed to be for the purpose of securing the public safety and the preservation of the State in time of war or armed rebellion, or to nullify any act done or purporting to be done in time of war or armed rebellion in pursuance of any such law, and the right of challenge under Articles 176 and 179 in respect of such law shall be limited accordingly.

114. Subject to this Part of the Constitution and to Articles 91–92, the Prime Minister may, acting in his or her own judgement, make emergency regulations if there is a serious threat to human welfare or the environment, or in case of war, armed rebellion or terrorism. Such emergency regulations will expire after seven days unless they are confirmed by Parliament.

115. Parliament may at any time enact a law under this Part of the Constitution conferring power on the Prime Minister acting alone or through Cabinet to proclaim a state of emergency in such circumstances and in such manner as the law permits. The law may include provisions conferring on the Prime Minister acting alone or through Cabinet the power to make regulations relating to the state of emergency and for such regulations to have effect for part or all of the period of the state of emergency. However, the law may not permit such regulations to remain in force after the state of emergency has expired in accordance with this Constitution.

116. A measure authorised by regulation or law referred to in Articles 114 and 115 (including measures taken under laws permitting such measures to be taken) may derogate from the rights and freedoms set out in this Constitution but only in accordance with this Constitution, only if the right or freedom in question is one which may be derogated from under this Constitution and only if the regulation or law or measure in question specifies in express terms that it is intended to derogate from specified rights and freedoms.

117. Upon a state of emergency being proclaimed in accordance with this Constitution the Head of State must, acting on the advice of the Prime Minister, summon a meeting of the Houses of the Parliament.

118. If the House of Representatives has been dissolved in accordance with this Constitution, the members of the Houses of the Parliament at the time when the House of Representatives was dissolved shall be summoned and those members shall have capacity to exercise all powers conferred on the Houses of the Parliament had the House of Representatives not been dissolved.

119. Once the state of emergency has expired in accordance with this Constitution the provisions of this Constitution shall re-engage as if a state of emergency had not been proclaimed. Time periods stipulated in this Constitution shall, even during a state of emergency, be complied with so far as is possible.

120. The Houses of the Parliament may at any time disallow the continuation of a state of emergency, or disallow or amend any regulations made by the Prime Minister under Article 114.

OBSERVATIONS AND EXPLANATORY NOTES

Overview—constitutional control of emergency powers   Most modern states rely on highly specific constitutional provisions that deal with what should happen in an emergency. This is because there is an ever-present danger that even the most liberal and well-intentioned executive will abuse its power when events can plausibly be argued to threaten the existence of the state itself. The legislative responses of both the US government (Guantanamo) and the British government (detention without trial) in the aftermath of the attacks on the United States that occurred on 11 September 2001 provide an illustrative example of the dangers that lurk below the surface of ostensibly stable democracies.

Whatever the legitimacy of extreme measures such as these, unless they are carefully controlled by a law enforceable by the courts and higher than those generated by a possibly over-reactive executive, the citizen's only 'right' will, at best, be to look to a law that fails adequately to protect him.

It has sometimes been suggested that there is a *paradox of constitutionalism*[80] which is that the people who are supposed to confer power on government are never, in fact, sovereign because the institutions and mechanisms through which power is exercised are in reality established and maintained by a dynamic series of processes in which—whatever a particular Constitution may say—power is simply not capable of being exercised on a 'popular' basis.

The difficulties thrown up by this 'paradox' may in practice be reduced, though never eliminated, by a precisely drafted Constitution in which the people have a clear and recurrent constitutional role. That is one of the purposes of Part 10 of this Constitution, which includes provisions for a Citizens' Branch embodied in a Citizens' Council through which a real constituent power is retained by the people which entitles them to place substantive constitutional constraints on the exercise of governmental power.

However, in the context of the exercise of *emergency* powers the problem is more acute. The rationale behind such powers is that the ordinary conditions under which law operates do not pertain in certain circumstances. Whatever legal constraints are placed upon the executive, there may be circumstances, which are impossible to predict, in which extra-legal power not only *may* but *must* be assumed in order to preserve the rule of law embodied in the Constitution for the future. If that logic is correct, it would seem to follow that no constitutional provisions can operate to prevent executive government taking whatever measures it sees fit in a real emergency.[81]

This, however, would be the real paradox of constitutionalism. Under a Constitution the power of the executive might be limited to that which is expressly or by necessary implication permitted by the Constitution, but logic would compel the conclusion that such a careful scheme of control would be undermined at the precise point at which it is most needed, namely from the point at which the nature of exercisable power is not defined at all.

The underlying question is therefore whether or not democratic government can ever claim to be free of the constraints of law as set out in a written Constitution in a situation of true emergency. If not, then it is inevitably possible for a tightly drafted Constitution to give voice to all classes of crisis situation that may arise and to limit the power of the government during such crises. If, by contrast, extra-legal governmental power may, in substance, always be exercised in an emergency, then it must also be the case that the courts have little, if any, power of constitutional control over the executive in that context.

---

[80] See Martin Loughlin and Neil Walker (eds), *The Paradox of Constitutionalism* (Oxford, Oxford University Press, 2007).

[81] See eg Viscount Radcliffe in *Burmah Oil Co v Lord Advocate* [1965] AC 75 who observed that the essence of emergency prerogative power is 'to act for the public good, where there is no law, or even to dispense with or override the law where the ultimate preservation of society is in question'.

In the landmark wartime ruling in *Liversidge v Anderson*,[82] the House of Lords by a majority considered that in an emergency situation the executive was outside any effective legal control. That case involved the internment (in prison) by the Home Secretary under emergency regulations of a man the Home Secretary claimed to have 'reasonable cause' to suspect of having 'hostile associations'. The majority of the House of Lords held that, as a matter of legal interpretation of the emergency regulations, the Home Secretary was permitted to exercise the emergency power of internment if he was acting in good faith. On that footing, the Home Secretary did not have to provide reasons for internment and his actions were not justiciable in the courts.

In a powerful dissenting judgment, which has largely been followed by the UK courts in more recent times, Lord Atkin considered that the question of whether there was reasonable cause for the Home Secretary's actions was an objective matter to be evaluated by the courts.

For a very long time, the exercise of royal prerogative power in the UK was also thought to be unreviewable by the courts. Since (as explained above) prerogative power includes a number of sweeping powers obviously capable of being assumed in an emergency (such as going to war), there was in effect neither law governing nor parliamentary control over many potential instances of the use of emergency powers. The fact that it was in reality the Prime Minister exercising power as the delegate of the Crown (see above) is, for present purposes, neither here nor there because it is the fact that our current constitutional arrangements allow essentially dictatorial emergency power to be exercised that is the essential vice, rather than the question of who actually exercises the power.

Although the prerogative is no longer exempt from judicial control, it remains the case that only certain types of prerogative power may be the subject of judicial review in the courts. It seems safe to say that exercises of emergency prerogative power would not be supervised by the courts. For example, in the wake of the decision in 2003 to declare war on Iraq, challenges were mounted as to the legality of that war. None of those challenges were considered to be suitable for adjudication by the courts.

In reality, though, it may be thought that the scope of the law can be extended as far as those legitimately making the law (whether they are, in the relevant context, judges or Parliament) wish it to be extended. As can be seen from *Liversidge v Anderson* itself, the judges in that case were interpreting emergency regulations and they could as easily have interpreted the regulations so as to bring the Home Secretary within the control of the court (as Lord Atkin did) as exclude supervision by the court (as the majority did). The more recent willingness of the courts to exercise control over the use of asserted executive emergency powers in the name of the royal prerogative provides a similar illustration that the common law control of the courts may be (and is being) extended incrementally. Even the common law doctrine of necessity, which, at

---

[82] [1942] AC 206.

least in some guises, allows for the use of extra-constitutional emergency power, subjects the exercise of such power to the control of the common law.

This Constitution takes as a premise, therefore, the potential for unlimited constitutional control over the executive, in the form of parliamentary control and/or in the form of judicial control as stipulated in the Constitution. There is no doctrinal, *a priori* reason for suggesting that the use of emergency powers enables governmental power to be exercised in defiance of a Constitution if the Constitution contains provisions that are sufficiently tightly drawn to limit its exercise.[83]

Emergency powers in time of war or armed rebellion (Articles 112–13)   The starting point is to identify the circumstances, if any, in which a Constitution recognises the immunity of executive action from judicial control by virtue of its emergency nature. Article 113 is modelled on a similarly worded provision found in the Constitution of the Republic of Ireland but with significant differences. Its intention is to prevent the courts in *most* situations from interpreting or applying the Constitution in such a way as to invalidate laws passed during a crisis caused by war or armed rebellion. It does not include acts of terrorism since these are not considered to pose any general threat to the rule of law, even though they may constitute an 'emergency' and, hence, be subject to other provisions of this part of the Constitution. It is perhaps for debate whether there can ever, sensibly, be a 'war against terrorism' in the sense advocated by former President Bush, but, as is made clear in the interpretation provisions set out in Part 14, the expression 'in time of war' does not encompass emergency measures in response to acts of terrorism.

Draconian as Article 113 is, however, there are a number of constraints. The first is that the combined effect of Articles 91–92 is to prevent a declaration of war without the approval of Parliament sitting as a single Assembly. The second constraint is that Article 113 is made subject to Article 180. This means that even emergency laws passed during a state of war or armed rebellion cannot interfere with the most fundamental rights, which may not be derogated from under any circumstances (as to which see Notes on Part 9 below and Article 180), This constraint has particular resonance in British society given the concerns over torture and rendition that have emerged in recent years. The third constraint is that no emergency law—even one subject to Article 113—may derogate from certain identified provisions of the Constitution (see Article 112, to which Article 113 is also subject). Thus, for example, no emergency law may—however temporarily—establish a dictatorship (see the definition of the expression 'fundamental provisions of the Constitution' in Article 246 and the provisions of the Constitution there referred to which permit or authorise derogation from certain fundamental rights).

---

[83] If the common law were to suggest otherwise, for example through the further development of the common law doctrine of necessity, then the common law itself would be susceptible to control by the provisions of the Constitution as the common law is capable of being abrogated or modified by Act of Parliament.

There is nonetheless an important difference between the emergency laws that may be passed if this country is at war or in a state of civil war and other emergency laws included in Articles 114–15. Provided that an emergency law passed in time of war or armed rebellion does not interfere with non-derogable rights or other fundamental provisions of the Constitution (as defined), it may not be invalidated and no act done pursuant to such laws will be capable of being nullified by the courts (see Article 113). Nor may any constitutional provision be interpreted to have such effect. This means that an otherwise defective law passed during the extreme conditions envisaged in Article 113 will continue to have legal effect if it does not infringe particular fundamental rights or fundamental constitutional provisions. The courts have traditionally been averse to statutory provisions purporting to oust their jurisdiction. However, Article 113 is a constitutional form of ouster provision and the courts would be acting in defiance of the Constitution (and hence unlawfully) if they purported to deny its effect (see Article 4).[84]

Other emergency powers (Articles 114–20)   Laws passed in other emergency situations are treated differently. A strict constitutional regime governs the passing of such laws, with an emergency power given to the Prime Minister to pass emergency regulations in prescribed circumstances (see Article 114). These broadly mirror the circumstances for the making of such regulations in the Civil Contingencies Act 2004, which (as with this Constitution) requires Parliament to confirm them after seven days, failing which the regulations will lapse. However, those provisions of the 2004 Act that permit the monarch to make such regulations are contrary to the Constitution and are therefore invalid (see Article 5).

Finally, an extended emergency regime is provided for in Articles 115 and 117–20. This allows Parliament to pass a law enabling the Prime Minister to proclaim a state of emergency and to make emergency regulations with legal effect during the period of such state of emergency.

As with emergency regulations or laws passed under Article 114, laws passed by Parliament under Article 115 and regulations made under such laws will be subject to judicial control (see Article 112).

---

[84] Importantly, however, the prerequisite for a law being passed under Article 113 is that there is in fact a 'time of war' or armed rebellion. It seems probable that the courts would reserve the right to inquire into whether that state of affairs (sometimes called 'precedent fact') actually existed.

PART 7
POLITICAL PARTIES

121. Subject to this Constitution and to the law[85], citizens have the right to form political parties and to join and to withdraw from them. However, this right may not be used to violate the fundamental liberties, the fundamental values, the democratic nature of the State or the sovereignty of the people (being the fundamental principles).[86]

122. Parties which violate the fundamental principles are unconstitutional and shall, on application duly made under this Constitution by the executive or by the Citizens' Council, where the Supreme Court has granted permission for the application to be made, be declared to be so by the Supreme Court. Such further relief as the Supreme Court considers within its jurisdiction to be necessary shall be granted by the Supreme Court if it makes a declaration of unconstitutionality[87], including the banning of a political party from operating for a period not exceeding six months, such period being capable of being renewed for further periods of six months on further application to the Supreme Court by the executive or by the Citizens' Council.

123. If the Supreme Court does not make a declaration of unconstitutionality, it must make a declaration of constitutionality[88] with such other relief acting within its jurisdiction as it considers necessary.

124. A declaration of constitutionality in respect of any political party may also be applied for in accordance with this Constitution by the Citizens' Council and must, where the Supreme Court has given permission for the application to be made, be granted by the Supreme Court with such other appropriate relief as, acting within its jurisdiction, it considers necessary if it is not, on such application, required to make a declaration of unconstitutionality by virtue of the conditions in Article 121 being satisfied and such other relief as, acting within its jurisdiction, it considers necessary.

125. Political parties and other public associations acting within the framework of this Constitution and laws shall have the right to use State mass media in accordance with law.

126. No political party shall be proclaimed or affirmed as a party or ideology of the State.

---

[85] There are, of course, a great many requirements of electoral law, including registration of political parties with the Electoral Commission and the maintaining of accounts pursuant to regulations laid down by the Commission. These detailed requirements should not, however, form part of a Constitution.

[86] The term 'fundamental principles' is defined in Part 14.

[87] This term is defined in Part 14.

[88] This term is defined in Part 14.

127. The State shall, subject to this Constitution, provide political parties acting within the framework of this Constitution and laws with adequate resources in a fair manner according to law. Political parties must account publicly for the sources and uses of their funds and for their assets which are permitted by law in accordance with a procedure determined by law.

OBSERVATIONS AND EXPLANATORY NOTES

Overview—problems with the modern party system   Political parties are the backbone of modern politics, in that, in substance, they control the political process. This is so for two basic reasons, which are closely connected. First, the majority party is able to dominate Parliament and thereby almost invariably ensure that the laws it wishes to pass are in fact enacted. Secondly, all parties in the UK are now highly organised through the whipping system, which, amongst other things, usually guarantees that party members attend Parliament and vote according to party policy.

The reason why whipping is so important is that if it works perfectly the majority party will always win a parliamentary vote. A carefully calibrated system of rewards and sanctions from the whips is directed towards achieving that objective. The narrower the majority, the more important effective whipping will be since a more tightly organised Opposition may otherwise defeat the Government and, in extreme circumstances, precipitate an election.

In practice MPs are sent a letter by the Chief Whip every week during a parliamentary session, detailing the week's debates. There appears alongside each debate a single sentence such as 'Your attendance is absolutely essential' or 'There will be a [one/two/three] line whip'. That sentence is underlined one, two or three times (hence the expression *three line whip*) depending on the importance attached by the whips to attendance and the severity of the sanction in the event of non-attendance. Sanctions are usually known (sometimes negotiated) in advance and are often tailored to the individual MP, about whose life and aspirations the whips will have considerable inside information.

The party system and the way in which Parliament is organised more generally raise serious questions about the nature of representative democracy at the present time. In reality, MPs follow the party line rather than engaging with the issues, not only because of the whips (see below) but also because it is only by following the party line that they will be 'given a job'.

Because the majority party dominates Parliament there is simply no alternative career progression in Parliament. As explained elsewhere (see Notes to Part 5), even membership of parliamentary select committees is in practice controlled by the whips. Further, if a three-line whip is defied, career demotion is inevitable, and effective expulsion from the party (by the whip being withdrawn)[89] is highly likely.

---

[89] Losing the party whip does not prevent an MP from attending Parliament. However, in practice an MP is highly unlikely to retain his or her seat if not adopted as a party candidate. The result of the whip being lost is that the MP no longer commands the support of the party in Parliament and is in effect expelled from the party.

The aspiring MP, minister or shadow minister is therefore overwhelmingly likely to look to the party machine rather than to his or her conscience when deciding how to vote. As one seasoned observer (and MP) has put it with a degree of irony: 'Members of Parliament are bombarded with representations from pressure groups and others about all the issues of the day, especially in the context of legislation and votes, as though they were dispassionate and independent legislators rather than the willing slaves of the whips.'[90]

These are not the only obstacles to a more effective representative democracy thrown up by the current party system in the UK. By its very nature party politics reflects a struggle for power amongst the main parties. The election manifesto of each party is not in substance an attempt by that party to represent the electorate; it is rather only a statement of which policies it intends to implement if elected. Therefore, the claim that a party is elected on the basis of the policies set out in its manifesto is, whilst being true, misleading in terms of its supposed democratic credentials. The fuller truth is that a party is elected on the basis of what policies it *chooses* to include in its manifesto.

There may thus be policy areas where the major parties speak with the same voice despite the fact that the tide of public opinion is in favour of a different policy. Aspects of constitutional reform, particularly electoral reform of FPTP, may fall into this category. Equally, parties may have different policies and voters may agree with some of the policies of one party but prefer other policies of another. How are they to vote?

Under the current system, it may be thought that political parties cannot, sensibly, lay claim to being the only legitimate vehicle for a system of representative democracy and that a better form of representative democracy would be one in which constitutional devices reduced the dominance of the parties. This is all the more so when the rapidly declining membership of our political parties is taken into account. Membership has declined across the board since the 1950s, when Labour had over a million members and the Conservatives had nearly three million. In 1997, Labour had around 405,000 members. It now has about 150,000 members and the Conservatives currently have around 250,000.[91] In terms of not being truly representative, declining party membership is compounded by an FPTP electoral system in which minor parties are effectively squeezed out, preventing them from having any effective representative influence in Parliament (see Notes to Part 3).

This suggests that whilst a dwindling number of members of one of the two major parties might be properly represented by their party, the vast majority of the electorate are not adequately represented. For this reason there is a plausible case for open primaries to elect party candidates in which the general public, as well as party members, have a voice in choosing their MP and by which means, it might be hoped, a wider interest and engagement in the political

---

[90] See Tony Wright, *British Politics: A Very Short Introduction* (Oxford, Oxford University Press, 2003).

[91] These figures are taken from *The New British Constitution* by Vernon Bogdanor (Oxford, Hart Publishing, 2009).

process is engendered.[92] However, the argument for open primaries is by no means decisive and the question of whether they should be funded by the state (as opposed to the individual party choosing to do so) is probably a matter for legislation rather than constitutional provision. This Constitution therefore makes no separate provision for a system of state-funded open primaries based on the US model.

It can be seen from the above discussion that the issues regarding political parties overlap with other sections of this Constitution and are in some ways dependent for their effective resolution on being tackled as a whole. For example, a more representative electoral system engendered by PR will introduce greater pluralism into politics by reducing two-party dominance. The provisions set out in Part 5 of this Constitution, introducing changes to the relationship between Parliament and the executive, also necessarily reduce the dominance of the party in government. Paradoxically, perhaps, the weakening of parliamentary sovereignty under a written Constitution of this kind will therefore strengthen rather than weaken the power of Parliament as an institution. The creation of a Citizens' Branch and Council with specific provision for referendums on important constitutional issues is another indirect way of grappling with the present constitutional imbalance caused by a party political system that has, it is strongly arguable, become far too mechanistic and serves as much the interests of those in power as those they are there to represent.

Part 7 of this Constitution should therefore be read in the context of more general issues raised by the need to control political parties. What it addresses are more direct issues of control over the operation of the party system.

Banning political parties (Articles 121–24)   It is important to emphasise that, whatever their practical deficiencies, political parties are essential to a healthy, functioning democracy. Without them, representation would simply not be possible. That is why some Constitutions state this expressly. For example, Article 8 of the Romanian Constitution provides, under the heading *Political Parties,* that 'pluralism … is a condition and safeguard of Constitutional democracy'.

The overarching question is whether—given their importance—there should be direct prohibitions on the operation of political parties in a democracy, especially restrictions allowing for such parties to be banned. In principle, Article 10 of the ECHR permits the banning of political parties and there is recent precedent for the outlawing even by some liberal democracies of religious and radical parties considered to be undemocratic. The Spanish Law of 2002 banning Basque separatist parties is one such example.

As a general principle it is intrinsic to a liberal, and hence pluralist, society that diversity of views must be tolerated, however objectionable those views may be.[93] Yet, there may be a danger in not restricting the scope of that principle in exceptional cases. A party that has a fundamental objection to the very exis-

---

[92] In *Tribune* (7 August 2009) David Milliband argues the case for open primaries; see www.tribunemagazine.co.uk. The Conservatives held an open primary in the Totnes by-election in 2009.

[93] An illustration of the dilemmas this may pose was provided by the BBC inviting Nick Griffin, the leader of the BNP, onto its *Question Time* panel on 22 October 2009.

tence of democracy could, once elected, proceed to demolish those institutions it had relied upon to secure power. There is a parallel difficulty in the right of freedom of expression, which is discussed in greater detail later (see Notes to Part 9). The difficulty is that the benefits of permitting free expression may sometimes be outweighed by the damage that free expression causes. A similar difficulty attends the issue of emergency powers (see Notes to Part 6). Is the rule of law always sufficient to protect the state from destruction? Are there not at least some crisis situations in which the law itself must step back?

This Constitution starts from the premise that there are exceptional circumstances in which there should be some judicial control over the operation of political parties. Those circumstances (see Article 121) exist where a party is acting in violation of certain fundamental principles as defined which materially threaten representative democracy (see Notes to Part 14 on Interpretation).

However, whereas some Constitutions impose conditions on political parties as a *sine qua non* of their continued operation, this Constitution adopts (with some modification) a device used in the German Constitution and leaves effective control with the Supreme Court provided that an application is made to it by either the executive or the Citizens' Council (see Articles 122–24).

The Supreme Court may only act within its jurisdiction (which is further discussed in Part 8), but, beyond being required to declare a party to be unconstitutional if the requisite conditions are satisfied, it may decide what further relief, if any, to grant. In particular, it need not necessarily ban a party outright but may impose conditions under which that party is permitted to continue to operate. Banning orders (see Article 122) may not be for more than six months at a time but such orders may be renewed on application to the Supreme Court. Such a power is not unheard of; the Israeli and Turkish courts have similar powers. However, given the intense political nature of the question, some may think it more desirable to give the courts a secondary rather than a primary role. A possible alternative to the proposals set out here would be for an independent commission (with no affiliation to existing parties) to be set up in order to determine the constitutionality of political parties in accordance with the 'fundamental principles' mentioned in Article 121, and the Supreme Court could then be given the power to judicially review the decisions of such a commission.

Whether by the method proposed in Article 122 or a suitable alternative such as that canvassed immediately above, the rival dangers of, on the one hand, the state abusing the constitutional mechanism for control of political parties and, on the other, parties flouting minimum democratic standards are sought to be reduced. A further attempt at reducing risk within the Article 122 mechanism is the above-mentioned provision that enables the Citizens' Council to seek a declaration of constitutionality (as well as unconstitutionality) in respect of political parties, either of which the Supreme Court must grant if the conditions for their granting are satisfied. In this way, the Citizens' Council can act independently of the executive and seek appropriate relief from the Supreme Court.

Use of mass media and party funding (Articles 125, 127)   Of course, political parties are also subject to the general law, where applicable, and Articles 125 and 127 grant parties operating within the framework of the law the specific rights there referred to. Conformity with the law is, however, a precondition of such rights being conferred. Thus, a party such as the BNP, which has had a controversial membership policy and which was the subject of legal action instituted by the Equality Commission alleging it to be in breach of race relations laws, would not, if that action had succeeded—however large it became—have any right to use the mass media (Article 125) or to receive state funding (Article 127), both of which are proposed under this Constitution. At present the BNP has agreed to reconsider its membership policy in the light of that legal action.

State funding of political parties is a somewhat controversial area. The costs of political campaigning are increasingly high and are not met by a system of state funding, although a few state grants (to opposition parties) are available and indirect costs (such as expenditure on party political broadcasts) are defrayed by the state. The result of insufficient state provision (perhaps paralleled in the arena of MPs' relatively low salaries and the expenses scandal) has been a lack of transparency over how parties are being financed and the true extent of loans and donations comprising important elements of funds and assets.

The law has moved quite quickly in response to increased public concern. Thus, initially, Parliament enacted the Political Parties, Elections and Referendums Act 2000, which amongst other provisions[94] required details of parties' income and expenditure and donations to be disclosed. However, the parties effectively circumvented these provisions by taking out *loans* (as opposed to receiving *donations*). This led to amendments being introduced to the Electoral Administration Act 2006 mandating the disclosure of donations as well as loans.

A police investigation was conducted with regard to whether criminal offences might have been committed by the promising of honours in return for loans. While this investigation did not result in any prosecutions, it took place in a climate of hostile public opinion reminiscent of the expenses furore that later occurred in the early summer of 2009.

It is against this unsatisfactory historical background that the need for state funding of parties is being advocated. There are advantages and disadvantages. The advantages lie in the fact that, as noted above, political parties are an essential part of the democratic process. Absence of state funding carries with it risks such as business interests exerting control over party policy and a loss of public confidence in the honours system, which is particularly susceptible to abuse in this context. The main disadvantages of state funding are (in the present financial climate) the increased burden on public spending and, perhaps, concerns over whether it is appropriate to force the taxpayer to support a party financially when he does not support that party.

In this Constitution there is a proposal for state funding of political parties (see Article 127). The requirement is, however, couched in the most general terms.

---

[94] These included the establishment of an Electoral Commission to oversee the new rules. However, the Commission had no powers of prosecution.

A number of studies investigating possible funding mechanisms have recently been undertaken. The most authoritative is the review conducted by Sir Hayden Phillips, which was published in 2007. The principal recommendations were that donations should be capped at £50,000, that there should be increased state funding as the present situation was unsatisfactory, that there should be greater regulation and transparency with stricter control of donations and loans from third parties, and that there should be a reduction in allowable expenditure on general elections.

However, Sir Hayden Phillips' proposals have not resulted in consensus. This is unsurprising. Whilst capping donations seems sensible in principle and would eliminate scandals such as the Ecclestone affair,[95] there is asymmetry between the parties, which makes the practical detail of party funding—even if accepted in principle—significant. For example, Labour derives around 30 per cent of its income from trade union donations and, though there may be ways of structuring a cap on the political levy paid by individual members,[96] a simple £50,000 cap on union donations as a class would not seem to be equitable. The size of any cap is also controversial. Some, such as James Purnell MP, argue that it should be in the hundreds of pounds in order to encourage small donors, in the spirit of those who swept Barack Obama to power in the 2008 US presidential election. Others argue that this is simply unrealistic and too uncertain to produce an adequate level of funding.

Matters of detail such as these, although extremely important, do not obviously raise issues of constitutional principle. This is why Article 127 leaves the details to be worked out in legislation.

PART 8
THE JUDICIARY

JUDICIAL POWER

128. The structure, powers and functions of the courts and judges of the United Kingdom at all levels shall be as prescribed by this Constitution.[97]

129. Subject to this Constitution, judges shall hold their office during good behaviour for such period as shall be laid down by law except that the maximum

---

[95] This involved a £1 million donation to the Labour Party by Bernie Ecclestone, which was made just before the announcement that Formula One (Ecclestone's company) would be exempt from the ban on smoking in sport.

[96] As suggested by James Purnell MP (see 'It's All About the Money' *The Guardian*, 29 May 2009).

[97] Some Constitutions contain specific provisions as to the structure of the judiciary. Such detailed provisions are not considered appropriate for a written Constitution (and in any event, the structures differ as between the different nations of the UK). As can be seen, the general intention is not to disturb the overall judicial structure but to leave that to be addressed in legislation if necessary.

age, if any, at which the law may stipulate compulsory retirement for any judge shall not be lower than 65 years of age. Judges shall be paid a salary and pension to be determined by law for their services.

130. Subject to this Constitution, the appointment and removal from office of judges shall be governed by law.

131. In the exercise of its jurisdiction, the judiciary is independent of the legislative and executive branches of government and is also independent of the Citizens' Branch.

132. Judges must, within their jurisdiction, interpret and apply the provisions of this Constitution and law compatibly with this Constitution.

133. The judiciary shall, as prescribed by law, be accountable both in terms of the individual judges and as an institution for the undertaking of functions under this Constitution and the law.

134. As an institution, the judiciary derives its constitutional status from this Constitution and from such laws as may be, and are, made that are compatible with this Constitution.

135. The rights and obligations of the United Kingdom from time to time under international treaties that have been ratified by the United Kingdom (including those under European Union law and under the European Convention on Human Rights) shall form part of this Constitution to the extent that such rights and obligations shall inform the judicial interpretation of the provisions of this Constitution and of the law. However, rights and obligations under international treaties shall not, save as otherwise provided for by this Constitution, be enforceable at the suit of parties in the courts.

136. In the case of European Union law that law will have the same force and effect in this Constitution as under the European Communities Act 1972 and laws that violate European Union law shall violate this Constitution.

137. In the case of the European Convention on Human Rights the rights and obligations therein contained shall, subject to this Constitution, be directly enforceable in the courts against public authorities within the meaning of the Human Rights Act 1998, and laws that violate the European Convention on Human Rights shall also violate this Constitution to the extent prescribed by this Constitution.

138. If and to the extent that there is any conflict between the provisions of European Union law and the other rights protected by this Constitution, including those contained in the European Convention on Human Rights,[98] the courts

---

[98] The European Convention on Human Rights holds a special place in EU law but is not binding on the European Court of Justice in Luxembourg. Conflicts between the two systems of law can therefore occasionally occur, although in practice both the European Court of Justice and the European Court of Human Rights (which sits in Strasbourg) try to avoid direct conflicts.

shall give priority to applying the other rights protected by this Constitution but must in such a case refer a question or questions to the European Court of Justice for a preliminary ruling. The preliminary ruling of the European Court of Justice will then bind the Court whatever the result. However, if and to the extent that European Union law would otherwise be in breach of this Constitution the Court shall make a declaration of incompatibility[99] that the provision of European Union law in question is incompatible with this Constitution. Such declaration shall not affect the validity of the European Union law provision in question.

139. The highest judicial power and jurisdiction shall vest in the Supreme Court established by this Constitution. The composition, constitutional power and jurisdiction of the Supreme Court are derived solely from this Constitution and must be exercised subject to this Constitution. However, nothing appertaining to the constitutional power and jurisdiction vested in the Supreme Court affects the distinctions between the separate legal systems of the parts of the United Kingdom.

140. Judicial power shall otherwise vest as prescribed by this Constitution and by law provided that such laws are compatible with this Constitution.

141. Laws shall make provision, or continue to make provision, for both superior courts of record and inferior courts and tribunals in the United Kingdom and for a comprehensive system of appeals. No court or tribunal below the level of the Supreme Court shall have greater power than the Supreme Court in the application of the law to the proceedings before it. No court or tribunal below the level of the Supreme Court shall have the constitutional powers conferred on the Supreme Court in Articles 12, 122–24 or this Part of this Constitution, or the power to declare primary legislation to be unconstitutional.

THE SUPREME COURT

142. The permanent judges of the Supreme Court comprise the President and eleven Justices. One of the permanent judges who is not the President shall be appointed Deputy President by majority vote of the other permanent judges in accordance with a procedure determined by the President.

143. The Court is to be taken to be duly constituted despite any vacancy among the judges of the Court or in the office of President. However, in order to be duly constituted the Court must consist of at least seven judges,[100] there must

---

[99] This term is defined in Part 14.

[100] There is a strong case for a greater number of Supreme Court judges hearing the most important cases, which by definition come to the Supreme Court: see David Pannick QC, '"Better that a Horse should have a Voice in that House [of Lords] than that a Judge should" (Jeremy Bentham). Replacing the Law Lords by a Supreme Court Lord' [2009] *Public Law* 723, 733–34.

be an uneven number of judges and more than half must be permanent judges of the Court.

144. Each permanent judge of the Court must, before assuming office and as a condition of exercising office, take an oath of allegiance to this Constitution as set out in Schedule [ ] and in the manner there prescribed.

145. Additional members of the Supreme Court may at the request of the President or, if the President is not available, the Deputy President, and provided that the Court is duly constituted, sit on the Supreme Court as non-permanent judges if they fulfil the qualifications specified by law, and may sit on the Supreme Court for such periods as may be specified by law.

146. The Supreme Court shall, subject to this Constitution, have final responsibility for interpreting this Constitution and shall accept references on questions of constitutional interpretation that are made to it in accordance with this Constitution by other inferior courts or tribunals. Where such a question is raised before any such court or tribunal, that court or tribunal may, if it considers that a decision on the question is necessary to enable it to give judgment, request the Supreme Court to give a ruling thereon provided that it considers that the conditions for exercise of the jurisdiction of the Supreme Court as set out in Article 162 are satisfied.

147. Where any such question is raised in a case pending before an inferior court or tribunal against whose decisions there is no judicial remedy, that court or tribunal shall bring the matter by way of request for a preliminary ruling before the Supreme Court provided that it considers that the conditions for exercise of the jurisdiction of the Supreme Court as set out in Article 162 are satisfied. There shall be a right to seek permission to appeal to the Supreme Court from a court or tribunal required to seek a preliminary ruling by any party whose application for a referral to the Supreme Court has been refused and who contends that such referral ought to have been made.

148. If the Supreme Court needs to interpret the provisions of this Constitution concerning affairs which are the express responsibility of the Prime Minister or executive under this Constitution and if such interpretation would otherwise determine the result in a manner adverse to the Prime Minister or executive, the Supreme Court shall, before making any final judgment, ruling or opinion which is not appealable, seek an interpretation of the relevant provisions from the Cabinet. The Supreme Court shall take such interpretation into account when giving its judgment, ruling or opinion.

149. Where a reference is made to the Supreme Court by another court or tribunal in accordance with this Constitution or on appeal by a party entitled to seek permission to appeal under Article 147, the Supreme Court shall, if it grants permission for the making of such reference, give a preliminary ruling on the questions referred to it.

150. The Prime Minister may in the public interest and on the advice of the Cabinet refer to the Supreme Court for its opinion any question as to the effect of a provision of this Constitution that has arisen or appears likely to arise, and the Supreme Court must, if the application is properly brought and it has given permission for the reference to be made, state its opinion on the question.

151. The Citizens' Council may in the public interest and subject to this Constitution refer to the Supreme Court for its opinion any question as to the effect of a provision of this Constitution that has arisen or that appears likely to arise, and the Supreme Court must, if the application is brought in accordance with this Constitution and it has given permission for the reference to be made, state its opinion on the question.

152. Bills proposed to be enacted by Parliament must, if the Attorney-General advises that a question arises as to the compatibility of the Bill with this Constitution, be referred by the Prime Minister to the Supreme Court for a declaration that such Bill would, if enacted, be compatible with this Constitution. If, on such reference made in accordance with this Constitution, the Supreme Court considers, having given permission for the reference to be made, that such Bill would, if enacted, not be compatible with this Constitution it must make a declaration to that effect.[101]

153. The Supreme Court shall have jurisdiction to hear appeals from other courts and tribunals according to law. Laws made which provide for appeal to the Supreme Court shall not provide for any lesser access to the Supreme Court from a lower court or tribunal than was available in laws existing immediately prior to the coming into force of this Constitution. In any case where the Supreme Court is entitled by law to refuse permission for the making of an appeal and does refuse permission it shall state its reasons for refusing permission to appeal.

154. Nothing in the content or legal effect of the jurisdiction of the Supreme Court under the Constitutional Reform Act 2005 in relation to devolution matters as defined in the Constitutional Reform Act 2005 shall be affected by this Constitution save insofar as it is amended by law. However, exercise of the jurisdiction of the Supreme Court in respect of devolution matters must otherwise conform to this Constitution and be consistent and compatible with the powers granted by this Constitution.

---

[101] The Supreme Court here grants a declaration of *incompatibility* rather than a declaration of *unconstitutionality* as the Bill, not having received assent under Article 12, is not yet law.

155. The Supreme Court shall have power to determine any question necessary to be determined for the purpose of doing justice in proceedings before it.[102]

156. Apart from its jurisdiction conferred by this Constitution, including the power to grant preliminary rulings on questions of law referred to it by other courts or tribunals, declarations of constitutionality and declarations of unconstitutionality under specific provisions of this Constitution, and to give advisory opinions, the Supreme Court shall have power to grant any relief in proceedings before it which the Supreme Court as defined in the Constitutional Reform Act 2005 could have granted, or would have been required to grant, immediately before the coming into force of this Constitution.

157. In any other case before it the Supreme Court must grant a declaration of unconstitutionality in respect of legislation, including primary legislation, and any other measure, act or omission which it finds to be in breach of this Constitution except that in the case of a provision of European Community law which it finds to be in breach of this Constitution it must make a declaration of incompatibility and the validity of the Community law provision in question shall not be affected.

158. Administrative arrangements for the Supreme Court, including the payment of judicial salaries and pensions, and all other matters relating to that Court which are not otherwise regulated by this Constitution, shall be governed by law.

CONSTITUTIONAL APPLICATIONS AND REFERENCES TO THE
SUPREME COURT

159. No application or reference permitted to be made direct to the Supreme Court as provided for in this Constitution may be entertained by the Supreme Court unless the Supreme Court has granted permission for the making of the application or reference.

160. The Supreme Court may refuse permission for the making of any such application or reference made to it but must give its reasons for declining to entertain such application or reference. However, permission for the making of any such application or reference may only be refused in accordance with this Constitution.

---

[102] Article 155 is quite open-ended and may lead to complicated debate and discussion during court proceedings, especially with regard to its relationship with other specific provisions that set out the basis for the exercise of the Supreme Court's powers. It is for consideration whether such a provision is necessary.

161. The Supreme Court must refuse permission for the making of such application or reference unless the conditions for the exercise of its jurisdiction are satisfied.

162. The conditions for the exercise of the Supreme Court's jurisdiction are that the application or reference in question involves a question or questions of interpretation of this Constitution, or of the validity under this Constitution of acts or omissions which give rise to constitutional obligations or rights.[103]

163. The Supreme Court may refuse to allow such application or reference to be made unless it considers that the application or reference in question raises issues of constitutional importance or that it is in the public interest that the application or reference in question should be determined.

APPOINTMENT AND REMOVAL OF JUDGES. ADMINISTRATIVE PROVISIONS

164. Provision shall be made in law for the appointment of judges of courts and tribunals at all levels by an independent Judicial Appointments Commission. The composition and manner of selection of the members of the Commission shall be determined by law but it must be independent of the legislative, executive and judicial branches of government.

165. The procedure for making judicial appointments by the Commission shall be specified in law but must be independent of the legislative, executive and judicial branches of government. In making decisions on judicial appointments the Commission must follow a fair and transparent process and shall make the final decision as to which judges are to be appointed. The Commission shall select only the best candidates in terms of merit by reference to selection criteria which must give priority to independence of mind, high intellect, excellent judgement and integrity, and also taking into account any other general obligations under this Constitution. However, no candidate may be considered who fails to fulfil the qualifications prescribed by law in terms of legal experience.

166. Subject to this Constitution, judges shall not be dismissed, or retired before the age prescribed by this Constitution, nor shall they be deprived in real terms of the whole or part of their salaries, allowances or other rights relating to their status.

---

[103] Some jurisdictions (eg the USA) have adopted the *doctrine of constitutional avoidance*, which provides that the court should avoid interpreting statutes etc in a way that would raise constitutional questions. The motivation is to avoid making issues constitutional issues if they can be dealt with in some other way. Consideration should perhaps be given to entrenching such a doctrine in the Constitution as a canon of interpretation in order to avoid unnecessary disputes under provisions such as these.

167. Exceptions may be indicated in law relating to those convicted of an offence requiring dismissal from the profession, those who are established as unable to perform their duties on account of ill-health, and those determined to be unfit to continue in judicial office.

168. The manner by which judges may, subject to this Constitution, be removed from office shall be specified by law except that judges of the Supreme Court or of any Superior Court of Record may only be removed by the Head of State on an address[104] by both Houses of the Parliament.

169. Administrative arrangements for courts, tribunals and judges including the payment of judicial salaries and pensions, and all other matters relating to those courts, tribunals and judges which are not otherwise regulated by this Constitution, shall be governed by law.

OBSERVATIONS AND EXPLANATORY NOTES

Overview—constitutional role of judges Some constitutional tensions arise when considering what the constitutional position of judges should be in society. Judges are not legislators. This is a necessary consequence of the doctrine of separation of powers. Nonetheless, the judiciary is an important branch of government because it interprets and applies the laws that the legislature enacts and the executive enforces.

The first tension is that between *making* law and *deciding* law. The reality is that in interpreting and applying laws, judges are being forced into something of a political role. It is hard to deny that one of the consequences of the introduction of recent legislation, including devolution statutes and the HRA 1998, is that a measure of political power has passed from Parliament and the executive to the judiciary.

Though classed as legal rulings, many of the judgments made in court are now capable of overturning parliamentary legislation or executive acts. In recent years there have been challenges in court to highly politically controversial government decisions such as the legality of the Iraq war, the validity of the Parliament Act and the internment without trial of foreign terrorist suspects.

Law is not an abstract entity with an identity always easily separable from that of political and executive decision-making. In substance, when judges decide that legislation is contrary to law, one constitutional body (the judiciary) is usually making a value judgement as to the appropriateness of a set of rules decided on by another constitutional body (the executive) and (because we have an over-strong executive) only formally legislated for by a third constitutional body (the legislature—Parliament).

Judges are empowered to make such value judgements because the language of the law is, in such a context, largely open-ended. Interferences with many

---

[104] An 'address' in the sense used here means a statement or opinion of one or both of the Houses of Parliament that is sent to the sovereign.

fundamental rights, for example, are unlawful under the ECHR if they are not *necessary in a democratic society.* Yet whether a measure is or is not necessary in a democratic society is not a hard-edged question of law. It represents a subjective decision with implicit policy content.

Responses to these tensions are not always logical. It is sometimes suggested that there is a conflict between unelected judges and an elected Parliament which is contrary to democracy. Yet, as has been seen, the process by which laws come to be made is largely executive-driven, with, for reasons already discussed (see Notes to Part 7), an essentially complaisant Parliament. Judges, it may be argued, provide an essential check on an over-mighty executive which is not otherwise effected in an organic fused-powers constitution of the kind we currently have in the UK. Nonetheless, even if this is true—and whatever the imperfections of our present electoral system—it leaves a wholly unelected body potentially capable of interfering with the decisions of an elected body on a basis that is arguably too imprecise and too uncertain.

A second tension arises from the fact that the doctrine of parliamentary sovereignty—the doctrine used to explain the judges' limited constitutional role (Parliament legislates, judges interpret)—no longer provides either a complete or a satisfactory constitutional basis for the different roles now played by the different branches of government and, in particular, by the judiciary.

A series of body-blows to the principle of parliamentary sovereignty, even in terms of constitutional theory, can now be seen to have been delivered by various events over the past 30 years or so. Accession to the EU and the enactment of the European Communities Act 1972 were the first of these events. The clear result of the incorporation of EU law into national law is that—because of the well-established EU principle of European Union law supremacy over national laws—parliamentary legislation can no longer be applied if it is found by the domestic court to breach EU law. Although efforts have been made to explain why this is not an abandonment of sovereignty,[105] the reality is that EU law prevails over laws enacted by Parliament whenever there is a conflict.

Another development that has made it difficult to rely on parliamentary sovereignty as an explanation for what judges actually do is the expansion of judicial review to encompass control by the judiciary over bodies which have not been created by Parliament at all. This development was introduced in 1987 by the Court of Appeal's ruling in the *Datafin* case,[106] in which a non-statutory body (the Panel on Takeovers and Mergers) was held to be amenable to judicial review. The difficulty, as many commentators noted at the time, was that this otherwise welcome judicial activism had no obvious constitutional source of authority and certainly could not be explained by invoking parliamentary sovereignty.

---

[105] See eg Lord Bridge in *R v Secretary of State for Transport, ex p Factortame Ltd* [1990] 2 AC 85 who suggested that the exercise of sovereignty lay precisely in the fact that Parliament chose when passing the 1972 Act to permit European Union law to have supremacy over parliamentary law.
[106] *R v Panel on Takeovers and Mergers plc, ex p Datafin* [1987] QB 815.

A more recent body-blow to the supposed axiom of sovereignty came, perhaps ironically, from the constitutional reforms introduced by the Blair Government from 1997, and especially from the enactment of the HRA 1998. Taking that Act as the best example, ingenious attempts were made in its drafting to preserve parliamentary sovereignty by not allowing the courts to strike down legislation in the manner of the US Supreme Court. Instead, the courts could only grant a declaration of incompatibility between laws found to offend against human rights and the requirements of the ECHR.

However, nearly all declarations of incompatibility made by the courts have either been complied with or are intended to be complied with.[107] They could, it may be thought, hardly not be. It would be impossible, politically, for a government to defy such a declaration. In this context it may therefore be seen that whilst parliamentary sovereignty survives with its analytic integrity intact, we are left with more words than substance.

The absence of an adequate explanation in constitutional terms for what judges are doing is easily solved by a written Constitution. This is because in a written Constitution the source of authority for what each of the different branches of government may do is the Constitution itself. The more difficult question is what to include in such a Constitution, since the tension between unelected judges and elected politicians remains, has the potential for friction, and needs to be carefully addressed.

It should first be noted that the very fact of a written Constitution should eliminate the prospect (whether heretical or not) of continued judicial assertion of some undefined common law control over Parliament. In recent years some senior judges have made statements to the effect that parliamentary sovereignty may itself be a construct of the common law rather than a separate constitutional doctrine.[108] The result, if this were correct, would be that the judges would enjoy uncontrolled power despite being wholly unelected. This is on any view antithetical to the idea of a representative democracy. In a Constitution this could not happen because common law (which provides the only basis for such assertion of power) is, necessarily, subordinate to the terms of the Constitution.

What a written Constitution must do is grapple with the fact that judges are not elected. There are different means of addressing this. One possibility is to provide for the election of judges, as in the US system below the federal Supreme Court. The advantage of an elected judiciary is that it would be less likely to lose touch with the people. Moreover, it would, on one view, lend legitimacy to judicial rulings precisely because they would be the rulings of an elected body.

But the disadvantages of allowing judges to be elected are, it is suggested, fundamental. The essential requirement of a judiciary at all levels is that it is both independent and impartial (as well as being perceived to be so). It is often be-

---

[107] The very few exceptions to this are immaterial for the purpose of the point being made here.
[108] See *Setting the Scene*, p 19.

lieved that judicial independence requires only a guarantee of independence from the executive and impartiality in the individual case.

However, independence of the people is equally important. The systemic dangers of judges having to campaign for election or re-election whilst sitting on a controversial case are graphically illustrated by the observation of a former California Supreme Court Justice who described it as 'like finding a crocodile in your bathtub when you go in to shave in the morning. You try not to think about it, but it's hard to think about much else while you're shaving.'[109]

It is important, therefore, to view the non-electability of judges as a component of judicial independence rather than as evidencing a democratic deficit. Representative democracy is served better by an integrated system, endorsed by the people and reflected in a Constitution in which the different branches of government and civic activity can readily be justified and harmonise with each other.

In order to achieve these objectives, the starting point is an independent judiciary constitutionally entrenched by constitutional guarantees of full independence from all other branches of a constitution. Then, the greatest care needs to be taken in appointing judges. Those who are selected must be independent-minded, must be of the highest intellectual calibre, must possess excellent judgement and common sense, and must be in touch with contemporary ideas and values. It is important, too, that judges are, to a material extent, representative of the society in which we live.

Providing the necessary constitutional guarantees of independence once judges have been appointed to office is relatively easy and is a feature of most written Constitutions. However, such guarantees are empty words unless an objectively independent and transparent appointments system is established in which selection criteria are fairly and consistently applied.

The key issue here is the extent, if any, to which judges, executive government and Parliament should be able to participate in a judicial appointments process. In the US Supreme Court justices are appointed by the President but have to undergo extensive and potentially gruelling confirmation hearings by the Senate before the appointment is confirmed.

During these confirmation sessions the personal life and judicial record of the potential candidate is exposed to exhaustive public scrutiny. The problem is that the dynamics of such a process can lead to (and have been argued to have led to) not much more than an extension of the legislative work of the Senate as well as being 'an arena for competition among warring factions of interest groups and senators'.[110] In other words, the appointments process itself is vitiated by a breach of the separation of powers principle.

---

[109] Cited in John D Fabian, 'Paradox of Elected Judges—Tension in the American Judicial System' (2001) 15 *Georgetown Journal of Legal Ethics* 155.

[110] LC Bell, *Warring Factions: Interest Groups, Money and the New Politics of Senate Confirmation* (Columbus OH, Ohio State University Press, 2002).

There is arguably no principled basis for permitting any of the other constitutional branches of government (including the judiciary itself) to intrude into the process of selecting judges. It is sometimes contended that an appointments commission will produce bland appointments, but there is no reason of principle why this should be so, especially if the selection criteria are sufficiently tightly drawn.

Finally, the logical consequence of having a written Constitution is that provisions need to be made for its interpretation and application. Such provisions are likely to require the creation of effectively a Constitutional Court with special principles relating to its composition and jurisdiction.

Judicial independence (Articles 128–31) Against the background of these considerations (few of which are confronted in the Constitutional Reform Act 2005 which, nonetheless, made some extremely important changes to the running of the judicial system, including the creation of a Supreme Court and a new judicial appointments system), the section of this Constitution dealing with the judiciary (Part 8) begins by laying down certain general principles relating to the holding of judicial power in the UK.

Articles 128–31 are directly concerned with judicial independence. For the reasons set out earlier, Article 131 states in terms that the judiciary is independent not merely of the executive and legislative branches of the Constitution but also of the Citizens' Branch.

Judicial independence is thus an express guarantee of this Constitution (as it is of most Constitutions and, indeed, as it is currently enshrined in statute: see s 3 of the Constitutional Reform Act 2005). But it is indirectly backed up by a number of other provisions. Article 130 prevents all restrictions on judges that are not grounded in law. Importantly, therefore, Article 130 implicitly makes clear (as some written Constitutions do not) that emergency powers do not apply to the judiciary. This provision is designed to avoid situations such as the dismissal and detention of judges in Pakistan in 2007 under the regime of former President Musharraf during a national state of emergency.[111]

An indirect aspect of judicial independence is the question of salary and other benefits. This is foreshadowed in Article 129 (see, further, Notes to Articles 164–66 below which also address the question of removal of judges).

Accountability of judges (Article 133) The Constitutional Reform Act 2005 introduced other constitutional reforms besides the creation of a Judicial Appointments Commission. As well as creating a Supreme Court (discussed below), it displaced the Lord Chancellor as head of the judiciary. In doing so, it altered the traditional mechanism by which the judiciary were accountable as an institution. As a government minister, the Lord Chancellor was formerly accountable to Parliament in the normal way for the acts and omissions of the judiciary.

---

111 This action was declared to be unlawful by the Supreme Court of Pakistan in 2009.

Article 133 deals, therefore, with the related, but often neglected, topic of judicial accountability by requiring laws to ensure the accountability of individual judges and of the judiciary as an institution. Accountability should be distinguished from the separate laws governing the effective running of the court system and deployment of resources, which are currently regulated by law and continue to be so regulated under the Constitution (see eg Articles 128 and 169).

The accountability of *individual* judges causes few constitutional problems. Apart from the appeal system whereby higher courts oversee how specific cases have been handled, there is an Office for Judicial Complaints (OJC) which is part of the Ministry of Justice and addresses complaints about the conduct of individual judges.

However, the judiciary *as an institution* causes more problems. If it is accepted as a principle that, to ensure the rule of law, there must be an independent and unelected judiciary capable, at least at the highest level, of wielding considerable political power, it ought to follow logically that there should be a substantial degree of judicial accountability in terms of the performance of the judiciary as a whole. However, this is not universally accepted. For example, the late Lord Cooke of Thorndon argued that external accountability and judicial independence were contradictions in terms and that accountability could only properly take the form of self-policing.

It may depend on what one means by *accountability*. This is sometimes thought of in terms of what Professor Vernon Bogdanor calls *sacrificial* accountability,[112] which is the political doctrine that ministers are accountable to Parliament for the mistakes of their department. Any such doctrine applied by analogy to the judiciary would compromise its independence.

In a different application of accountability, though, Professor Bogdanor suggests that judges may be accountable in an *explanatory* sense. What this means is that the judiciary ought, as a matter of principle, to enter into a dialogue with other branches of government. By this means its distinct role in the constitution will be better understood. Added to this, however, it is suggested that the judiciary needs to be accountable in being *required* to explain to the other branches of government (which are electorally accountable) how it has exercised its functions; otherwise, the judiciary is accountable only to itself.

The ways in which accountability in this sense is guaranteed will (as Article 133 recognises) require special legislation. Central to that legislation will be a need to ensure that the mechanisms of accountability do not in any way impinge on judicial independence and that the judiciary is made accountable only for those matters for which it and not another entity (such as the Lord Chancellor) has been made separately responsible. Legislation that fails to make these distinctions will, to that extent, be invalid under the Constitution (see Article 5).

---

[112] See Vernon Bogdanor, *Accountability and the Media: 'Parliament and the Judiciary: The Problem of Accountability'*, 2006 Sunningdale Lecture, www.ukpac.org/bogdanor_speech.htm.

Hierarchy of judicial control (Articles 134–41)   Articles 134–41 address the different legal regimes that affect judicial decision-making in the UK. Article 134 makes it clear that judges in the UK derive their constitutional status from the Constitution and any laws made under it. Articles 135–38 deal with possible conflicts between EU law and laws that violate rights protected by the Constitution, including those contained in the ECHR. All courts are subject to EU law. Legislation that is incompatible with EU law, even primary legislation, cannot be applied by a court. That is the result of acceding to the EU and it is not altered by this Constitution (see Article 136).

However, Article 138 requires *initial* priority to be given to an interpretation of the law that is human rights compliant over one which is only compliant with EU law. In the unlikely event of a conflict the national court must make a reference to the European Court of Justice (ECJ) for a preliminary ruling on the question and the national court must follow the ECJ's ruling save that it must, where EU law violates the Constitution, declare it to be incompatible with the Constitution. This does not affect the validity of the EU law provision in question. Unsatisfactory as it may seem to accord EU law constitutional supremacy over all other law, there is no way of avoiding this short of withdrawing from the EU altogether.

Alongside certain specific international treaties such as the Treaty of Accession to Europe and the ECHR that have been incorporated into national law, international treaties that have not been incorporated can be used to inform judges' interpretation of legislation but (unlike treaties that have been incorporated) are not otherwise binding (Article 135).

Articles 139 and 141 preserve the status quo in terms of devolution (Article 139) and the overall structure of courts (Article 141).

The Supreme Court (Articles 142–63)   A Supreme Court has only recently (as from October 2009) been established, under the Constitutional Reform Act 2005. However, the reason for creating it was to avoid the continuation of a breach of the separation of powers principle (see above), not to invest it with new powers. In the absence of a written Constitution, this would have required primary legislation. The Supreme Court that we currently have is simply a merger of the two committees that the 12 former Law Lords used to sit on in the House of Lords, which were the Appellate Committee of the House of Lords (which dealt with final appeals in domestic civil and criminal cases) and the Judicial Committee of the Privy Council (which dealt mainly with overseas appeals and devolution questions). There are a number of modern features, such as updates on hearings via the internet and televised proceedings, but there is no essential difference between the Supreme Court sitting in the newly renovated Middlesex Guildhall and the former judicial committee of the House of Lords that sat in Westminster.

However, as noted above, the logic behind a written Constitution is that a *real* Constitutional Court should be established. This is because, amongst other things, the Constitution takes primacy and all branches of government are therefore subject to it. The consequence of this is that enforcement powers must be vested in such a court to decide, where necessary, that laws passed by the government are invalid and to make such orders as may be necessary to secure enforcement of the Constitution against (even) the government itself.

This creates an entirely new jurisdiction and one that is logically inconsistent with the notion of parliamentary sovereignty, which underpins our present constitutional settlement. The strong new powers that are required should, it may be thought, be vested at the highest level in a new Supreme Court with a special constitutional jurisdiction. That is the aim of Article 139 and of the specific provisions in this Constitution that confer discrete powers of a constitutional nature on the Supreme Court (see especially Articles 12, 122–24, and those conferred in this Part). None of these special powers is to be exercisable by any other court and no court or tribunal below the level of the Supreme Court may declare primary legislation to be unconstitutional (see Article 141).

Leaving out consideration of the supremacy of EU law over all other constitutional protections (discussed above) to which the following is necessarily subject, the main features of the proposed changes insofar as they affect the powers of the Supreme Court (subject to the detail of specific laws passed separately) are essentially as follows:[113]

- The Supreme Court retains its current appellate jurisdiction (Article 153). This includes its existing jurisdiction over devolution issues, which was transferred to it under section 40 of the Constitutional Reform Act 2005 and is expressly preserved (see Article 154). The principles governing composition (see Articles 143–45) are very similar to those contained in the Constitutional Reform Act 2005.

- The present jurisdiction to grant declarations of incompatibility under the HRA 1998 remains, but where such a human rights case reaches the Supreme Court that Court is under a duty to make a declaration of unconstitutionality as opposed to a declaration of incompatibility if primary legislation, by breaching a fundamental right, contravenes the Constitution (see Article 157).

- The Supreme Court is invested with a duty to make declarations of unconstitutionality if it considers that an existing legislative provision, act or omission is unconstitutional; sometimes, alternatively, it is required to make a declaration of constitutionality (see Article 157; see also Article 123).

- Article 148 is a much softer version of a provision contained in the Hong Kong Basic Law which requires the Supreme Court to refer the interpretation of certain sensitive legislation to a central government committee which provides an 'authoritative' interpretation that the courts must follow. Such a provision would not be acceptable in most democracies underpinned by the rule of law where questions of law are treated as matters solely for the judiciary. However, what Article 148 does is to mandate the referral by the Supreme Court of a proposed

---

[113] Different powers from those proposed in this Constitution may also be envisaged; for example, a Supreme Court might be given a power to dis-apply legislation without invalidating it or, consistent with the Canadian approach, to declare a measure to be incompatible with the Constitution but with the legislature being able to override such declaration for a limited period.

judicial interpretation of a constitutional provision which impinges on expressly defined executive functions in order to obtain the executive's view of the matter which the Court must take into account before deciding the matter. This provision is designed to strengthen the links between the Supreme Court and the executive rather than (as in the Hong Kong model) to tie the Court's hands, and is considered to be useful in that it affords the Supreme Court a somewhat better insight into the thought processes of executive government in sensitive areas.

- New regimes, not dissimilar to those adopted in the German Constitution, are created for the Supreme Court to determine the constitutionality or otherwise of political parties (see Articles 122–24). There is also a power granted to the Supreme Court to give preliminary rulings and opinions (see Articles 146 and 149). The preliminary ruling procedure has obvious and intended affinities with the reference procedure to the ECJ by national courts and tribunals, although references on constitutional questions will effectively be compulsory where the lower court or tribunal (even if not a court or tribunal 'of last resort') needs a ruling on whether a legislative provision or other act or omission is unconstitutional, since only the Supreme Court may make a declaration of unconstitutionality.

- The power in Article 152 to review the constitutionality of bills is a significant enhancement of the Supreme Court's powers and needs to be carefully considered in terms of its potential implications for representative democracy. The argument against conferment of such power is that the will of the elected Parliament ought not to be capable of being stifled by an unelected court. However, if proposed legislation is indeed unconstitutional, a power to declare it to be so before it is enacted may be thought to be valuable. Both the Irish Supreme Court and the French Conseil Constitutionnel have such a power.

- However, the proposed scope for further constitutional references and applications to the Supreme Court under the Constitution is much wider than permitting/requiring lower courts to make references. It enables (and sometimes requires) references and applications to be made direct to the Court not only by courts and tribunals but also by the executive and by the Citizens' Council on questions of constitutional importance (see especially Articles 150–51).

- Nonetheless, in all constitutional cases coming directly before the Supreme Court, it must give permission for the application or reference to be heard before it may be entertained on a full hearing (see Articles 159–63). These provisions are designed to prevent abuse by the bringing of wholly unmeritorious applications. However, the Supreme Court must give permission on matters of constitutional importance (Article 163). Unlike the present situation in relation to its appellate jurisdiction, the Supreme Court must give its reasons for declining to grant permission for the making of a constitutional application or reference (see Article 160). It would seem desirable that the Supreme Court should give its reasons for declining permission even in respect of its appellate jurisdiction. However, such a requirement is less important (though is currently included in Article 153) where issues are raised that do not affect the interpretation of the Constitution or are not of fundamental constitutional importance.

Overall, the new Supreme Court created by this Constitution has the widest constitutional powers—both in relation to proposed legislation and to existing measures including administrative acts and omissions—to ensure that the Constitution is being interpreted and implemented lawfully. It has the widest power to entertain applications from the executive, and from the Citizens' Council. There is much scope for debate as to the exact nature of the constitutional jurisdiction that could or should be conferred on the Court, but it is suggested that it is intrinsic to the nature of a Constitution embodying the values of a representative democracy that some form of constitutional jurisdiction of this kind is both necessary and desirable.

Appointment and removal of judges and administrative provisions (Articles 164–69)   Articles 164–66 address the question of the appointment and removal of judges as well as salary and other financial benefits, together with issues relating to salary and other benefits.

The process of appointing judges also raises important issues as to judicial independence. Here, the requisite considerations include not merely the provision of objective protections but must also include devising mechanisms for ensuring that persons of independent mind are selected and that pressure is not brought to bear in the selection process from other branches of the Constitution.

Articles 164–65 are designed to give effect to these considerations. Article 164 entrusts the appointment of judges to an independent Judicial Appointments Commission, which must (see Article 165) make its decisions in such a way as to be independent of the legislative, executive and judicial branches of government.

The composition of the current Judicial Appointments Commission (JAC) set up under the Constitutional Reform Act 2005 is, it is suggested, entirely independent. Neither the executive nor Members of Parliament take part in the selection process. There is a requirement that the JAC include five *judicial* members. But since the number of Commissioners is 15 there is no issue of *composition* relating to its independence from the judiciary. This is all the more so given the current statutory requirement that the Chairman must be a layperson.

There are, however, issues relating to the nature and 'reach' of the current decision-making process of the JAC contained in the 2005 Act that are arguably relevant to judicial independence.

First, under the Constitutional Reform Act 2005 the JAC's decisions may be rejected by the Lord Chancellor. Although, following such rejection, the Lord Chancellor cannot make the appointment himself but must remit the decision to the JAC, the reality is that executive influence is built into the statutory framework.

Secondly, judicial influence is also present. Even at the level of the High Court, senior members of the judiciary must, under the 2005 Act, be consulted, and their views will sometimes determine whether an appointment is made.[114] At higher levels, senior members of the judiciary are required by the same Act to be on the selection panel and have a potentially decisive influence on the appointment that is made. Whilst it is arguable that judges ought to have an influence on who is appointed, the perception that an elitist 'club' will select by a tap-on-the-shoulder those conforming to a male, middle-aged, Oxbridge stereotype with out-of-touch values continues to prevail in the popular press.[115] There may, on present evidence, be some truth in this and, in any event, it may be that perception is extremely important in this sensitive area. It may be that reducing the possibility of judicial influence of this kind will provide better protection against less good appointments than a specific diversity requirement.

Thirdly, the JAC has no direct remit in the selection of justices of the Supreme Court. At first sight at least, this is a surprising omission. Instead of involving the JAC (and its other UK counterparts) directly, the Constitutional Reform Act 2005 establishes a *selection commission* which consists of the President and Deputy Chairman of the Supreme Court as well as individual members of the respective JACs for the UK. The appointments process requires recommendations to be made to the Prime Minister, who must choose one of the names notified. This means that in practice there is heavy judicial input in the selection process from the very body into which the new appointment is to be made. Given the small size of the Supreme Court it may be difficult, in practice, to avoid giving the impression that new appointments are decided from the 'inside' rather than by a transparently fair process. This is perhaps even more important given that Supreme Court justices may now be appointed from outside the serving judiciary altogether.

Amongst other things, Article 165 does away with the currently heavy behind-the-scenes judicial influence in the decision-making process leading to the selection of judges at all levels. It also requires decisions to be made in all cases by the JAC.

Article 165 sets out the general criteria by which judges are to be selected. These are necessarily general, and because they cannot be precisely quantified in isolation let alone in relation to each other they are not expressed to be determinative. The JAC must 'give priority to' independence of mind, high intellect and excellent judgement, and must take into account any other requirement of the Constitution. Most notable of these will be the requirement (see Article 8)

---

114 There is, for example, strong anecdotal evidence of instances (a specific incident occurring most recently in the 2008 appointment process for High Court judges) where the JAC has, following interview, assessed a candidate as fully meeting the requirements for appointment to the High Court and prepared a report 'recommending' such candidate, but following 'consultation' the judges statutorily required to be consulted have in practice had an effective veto over the appointment. The process operates unfairly in that the rejected candidate has no opportunity to learn of the reasons for the veto or to know the case against him or her. As importantly, the senior judges with the 'veto' do not hear the tape of the interview with the rejected candidate.

115 See eg Clare Dyer, 'First 10 High Court Judges under New Diversity Rules' *The Guardian*, 28 January 2008.

to appoint more women to these positions provided that doing so is consistent with the specific selection criteria. However, the central requirement for selection is that the 'best' candidate 'in terms of merit' is selected. This is effectively the present position under the Constitutional Reform Act 2005, which requires candidates to be selected on 'merit'.

Judicial selection has been the subject of much recent academic work, particularly the question whether appointment on merit needs to be rethought having regard to the requirements of diversity in a modern and pluralistic society.[116] However, the approach adopted in this Constitution is to emphasise that merit in terms of individual excellence (irrespective of gender or race) is the overriding criterion. There will be those who disagree with this approach,[117] but the danger is that an appointments system based on diversity or gender[118] rather than merit would be more likely to reduce the high regard in which the judiciary must be held if the rule of law is to be preserved.

As to removal of judges, the present position is essentially preserved but with more uniformity across all levels of the judiciary in terms of the criteria for removal (see Articles 166 and 168 but with the exceptions contained in Article 167). The current position is that judges of the Supreme Court, the Court of Appeal and the High Court may only be removed if they misbehave, and only then by the Crown on an address by both Houses of Parliament. However, this little-used procedure has not been invoked since 1830 (when it was used to remove an Irish judge found to have misappropriated funds). Below that level the Lord Chancellor may remove circuit judges on grounds of misbehaviour or incapacity. Other similar but less stringent provisions apply to the removal of stipendiary and lay magistrates.

The US Constitution expressly prohibits reduction of salary whilst in office and a similar provision is contained in Article 166. This provision, once perhaps uncontroversial, may be more contentious in times of economic recession, and there have recently been calls for pay and pension cuts in the public sector and even in government.

Nonetheless, the purpose of maintaining the level of judicial salary in real terms (an expression used in Article 166 which may arguably require greater precision) is to ensure not only that judges remain in office and are not deterred from seeking office but also to avoid judicial corruption in the form of bribes and other inducements where salaries are very low. This danger, happily rare at present in the UK, is a real and current problem, especially in some African countries.

---

[116] Most notable perhaps in this area is the work of Professor Kate Malleson at Queen Mary University of London. See especially her 'Rethinking the Merit Principle in Judicial Selection' (2006) 33 *Journal of Law and Society* 126.

[117] Baroness Hale in particular has argued that without a more diverse judiciary, judicial decisions will, amongst other things, lack democratic legitimacy and will not command public confidence: see Brenda Hale, 'Equality and the Judiciary: Why Should We Want More Women Judges?' [2001] *Public Law* 495.

[118] The South African Constitution contains an express requirement that the judiciary should reflect the racial and gender composition of the nation.

PART 9
FUNDAMENTAL RIGHTS, FREEDOMS
AND RESPONSIBILITIES

CONSTITUTIONAL EFFECT OF RIGHTS, FREEDOMS AND
RESPONSIBILITIES

170. This part of the Constitution is subject to the provisions of Part 6.

171. Subject to the terms of this Constitution, the provisions of the European Convention on Human Rights and the European Charter of Fundamental Rights and the rights contained in them are guaranteed by this Constitution in their entirety whatever their status as international obligations imposed on the United Kingdom.

172. In particular, the fundamental rights and freedoms contained in this Constitution which correspond with rights guaranteed by the European Convention on Human Rights and the European Charter of Fundamental Rights shall be interpreted as having at least the same scope as those Convention and Charter rights. However, nothing in this Constitution shall prevent the fundamental rights and freedoms contained in this Constitution from being interpreted as providing more extensive protection than the corresponding Convention and Charter rights.

173. Nothing in the provisions of this Part of the Constitution shall prevent the rights and responsibilities recognised by this Constitution from being developed further by law or so as to provide additional rights and responsibilities through the devolved government institutions of the United Kingdom enacting legislation within the limits of their jurisdiction, provided that nothing in the recognition of any additional responsibilities shall affect either the existence or the availability of the fundamental rights and freedoms under this Constitution.

174. Nothing in the provisions of this Part of the Constitution shall affect the rights, remedies and obligations contained in the Human Rights Act 1998 which shall form part of this Constitution. However, any limitation of rights and remedies contained in that Act as are incompatible with the provisions of this Constitution shall no longer apply.

175. Nothing in this Constitution denies the existence, or restricts the scope, of any other rights or freedoms recognised or conferred by European Union law, common law, statute, or customary international law, to the extent that they are consistent with the rights and freedoms contained in this Constitution.

176. Any person or body who has a sufficient interest in a matter may bring legal proceedings in the appropriate court or tribunal concerning the alleged breach of any provision of this Constitution.

177. No derogation from any of the rights and freedoms in this Constitution shall be lawful unless emergency powers are lawfully exercised under Part 6 of this Constitution. Any legislation enacted in consequence of the exercise of emergency powers may derogate from any right or freedom in this Constitution only as permitted under this Constitution and only then to the extent that the derogation is strictly required by the emergency and is consistent with the UK's other international obligations.

178. Subject to this Constitution the rights and freedoms contained in this Constitution may, where capable of being restricted, be subject only to such reasonable limits,[119] provided for by law, as can be demonstrably justified in a society based on the values of liberty, democracy, fairness, civic duty and the rule of law, and to the extent compatible with international human rights treaties to which the UK is a party, taking into account all relevant factors, including—

    (i)   the nature of the right;

    (ii) the importance and legitimacy of the purpose of the limitation;

    (iii) the nature and extent of the limitation;

    (iv) the relation between the limitation and its purpose; and

    (v)   the availability of less restrictive means to achieve the purpose.

179. Any person or body who has a sufficient interest in a matter may bring legal proceedings in the appropriate court or tribunal challenging, to the extent permitted by Part 6 of this Constitution, the validity under this Part of the Constitution of—

    (i)   the exercise of emergency powers under Part 6 of this Constitution; or

    (ii) any legislation enacted, or other action taken, in consequence of the exercise of such emergency powers.

---

[119] This is one of various provisions in the draft Constitution that are likely to be the focus of extensive discussion as to how they should be interpreted (eg phrases such as 'sufficient interest' when interpreting standing to commence proceedings under the Constitution and 'consistently with the needs of a representative democracy in a modern and developing society' (Article 6(i)) as well as the general limitations clause for rights in Article 178. For such provisions it will be important to balance the need for flexibility (and therefore leaving the phrases open-textured) and the need for prescription to assist the courts in their adjudication of constitutional questions. For reasons of flexibility it may not be desirable to include too many definitions for such terms (indeed, it is not possible).

180. No legislation enacted in consequence of emergency powers under Part 6 of this Constitution may permit or authorise any derogation from the rights and freedoms contained in Articles 181–96 and Articles 200–02 of this Constitution except in respect of deaths resulting from lawful acts of war, which shall be deemed not to constitute a derogation from the right to life under Article 183 of this Constitution.

CIVIL AND POLITICAL RIGHTS AND FREEDOMS

181. All persons shall be equal before the law. Everyone is equal before the law and has the right to equal protection and benefit of the law. Equality includes the full and equal enjoyment of all rights and freedoms under this Constitution. To promote the achievement of equality, legislative and other measures designed to protect or advance persons, or categories of persons, disadvantaged by unfair discrimination may be taken.[120] The state may not unfairly discriminate directly or indirectly against anyone on one or more grounds, including race, gender, sex, pregnancy, marital status, ethnic or social origin, colour, sexual orientation, age, disability, religion, conscience, belief, culture, language and birth. National legislation must be enacted to prevent or prohibit unfair discrimination. Discrimination on one or more of the grounds listed in this Article is unfair unless it is established that the discrimination is fair.

182. Human dignity is inviolable.[121] It must be respected and protected.

183. Everyone's right to life shall be protected by law. No one shall be deprived of life intentionally. No one shall be condemned to death or executed. Deprivation of life shall not be regarded as inflicted in contravention of this Constitution when it results from a use of force which is no more than absolutely necessary in defence of any person from unlawful violence, in order to effect a lawful arrest or to prevent the arrest of a person lawfully detained or in action lawfully taken for the purpose of quelling a riot or insurrection.

184. Everyone has the right to respect for his or her physical and mental integrity. In the fields of medicine and biology, the following must be respected in particular—

   (i)   the free and informed consent of the person concerned, according to the procedures laid down by law;

---

[120] Some instruments (such as the UN's Convention on the Elimination of Racial Discrimination) include a time limit for affirmative action policies, such as 'for so long as necessary to achieve objectives'. This is a useful limit as it provides a balance between the interests of the various affected parties.

[121] 'Dignity' is an interesting contemporary inclusion in modern Constitutions. Such guarantees are a difficult basis for adjudicating claims (see C McCrudden, 'Human Dignity and Judicial Interpretation of Human Rights' (2008) 19(4) *European Journal of International Law* 655). As a result of these difficulties, some have suggested that guarantees of dignity may be better placed in a preamble rather than as a norm within the operative provisions of a Constitution.

(ii)   the prohibition of eugenic practices;

(iii) the prohibition of making the human body a source of financial gain; and

(iv)   the prohibition of reproductive cloning of human beings.

185. No one shall be subjected to torture or to inhuman or degrading treatment or punishment.

186. No one shall be held in slavery and servitude or required to perform forced or compulsory labour. Trafficking in human beings is prohibited. However, the term "forced or compulsory labour" shall not include any work required to be done in the ordinary course of lawful detention, or during conditional release from any such detention, or as part of legitimate punishment imposed by a court or tribunal according to law, or as part of any service of a military character or, in case of conscientious objectors in countries where they are recognised, service exacted instead of compulsory military service, or any work or service which forms part of normal civic obligations including as part of the responsibilities under this Constitution.

187. Everyone has the right to liberty and security of person. No one shall be deprived of his or her liberty save in the following cases and in accordance with a procedure prescribed by law—

(i)   the lawful detention of a person after conviction by a competent court;

(ii)   the lawful arrest or detention of a person for non-compliance with the lawful order of a court or in order to secure the fulfilment of any obligation prescribed by law;

(iii) the lawful arrest or detention of a person effected for the purpose of bringing him or her before the competent legal authority on reasonable suspicion of having committed an offence or when it is reasonably considered necessary to prevent his or her committing an offence or fleeing after having done so;

(iv)   the detention of a minor by lawful order for the purpose of educational supervision or his or her lawful detention for the purpose of bringing him or her before the competent legal authority;

(v)   the lawful detention of persons for the prevention of the spreading of infectious diseases, or of persons of unsound mind, alcoholics or drug addicts or vagrants;

(vi)   the lawful arrest or detention of a person to prevent his or her effecting an unauthorised entry into the country or of a person against whom action is being taken with a view to deportation or extradition.

188. Without prejudice to the specific provisions of Articles 197–99 and Articles 203–04,[122] all persons who are arrested shall be informed promptly, in a language they understand, of the reasons for their arrest and of any charge against them. All persons arrested or detained in accordance with the provisions of Article 187(iii) of this Constitution shall be brought promptly before a judge or other officer authorised by law to exercise judicial power and shall be entitled to a trial within a reasonable time or to release pending trial. Release may be subject to a requirement of guarantees from third parties that an accused person will appear for trial. All persons who are deprived of their liberty by arrest or detention shall be entitled to take proceedings by which the lawfulness of their detention shall be decided speedily by a court and their release ordered if the detention is not lawful. All persons who have, since the coming into force of this Constitution, been the victim of arrest or detention which is judged to be unlawful shall have a right to compensation.

189. Everyone has the right to respect for his or her private and family life, his or her home and his or her communications. There shall be no interference by a public authority with the exercise of this right except such as is in accordance with the law and is necessary in a democratic society in the interests of national security, public safety or the economic well-being of the country, for the prevention of disorder or crime, for the protection of health or morals, or for the protection of the rights and freedoms of others.

190. Everyone has the right to freedom of thought, conscience and religion. This right includes a person's freedom to change his or her religion or beliefs, and freedom, either alone or in community with others and in public or private, to manifest his or her religion or beliefs, in worship, teaching, practice and observance. Freedom to manifest one's religion or beliefs shall be subject only to such limitations as are prescribed by law and are necessary in a democratic society in the interests of public safety, for the protection of public order, health or morals, or for the protection of the rights and freedoms of others. The right to conscientious objection is recognised, in accordance with the national laws governing the exercise of this right.

191. Everyone has the right to freedom of expression. This right shall include freedom to hold opinions and to receive and impart information and ideas without interference by public authority and regardless of frontiers. This article shall not prevent States from requiring the licensing of broadcasting, television or cinema enterprises. The exercise of these freedoms, since it carries with it duties and responsibilities, may be subject to such formalities, conditions, restrictions and penalties as are prescribed by law and are necessary in a democratic society, in the interests of national security, territorial

---

[122] The rights here are non-derogable, whereas the more specific provisions of Articles 197–99 and Articles 203–04 may occasionally be derogated from: see Article 180.

integrity or public safety, for the prevention of disorder or crime, for the protection of health or morals, for the protection of the reputation or the rights of others, for preventing the disclosure of information received in confidence, or for maintaining the authority and impartiality of the judiciary. The freedom and pluralism of the media shall be respected.

192. Everyone has the right to hold unarmed and peaceful demonstration marches, the right of freedom of peaceful assembly and of freedom of association with others, including the right to form and to join trade unions for the protection of his or her interests. No restrictions shall be placed on the exercise of these rights other than such as are prescribed by law and are necessary in a democratic society in the interests of national security or public safety, for the prevention of disorder or crime, for the protection of health or morals, or for the protection of the rights and freedoms of others. However, this Article shall not prevent the imposition of lawful restrictions on the exercise of these rights by members of the armed forces, of the police or of the administration of the State.

193. Men and women of marriageable age have the right to marry and to found a family, according to the national laws governing the exercise of this right. The right to marry shall not be restricted to marriage between members of the opposite sex.

194. Every natural or legal person is entitled to the peaceful enjoyment of his or her possessions. No one shall be deprived of his or her possessions except in the public interest and subject to the conditions provided for by law and by the general principles of international law. These provisions shall not, however, in any way impair the right of a State to enforce such laws as it deems necessary to control the use of property in accordance with the general interest or to secure the payment of taxes or other contributions or penalties. Intellectual property shall be protected under the same terms.

195. Everyone lawfully within the territory of the United Kingdom shall, within that territory, have the right to liberty of movement and freedom to choose his or her residence. Everyone shall be free to leave the United Kingdom. No restrictions shall be placed on the exercise of these rights other than such as are in accordance with law and are necessary in a democratic society in the interests of national security or public safety, for the maintenance of public order, for the prevention of crime, or for the protection of the rights and freedoms of others. These rights may also be subject, in particular areas, to restrictions imposed in accordance with law and justified by the public interest in a democratic society.

196. The right to asylum shall be guaranteed with due respect for the rules of the Geneva Convention of 28 July 1951 and the Protocol of 31 January 1967 relating to the status of refugees and in accordance with the Treaty establishing the European Community.

FAIR PROCESS RIGHTS

197. Everyone who is arrested for allegedly committing an offence has the right—

    (i)   to remain silent;

    (ii) to be informed promptly—

        (a) of their right to remain silent, and

        (b) of the consequences of not remaining silent;

    (iii) not to be compelled to make any confession or admission that could be used in evidence against that person;

    (iv) at the first court appearance after being arrested, to be charged or to be informed of the reason for the continuation of the detention, or to be released; and

    (v) to be released from detention if the interests of justice permit, subject to reasonable conditions

198. Everyone who is detained, including every sentenced prisoner, has the right—

    (i)   to be informed promptly of the reason for the continuation of the detention;

    (ii) to choose, and to consult with, a legal practitioner, and to be informed of this right promptly;

    (iii) to have a legal practitioner assigned by the state and at state expense, if substantial injustice would otherwise result, and to be informed of this right promptly;

    (iv) to challenge the lawfulness of the detention in person before a court and, if the detention is judged to be unlawful, to be released;

    (v) to conditions of detention that are consistent with human dignity, including at least reasonable exercise and the provision, at state expense, of adequate accommodation, nutrition, reading material and medical treatment; and

    (vi) to communicate with, and be visited by, that person's—

        (a) spouse or partner,

        (b) next of kin,

        (c) chosen religious counsellor, and

        (d) chosen medical practitioner.

199. In the determination of civil rights and obligations or of any criminal charge, everyone is entitled to a fair and public hearing within a reasonable time by an independent and impartial tribunal established by law. Judgment shall be pronounced publicly. The press and public may be excluded from all or part of the trial or hearing in the interest of morals, public order or national security in a democratic society, where the interests of juveniles or the protection of the private life of the parties so requires, or to the extent strictly necessary in the opinion of the court in special circumstances where publicity would prejudice the interests of justice.

200. Everyone charged with a criminal offence shall be presumed innocent until proved guilty according to law. Everyone charged with a criminal offence has the following minimum rights—

    (i)   to be informed promptly, in a language he or she understands and in detail, of the nature and cause of the accusation against him or her;

    (ii)   to have adequate time and facilities to prepare his or her defence;

    (iii) to defend himself or herself in person or through a legal representative of his or her own choosing or, if he or she has not sufficient means to pay for legal assistance, to be given legal assistance without charge when the interests of justice so require;

    (iv)   to examine or have examined witnesses against him or her and to obtain the attendance and examination of witnesses on his or her behalf under the same conditions as witnesses against him or her;

    (v)   to have the free assistance of an interpreter if he or she cannot understand or speak the language used in court.

201. No one shall be held guilty of any criminal offence on account of any act or omission which did not constitute a criminal offence under national or international law at the time when it was committed. Nor shall a heavier penalty be imposed than the one that was applicable at the time the criminal offence was committed. If subsequent to the commission of a criminal offence the law provides for a lighter penalty, that penalty shall be applicable. This Article shall not prejudice the trial and punishment of any person for any act or omission which, at the time it was committed, was criminal according the general principles of law recognised by civilised nations. The severity of penalties must not be disproportionate to the criminal offence.

202. Everyone whose rights and freedoms as set forth in this Part of the Constitution are violated shall have an effective remedy before a national authority notwithstanding that the violation has been committed by persons acting in an official capacity.

203. Everyone has a right of access to any information held by the State, and any information that is held by another person, that is required for the exercise or protection of any of their rights protected by this Constitution. Laws must be enacted to give effect to this right, and may provide for reasonable measures to alleviate the administrative and financial burden on the State.

204. Everyone has the right to receive administrative treatment that is lawful, reasonable and procedurally fair. Everyone whose rights have been adversely affected by administrative action has the right to be given written reasons. Laws must be enacted to give effect to these rights, and must—

   (i)   provide for the review of administrative action by a court or, where appropriate, an independent and impartial tribunal; and

   (ii) impose a duty on the state to give effect to these rights and promote an efficient administration.

DEMOCRATIC RIGHTS

205. There shall, subject to this Constitution, be provision by law for the acquisition and termination of citizenship and all other matters relating to citizenship.

206. Every citizen shall have the right and the opportunity—

   (i)   to take part in the conduct of public affairs, directly or through freely chosen representatives;

   (ii) to vote and to be elected at genuine periodic elections which shall be by universal and equal suffrage and shall be held by secret ballot, guaranteeing the free expression of the will of the electors; and

   (iii) to have access, on general terms of equality, to public service in his or her country.

RIGHTS OF SPECIAL GROUPS

207. A child's[123] best interests are of paramount importance in every matter concerning the child and must be identified and protected with the minimum of delay. Every child has the right—

   (i)   to a name and a nationality from birth;

   (ii) to parental care, or to appropriate alternative care when removed from the family environment;

---

[123] The word 'child' is defined in Part 14.

(iii) to basic nutrition, shelter, basic health care services and social services;

(iv) to be protected from maltreatment, neglect, abuse and degradation;

(v) to be protected from exploitative labour practices;

(vi) not to be required or permitted to perform work or provide services that—

(a) are inappropriate for a person of that child's age, or

(b) place at risk their well-being, education, physical or mental health or spiritual, moral or social development;

(vii) not to be detained except as a measure of last resort, in which case, in addition to the rights a child enjoys as a detained person under this Constitution, the child may be detained only for the shortest appropriate period of time, and has the right to be—

(a) detained separately from persons over the age of 18 years, and

(b) treated in a manner, and kept in conditions, that take account of the child's age;

(viii) to have a legal practitioner assigned by the state, and at state expense, in civil proceedings affecting the child, if substantial injustice would otherwise result; and

(ix) to be protected in times of armed conflict.

208. This Constitution recognises and guarantees, subject to its other provisions, the right of persons belonging to national minorities to the preservation, development and expression of their ethnic, cultural, linguistic and religious identity and to the right of such persons to be treated in conformity with the principles of equality and non-discrimination in relation to other citizens of the United Kingdom.

209. This Constitution recognises the equal right of all persons with disabilities to live in the community, with choices equal to others, and laws shall facilitate full enjoyment by persons with disabilities of this right and their full inclusion and participation in the community, including by ensuring that—

(i) persons with disabilities have the opportunity to choose their place of residence and where and with whom they live on an equal basis with others and are not obliged to live in a prescribed arrangement;

(ii) persons with disabilities have access to a range of in-home, residential and other community support services, including personal assistance necessary to support living and inclusion in the community, and to prevent isolation or segregation from the community;

(iii) community services and facilities for the general population are available on an equal basis to persons with disabilities and are responsive to their needs. Laws shall also ensure personal mobility with the greatest possible independence for persons with disabilities, including by—

   (a) facilitating the personal mobility of persons with disabilities in the manner and at the time of their choice, and at affordable cost,

   (b) facilitating access by persons with disabilities to quality mobility aids, devices, assistive technologies and forms of live assistance and intermediaries, including by making them available at affordable cost,

   (c) providing training in mobility skills to persons with disabilities and to specialist staff working with persons with disabilities, and

   (d) encouraging entities that produce mobility aids, devices and assistive technologies to take into account all aspects of mobility for persons with disabilities.

210. The rights of persons who have sustained harm as a result of crimes shall be protected by law. In particular, the rights of such persons to access to justice and to compensation for damage are guaranteed by this Constitution.

ECONOMIC AND SOCIAL RIGHTS

211. Subject to this Constitution, all persons are entitled to an adequate standard of living sufficient for themselves and for their dependants. Everyone has the right to have access to—

   (i) sufficient food, water, clothing and housing; and

   (ii) social security, including, if they are unable to support themselves and their dependants, appropriate social assistance.

   Reasonable legislative and other measures, within the available resources of the State must be taken to achieve the progressive realisation of each of these rights.

212. Subject to this Constitution, everyone has the right to have access to appropriate health and social care services free at the point of delivery and within a reasonable time. No one may be refused emergency health treatment or emergency social care services. Reasonable legislative and other measures within the available resources of the State must be taken to achieve the progressive realisation of these rights.

213. This Constitution recognises the right of everyone to education. It recognises that education shall be directed to the full development of the human personality, the sense of its dignity, and the respect for human rights and fundamental freedoms. It also recognises that education shall be designed to enable all persons to participate effectively in a free society, promote understanding, tolerance and friendship among all nations and all racial, ethnic or religious groups, and further the maintenance of peace.

214. Subject to this Constitution, everyone of compulsory school age has the right to receive free, full-time education suitable to their needs and the right to have access to further education and to vocational and continued training.

215. Subject to this Constitution, everyone has the right to live in an environment that is not harmful to their health. Everyone has the right to access information that enables them to assess risks to their health from their environment. Everyone has the right to a high level of environmental protection, for the benefit of present and future generations, through reasonable legislative and other measures that—

     (i)   prevent pollution and ecological degradation;

     (ii)   promote conservation; and

     (iii) ensure that economic development and use of natural resources are sustainable.

RESPONSIBILITIES

216. Every person has both individual and civic duties towards his or her family and society, the State and other legally recognised communities as well as the international community. The rights and freedoms of each individual protected by this Constitution shall be exercised with due regard to the rights of others, collective security, morality and the just demands of general welfare in a democratic society.

217. Every individual shall have the duty to respect and consider his or her fellow beings without discrimination, and to maintain relations aimed at promoting, safeguarding and reinforcing mutual respect and tolerance.

218. Nothing in the provisions of this Part of the Constitution shall permit or be interpreted or applied as permitting or having the effect of permitting any person, group or body to engage in any activity or perform any act aimed at the destruction of any of the rights and freedoms contained in, or guaranteed by, this Constitution or at their limitation to a greater extent than is provided for in this Constitution.

219. The responsibilities recognised by this Constitution shall not affect the existence and availability of the fundamental rights and freedoms under this Constitution.[124]

220. No responsibility recognised by this Constitution shall be legally enforceable against individuals or create legal responsibilities of any kind.

OBSERVATIONS AND EXPLANATORY NOTES

Overview—the case for a domestic Bill of Rights   Part 9 represents what is sometimes referred to as a domestic Bill of Rights.

Of itself, the need for a domestic Bill of Rights is by no means self-evident. Underlying the enactment of the HRA 1998, which came into force on 2 October 2000, was the desire to 'bring rights home'. In essence, the rights in question were those to which the UK had subscribed by ratifying the ECHR. It could be said, therefore, that—at least by that stage—there was already a Bill of Rights and that to overlay it with further human rights provisions was both unnecessary and confusing.

This was the general view expressed by several witnesses who gave evidence to the Joint Committee on Human Rights in the course of its extensive inquiry during its 2007/2008 session into whether there was a good case for a domestic Bill of Rights.[125]

Explicit in many of the concerns expressed to the Committee was a suspicion that the real motive of the main political parties in espousing the need for a domestic Bill of Rights—possibly engendered by media highlighting of cases where it was suggested that rights protection was being given priority over public safety—was the wish to dilute existing fundamental rights protections in the HRA.

Whatever may have been the trigger for the initial political articulations of the desirability of a UK Bill of Rights, there is now broad party consensus that not only is it desirable to have such a Bill but at the very least a domestic Bill of Rights should not affect the UK's position as a party to the ECHR or result in the UK breaching its obligations under the Convention.[126]

There are in fact many arguments which support the idea that a domestic Bill of Rights should contain rights additional to those enshrined in the ECHR. Per-

---

[124]   The inclusion of responsibilities on the part of citizens is not without its difficulties. They have been incorporated in benign ways in some Constitutions, but there are also some more damaging inclusions (eg the Chinese Constitution, where it is argued that the emphasis is on responsibilities versus rights). There is a case to be made for emphasising more strongly than in the current version of Article 219—perhaps in the form of a presumptive interpretation principle—that it is *not* a question of responsibilities versus rights.

[125]   The Committee's Report *A Bill of Rights for the United Kingdom* was published on 21 July 2008.

[126]   At this stage it remains unclear exactly what effect a new UK Bill of Rights would have on the existing provisions of the HRA. For its part, the Government appears to have made a commitment that existing HRA protections will not be diluted: see Joint Committee on Human Rights, Twenty Ninth Report, Session 2007–08, para 54.

haps the most important consideration is that the ECHR was adopted as long ago as 1950 and arguably needs modernising and broadening to achieve maximal human rights protection.

The primary purpose of the ECHR, following the Holocaust, was to cement a *moral* foundation for protecting individuals against the tyranny of the state. Indeed, a general Enlightenment morality designed to protect individuals from state interference may be thought to have characterised earlier rights-driven landmarks of our constitutional history such as Magna Carta and the 1689 English Bill of Rights.

In more recent times a combination of higher living standards (at least in western liberal democracies) and the development of political and philosophical thought has led to a broader way of looking at human rights protection which encompasses, amongst other things, economic and social rights (which are not mentioned in the ECHR) often requiring state intervention that enable individuals to lead more fulfilling lives. Thinkers such as Isaiah Berlin, albeit drawing on Kantian political theory, have demonstrated that there is a significant distinction between *negative* liberty (the absence of constraint) and *positive* liberty (the potential to exercise personal autonomy).[127] International treaties—such as the International Covenant on Economic, Social and Cultural Rights—have increasingly focused on the protection of such economic and social rights.

It may be thought that the rationale for developing a Bill of Rights becomes more difficult to refute once the argument for a written Constitution is accepted. This is because, whatever view one takes of the current strength of fundamental rights protection under the HRA, the HRA is a statute and may be amended or repealed so as to weaken rather than strengthen rights protection. By contrast, in a written Constitution the desired level of rights protection is constitutionally entrenched because the Bill of Rights forms part of the Constitution. A Bill of Rights has the additional advantage that the drafting of such a Bill affords an opportunity to codify wider principles of administrative law such as a right to good administration as well as strengthening rights protection more generally.

It is interesting to note that many of the other arguments in favour of a domestic Bill of Rights, as expressed to the Joint Committee on Human Rights, are also arguments in favour of a written Constitution. Thus, witnesses to the Committee variously thought that amongst other things a Bill of Rights would provide 'human rights with superiority over all ordinary law', 'constitutional stability' and 'a unifying force in a diverse society', and that it would 'reinvigorate our democracy' and 'ingrain fundamental principles that otherwise might remain implied or implicit'.[128]

---

[127] I Berlin, 'Two Concepts of Liberty' in I Berlin, *Four Essays on Liberty* (Oxford, Oxford University Press, 1969). Even earlier, in his 'four freedoms' speech in 1941 President Roosevelt had emphasised the importance of freedom from want and freedom from fear, each of which could be viewed as giving rise to rights of an economic and social nature.

[128] See Joint Committee on Human Rights, Twenty Ninth Report, Session 2007–08, para 35.

This Constitution therefore proceeds on the basis that a constitutionally entrenched statement of fundamental rights is a considerable improvement on the present position. But a number of issues require consideration before such an entrenched rights model can be developed.

Constitutional mechanisms for a domestic Bill of Rights (Articles 170–80)   As explained above, it appears to be generally accepted that any new formulation of fundamental rights should not detrimentally affect the UK's adherence to the ECHR. It follows from this that neither the content nor the scope of the rights contained in this Constitution can be allowed to limit in any way the scope of the rights set out in the ECHR.

This is achieved by Articles 171–72, which in effect incorporate the ECHR into the Constitution (including, significantly, rights not ratified by the UK such as freedom of movement). Since there are many rights in the Constitution that are largely updates of ECHR rights or that contain only slightly modified wording of ECHR provisions[129] it is necessary to include a provision that enables constitutional rights that overlap with the ECHR to be interpreted as conferring at least as much protection as the ECHR version, and Article 172 (modelled on a similarly worded provision in the Joint Committee's outline of a Bill of Rights) makes it clear that the courts may interpret the constitutional provision in question as conferring *greater* protection than that conferred by the ECHR. It is questionable whether this result could have been achieved under HRA principles of interpretation, since the interpretative obligation on the courts under section 3 of the HRA is to interpret a statute so far as possible to be compatible with the ECHR.

Importantly, the ECHR is given domestic effect in the UK courts through the HRA. There is thus a significant question as to whether (and if so how) the HRA—as opposed to the ECHR—will be affected by a written Constitution (or, in fact, a domestic Bill of Rights). It is one thing to accept that the UK's international obligations under the ECHR will not be affected by new domestic legal provisions; it is quite another to make the same concession in respect of rights protection mechanisms in the HRA. It would, however, be a pyrrhic victory if the individual litigant were to have a brand new statement of rights which could not, in practice, be enforced save through having to petition the European Court of Human Rights in Strasbourg (a process that usually takes several years) because the HRA had been amended or repealed so as to weaken or even remove effective judicial domestic human rights protection.

However, in certain respects, the HRA is less than adequate. The Constitution is designed to strengthen rather than weaken existing judicial protection of fundamental rights. As already seen in the section on Judges, this Constitution proposes a radical new role for the new Supreme Court in terms of being empowered to strike down statutes. This is not possible under the HRA, which permits only (at the level of the High Court or higher) the granting of declarations of incompatibility in respect of primary legislation that breaches the Convention rights.

---

[129] See especially Articles 183, 185–91, 193–94, 197, 199–202.

For that reason, some limited changes to the HRA would be needed to give effect to the expanded constitutional powers of the Supreme Court. However, it is proposed that the other HRA mechanisms for protecting fundamental rights are left unchanged. Rather than repealing or amending the HRA, Article 174 adopts the simple expedient of leaving it in full force save and insofar as any statutory limitations set out in that Act are incompatible with the Constitution, in which case the Constitution trumps the Act.

In practice, the effect of this is that most HRA protections (including statements of compatibility with the Convention rights under section 19) will continue to be available. In particular, declarations of incompatibility will continue to be granted as at present by those courts having jurisdiction to award such relief. However, the Supreme Court is not subject to that limitation.

It should also be borne in mind that existing UK fundamental rights regimes are not necessarily confined to the ECHR. Such rights are sometimes given effect to (whether directly or indirectly) under the common law, under EU law and even by reference to customary international law, international human rights treaties and the European Charter of Fundamental Rights (EU Charter).

Article 175 is designed to address most of these regimes. In essence, it provides that any fundamental rights that are recognised in other existing UK legal rights regimes (including, most notably, EU law and the common law) remain in full force and effect save and insofar as they are incompatible with the Constitution.

International human rights treaties have sometimes afforded a basis for developing fundamental rights under the common law, and to that extent they continue to have identical legal effect under this Constitution. However, other than in respect of some rights under the ECHR which have not been incorporated into domestic law by the UK and other than in respect of the EU Charter, which is not part of domestic law (each of which are incorporated into the Constitution in their entirety), purely international obligations or other international provisions relating to fundamental rights have no separate force under the Constitution save, interpretatively, as provided for under Article 135.

The EU Charter is not binding in either UK law or EU law. It is a proclamation rather than a source of legal obligations. However, it refers to a number of social and economic rights and was 'solemnly proclaimed' in 2000 by the European Commission, the European Parliament and the European Council. It was incorporated into the abortive draft Constitution for Europe and was referred to in the Treaty of Lisbon. In practice, the (European) Court of First Instance (now called the General Court) has taken occasional account of the Charter in some of its judgments, as have the European Court of Human Rights and the High Court in England.

It seems likely, therefore, that the EU Charter will be increasingly relied upon before domestic courts and, in many instances, will be referred to by those courts. It contains a number of social and economic rights. As explained earlier, this is a logical development of the modern approach to human rights. For these reasons, this Constitution proposes to treat the EU Charter in the same fashion as the ECHR and to accord them equal status in the Constitution (see Articles 171–72).

Three further issues merit brief mention. The first is devolution. As is made clear by Article 173, nothing in the conferment of constitutional rights and recognition of civic responsibilities prevents additional rights from being conferred or additional responsibilities from being recognised through the devolved institutions of the UK acting within their jurisdictions.

The question of what role the devolved institutions might play in the creation of further fundamental rights (or responsibilities) raises difficult issues. One difficulty is that the current Convention rights do not include reserved matters (that is, matters over which power to legislate is reserved to the Westminster Parliament). However, at least some of the extended rights set out in this Constitution (or the UK Bill of Rights envisaged by the Joint Committee on Human Rights) are likely to intrude upon reserved matters. Article 173 does not confront these potential problems but leaves the way open for further discussion with the devolved institutions, which might even lead to some restructuring as to what might be included or excluded from the definition of 'reserved matters' in the context of fundamental rights.

The second issue is the question of restrictions on, and derogations from, the constitutional fundamental rights. This is linked to the last issue, which is concerned with the enforcement of the constitutional fundamental rights. As to *restrictions* on rights, Article 178 contains a general provision enabling those constitutional rights that can legitimately be restricted (an obvious exception is the right to life under Article 183) to be restricted by reference to the principle of proportionality. Some of these rights (see eg Article 189) specify their own limitation provisions and it is for consideration whether such provisions—which follow the language of the ECHR—are from a drafting perspective now otiose or whether there is a rationale for retaining them given the full retention of the ECHR where it is compatible with the Constitution. It is also for consideration whether other proposals in this Constitution (see eg the provisions regulating political parties) comply with Article 178.

Thirdly, a restriction on a fundamental right is to be distinguished from *derogation*. Derogation involves a breach of the right in question, whereas a legitimate restriction does not. It follows that derogation should only be permitted in very exceptional circumstances.

This Constitution envisages that derogation will only be allowed in a situation of true emergency. The concept of *emergency* has been discussed in the context of emergency powers under Part 6.

Parts 6 and 9 of the Constitution are therefore necessarily connected. Thus, Article 180 provides that, apart from deaths resulting from lawful war, the rights and freedoms set out in Articles 181–96 and 200–02 may not be derogated from in the exercise of any emergency powers under Part 6 of the Constitution. This goes much further than Article 15 of the ECHR, which only excludes derogation from the rights contained in Articles 2 (right to life—other than deaths resulting from lawful war), 3 (torture or inhuman or degrading treatment or punishment), 4 (servitude) and 7 (no punishment without law).

There is an important debate as to the extent to which other essential freedoms such as the right to freedom of expression may be derogated from (as opposed to being legitimately restricted) even in time of war or other emergency. This Constitution proposes that the distinction between legitimate restriction and derogation is important and that the scope for legitimate derogation from fundamental rights should be curtailed. It is also for consideration whether the prohibition on derogation should be extended (as this Constitution does) to certain rights and freedoms such as, most notably, the fair trial rights set out in Articles 200–02. This issue has created much recent controversy in the UK with the detention without trial and control order case law before the House of Lords. The position taken in the Constitution is that these fair trial rights should not be capable of being derogated from.

Other constitutional rights may be derogated from where emergency powers are being exercised under Part 6 of the Constitution. The limited circumstances in which derogation may occur even then are set out in Article 177.

The connection between, on the one hand, restricting fundamental rights or derogating from human rights and, on the other, enforcing compliance with fundamental rights is that without a clear enforcement process the restriction and derogation provisions arguably lack coherence. It is to be noted, in that context, that the Joint Committee on Human Rights would retain a provision in its Bill of Rights that allows Parliament to declare expressly in an Act of Parliament that the Act or any of its provisions 'shall operate notwithstanding anything contained in this Bill of Rights and Freedoms'. This is designed to preserve parliamentary sovereignty and is similar in nature to the mechanism detailed in the HRA which allows primary legislation to have full legal effect and validity notwithstanding that the Court has declared it to be incompatible with the ECHR.

However, as explained elsewhere, the concept of parliamentary sovereignty cannot stand beside a written Constitution. It follows that a constitutional provision that adopted the Joint Committee's proviso by simply allowing Parliament to override the Constitution in the case of primary legislation would be logically inconsistent with the overriding nature of the Constitution itself. This is why if the Supreme Court finds a breach of a fundamental right, then—as with any other breach of the Constitution—it has a general duty to make a declaration of unconstitutionality, the effect of which is (see Article 5) that the Act in question is invalid to the extent to which it violates the constitutional requirement.

Scope and content of a domestic Bill of Rights (Articles 181–215)   There is considerable scope for debate as to the precise rights that should be included in the Constitution and how they should be formulated. The Joint Committee suggested an outline Bill of Rights in its report. However, the rights themselves— with a few exceptions—were not drafted.

In the main, the rights drafted in this Constitution have taken the ECHR and the EU Charter as their starting point. Developing things further, it is proposed that in a modern Constitution it is appropriate to include, for the reasons advanced earlier, a number of social and economic rights that do not appear in the ECHR, and many of these are derived from the EU Charter. The Joint Committee considered that a savings clause was needed for such rights and suggested a statutory formulation that would have weakened their effect by not allowing them to be enforced by individuals against the government or any public authority. The reason for such a limitation is understandable and there is something to be said for it. However, this Constitution (borrowing from the South African Bill of Rights) proposes that instead of preventing legal enforcement altogether this class of rights should, rather, be qualified in two instances (see Articles 211–12) by requiring the state to progressively realise, within the state's available resources, these rights by legislation. It is perhaps undesirable to emasculate these rights further, especially with respect to free compulsory education and the very widely phrased series of environmental rights set out in Article 215.

The Joint Committee on Human Rights considered the difficult question of whether a UK Bill of Rights should contain some pre-eminently 'British' rights,[130] such as the right to trial by jury in the Crown Court, and concluded that it should. That suggestion has not been adopted in this Constitution because the ancient right of trial by jury in serious cases is regarded by many as anachronistic and time-consuming. In 2009 the Court of Appeal (Criminal Division) made legal history by ruling that a criminal trial in the Crown Court could take place without a jury.[131] In such a climate, it is considered that it is unwise to entrench jury trial as a constitutional right, whatever may be the merits of having separate laws that retain the absolute right of jury trial in the Crown Court. This appears to coincide with the current approach of the government, as foreshadowed in its Green Paper *Rights and Responsibilities: Developing our Constitutional Framework*.[132]

However, this Constitution adopts the general approach of the Joint Committee, which suggests that there is a need for a few more modern rights than those contained in the ECHR and even in the EU Charter. Thus, for example, the Constitution proposes a wide right of participation in public service on general terms of equality (Article 206), extensively-framed rights for children, persons with disabilities and victims of crime (Articles 207–10), a right to free social[133] (as well as health) care (Article 212), and broad environmental rights (Article 215). These rights are either not recognised in the ECHR or EU Charter or are framed in much wider terms.

---

[130]   However, there are difficulties in categorising even this right as 'British' since there is no established right to a jury trial in Scotland. See generally the discussion of devolution below.

[131]   The trial commenced on 12 January 2010.

[132]   Cm 7577, March 2009.

[133]   The arcane distinction between health and social care has been the subject of a number of court cases and was greatly muddied by the introduction of community care (for which charges may be levied) in 1993. Many consider it unfair that free treatment under the NHS becomes chargeable as social care once an individual's health has stabilised and they leave a long-stay hospital (where formerly they would have remained) and move into a residential care home setting. This is a subject that, it is suggested, deserves a full public debate.

Nonetheless, despite the importance of modernising rights and including, for the first time, specific social and economic rights, this Constitution does not, for the most part, go further and introduce so-called 'third generation rights', being rights which are internationally recognised fundamental rights (such as the right of self-determination). In this, again, the views of the Joint Committee are reflected. The inclusion of environmental rights in a UK Bill of Rights was treated by the Joint Committee as an exception to the omission of third generation rights. However, a level of environmental protection is recognised in the EU Charter and, indirectly, in the ECHR by means of the case law on Article 8; it is, I suggest, now more of a social right than a third generation right.

Given the specific inclusion of the ECHR and the EU Charter in the Constitution, the new rights introduced are relatively few, although the rights as expressed in the Constitution often differ considerably from one or both of the two European rights instruments.[134] The Table below sets out all the constitutional rights. These follow the general scheme of the outline Bill of Rights sketched out in the Twenty-Ninth Report of the Joint Committee on Human Rights, which is referred to above. Where the right in question derives from the ECHR or the EU Charter the source of the right is stated, along with any material differences. There is inevitably a degree of overlap, but incorporating the ECHR and the EU Charter into the Constitution should remedy any omission in the formulation of constitutional rights.

Should there be a statement of constitutional responsibilities? (Articles 216–20)   A constitutional statement of responsibilities is to be distinguished from the normal duties that may arise under the criminal law or other discrete legal regimes such as those of tort or contract. The difference is that a constitutional responsibility is a normative statement suggesting how individuals ought generally to behave towards each other.

In that context, it is perhaps a truism to state that rights may entail a degree of responsibility, certainly in the manner of their exercise. This is expressly recognised in parts of the ECHR, such as in Article 10(2), which—before stipulating the restrictions that may be imposed on the different aspects of the right of freedom of expression—provides that 'The exercise of these [Article 10] freedoms … carries with it duties and responsibilities'.[135]

---

[134]   A notable example is the new equality right contained in Article 181. There is now significant evidence that inequality in society is responsible for many social ills: see Richard Wilkinson and Kate Pickett, *The Spirit Level—Why More Equal Societies Almost Always do Better* (London, Allen Lane, 2009). The new Equality Bill, if it reaches the statute book, will be a further advance in this direction. It reflects what Amartya Sen refers to as the 'capability approach' by focusing more on the redress of substantive differences than on an impartial equality of opportunity (see Amartya Sen, *The Idea of Justice* (London, Allen Lane, 2009) esp 291).

[135]   See also the Preamble to the European Charter of Fundamental Rights.

TABLE OF CONSTITUTIONAL RIGHTS AND PARALLELS IN THE ECHR and EU CHARTER

CONSTITUTIONAL RIGHT (IF ANY)	ECHR SOURCE (IF ANY)	EU CHARTER SOURCE (IF ANY)
Art 181 Equality. This provision is modelled on a similar provision in the South African Bill of Rights	No direct parallel but the ECHR recognises equality of arms under Art 6.1 and non-discrimination in the enjoyment of Convention rights under Art 14	Art 20. Chapter III contains certain other requirements relating to equality (see Arts 21–26) which—although some of these requirements overlap with other constitutional rights—automatically become part of the Constitution (see Art 167 of the Constitution)
Art 182 Respect for human dignity	No direct parallel but many ECHR rights implicitly require respect for human dignity	Art 1
Art 183 Right to life (with specific exclusion of the death penalty)	Art 2. However, Art 2 includes lawful execution as an exception to the right to life	Art 2 (which excludes the death penalty)
Art 184 Respect for physical and mental integrity	No direct parallel but this is implicit in Art 8 (right to respect for private life)	Art 3. This also contains special provisions in relation to medicine and biology which are not included in the Constitution
Art 185 Freedom from torture, inhuman or degrading treatment or punishment	Art 3	Art 4
Art 186 Freedom from slavery and servitude including trafficking in people (excludes legitimate punishment such as unpaid work orders by the court)	Art 4. However, Art 4 does not include trafficking in people. Nor does it exclude legitimate punishment	Art 5. This does not exclude legitimate punishment
Arts 187–88 Right to liberty and security of the person	Art 5	Art 6. This merely states the right and is not elaborated further as it is in the ECHR
Art 189 Respect for private and family life, home and communications	Art 8. However, this refers to 'correspondence' rather than 'communications'	Art 7. There is also a right to protection of personal data which corresponds closely to the EU Data Protection Directive
Art 190 Right to freedom of thought, conscience and religion (including the right of conscientious objection)	Art 9. However, this does not ostensibly recognise conscientious objection as a right	Art 10 (which includes conscientious objection)
Art 191 Right to freedom of expression	Art 10	Art 11

TABLE OF CONSTITUTIONAL RIGHTS *contd*

CONSTITUTIONAL RIGHT (IF ANY)	ECHR SOURCE (IF ANY)	EU CHARTER SOURCE (IF ANY)
Art 191 Right to freedom of expression	Art 10	Art 11
Art 192 Right to freedom of association, assembly and peaceful demonstration	Art 11. However, this does not ostensibly recognise a right of peaceful demonstration	Art 13. However, this does not ostensibly recognise a right of peaceful demonstration
Art 193 Right to marry and found a family, including same-sex marriage	Art 12. However, this does not ostensibly recognise a right to same-sex marriage	Art 9. However, this does not ostensibly recognise a right to same-sex marriage
Art 194 Right to peaceful enjoyment of possessions. Intellectual property is protected under the same terms	Art 1 Protocol 1. There is no express reference to intellectual property	Art 17. Intellectual property is protected
Art 195 Right to freedom of movement	Art 2 Protocol 4. The UK is not currently bound by this right	Art 45
Art 196 Right to asylum	There is no right to asylum in the ECHR	Art 18
Arts 197–98 Rights of arrested and detained persons. The rights here are modelled on the South African Bill of Rights	There are no express rights of this kind in the ECHR, although Art 8 recognises a privilege against self-incrimination and Art 6 contains a number of relevant due process rights	There are no express rights of this kind in the EU Charter
Arts 199–200 Due process rights in civil and criminal cases	Art 6(1) (which Art 194 of the Constitution replicates) contains a general due process requirement in civil and criminal cases. Art 6(2)–(3) (which Art 195 of the Constitution replicates) contains specific safeguards in criminal cases	Arts 47–48
Art 201 Principles of legality and proportionality of criminal offences and penalties. This is concerned with no punishment without law and also with the proportionality of criminal penalty	Art 7. However, this provision is not concerned with the proportionality of penalties	Art 48. This provision, which Art 197 of the Constitution mirrors, is also concerned with the proportionality principle in relation to criminal penalties
Art 202 Right to an effective remedy	Art 13. Art 13 is not, however, a 'Convention right' under the HRA	Art 47

Art 203 Right of access to information. The right here is modelled on the South African Bill of Rights	This right is not recognised in the ECHR	Art 41 contains a right to good administration, which is partially concerned with a right of access to information. Art 42 is concerned with a right to access documents of EU institutions and bodies, offices and agencies of the Union
Art 204 Right to fair and just administrative action. The right here is modelled on the South African Bill of Rights	This right is not recognised in the ECHR	Art 41 contains a right to good administration
Arts 205–08 Democratic rights. Art 205 is taken directly from Art 25 of the International Covenant on Civil and Political Rights and includes not merely free and fair elections and the right to stand as a candidate and be elected but also the wider right to participate on an equal basis in the conduct of public affairs	Art 3 Protocol 1. This deals with free and fair elections	Art 40 deals with the right to vote and stand as a candidate in municipal elections
Art 207 Rights of the child. This statement of rights is modelled on the South African Bill of Rights	There are no express rights for children in the ECHR. However, Art 14 provides that there must be no discrimination in the enjoyment of Convention rights so that they apply equally to children	Arts 24, 32 and 33 contain a number of rights relating to children, although they are less extensive than the rights set out in Art 203 of the Constitution
Art 208 Rights of national minorities. This right is modelled on similar provisions in the Romanian Constitution	There is no express right of national and ethnic identity in the ECHR, although Art 8 (the right to respect for private life) has been held to include national and ethnic identity. Art 14 prohibits discrimination in the enjoyment of Convention rights on several grounds including association with a national minority	Art 22 contains a provision respecting cultural, linguistic and religious diversity
Art 209 Rights of persons with disabilities. This right entrenches Arts 19–20 of the UN Convention on the Rights of Persons with Disabilities, which was ratified by the UK on 8 June 2009	There are no express rights relating to disability in the ECHR. However, case law on Art 8 recognises the right of persons with disabilities to respect for their private life and the fact that this can create positive obligations. Art 14 implicitly encompasses such persons in the overall protection of enjoyment of the other rights	Art 26 contains a provision recognising and respecting the rights of persons with disabilities to benefit from measures designed to ensure their independence, social and occupational integration and participation in the life of the community

TABLE OF CONSTITUTIONAL RIGHTS *contd*

CONSTITUTIONAL RIGHT (IF ANY)	ECHR SOURCE (IF ANY)	EU CHARTER SOURCE (IF ANY)
Art 210 Rights of victims of crime and abuses of power	There is no explicit right in the ECHR	There is no explicit right in the EU Charter
Art 211 Right to adequate standard of living. This right is based in large part on a similar provision in the South African Bill of Rights	There is no such right in the ECHR	Art 34 recognises a right to social security and social assistance
Art 212 Right to free health and social care	There is no such right in the ECHR	Art 35 recognises a right to preventative health care and medical treatment
Arts 213–14 Right to free, full-time education. Art 212 is modelled on the 1948 UN Declaration of Human Rights	Art 2 Protocol 1 recognises a right not to be denied education and the right of parents to educate their children in accordance with their religious and philosophical convictions	Art 14 contains a similar right to that contained in the ECHR but includes the possibility of free compulsory education
Art 215 Right to a healthy environment. This replicates a drafting suggestion in the Twenty-Ninth Report of the Joint Parliamentary Committee in its Outline Bill of Rights	There is no such right in the ECHR, although the case law on Art 8 has established certain rights of environmental protection	Art 37 requires merely a high level of environmental protection in accordance with the principle of sustainable development

There is, though, a wider sense in which responsibilities are linked to the idea of fundamental rights protection. It is not necessary to embrace wholly Aristotle's view that it is the responsibilities of citizenship that give the fullest expression to the concept of the state to understand that rights are not exercised in a vacuum. They are exercised in a social context.

Without state responsibility there would be chaos. The same would be true if there were a complete absence of individual responsibility. Thus, even though there may be no *a priori* first principle compelling either the state or individuals within it to assume particular responsibilities, as a self-organising societal principle it is probably to be treated as axiomatic.

But should such responsibilities be given explicit voice in a Constitution? The main argument against so doing is that what are really moral responsibilities may be artificially limited by their being articulated. A linked argument is that moral responsibility may easily be confused with legal responsibility or, in a section of a Constitution addressing fundamental rights, as a *quid pro quo* of those rights being conferred.

As against these objections, it may be thought that there is strong symbolic value in having a statement of responsibilities. The statement of responsibilities here emphasises an older (mainly Greek) conception of civic virtue that, with the rise of impersonal computerised forms of communication, the decline of religion and few clear reasons for social bonding, leaves modern society looking strangely atomised and incomplete. As explained earlier, there are real risks involved in seeking to set out a statement of values that will always be less than comprehensive. But a general statement of civic responsibilities can double as an implicit endorsement of particular values and an overall reminder of what we owe to each other as human beings.

So, although some dangers exist, this Constitution opts for a short statement of constitutional responsibilities and their proposed effect (see Articles 216–20). The responsibilities themselves (see Articles 216–17) are expressed in the most general terms and cover both our relationships with each other and our relationship to the state as well as to more distant communities or bodies. Tragedies such as the Asian tsunami of 2004 provide exemplary reminders of the reciprocal relationships that we have with the global community.

The remainder of the 'responsibilities' section of the Constitution (Articles 218–20) is concerned to ensure that the responsibilities there set out are treated not as creating mechanistic legal responsibilities or as giving rise to restrictions on fundamental rights, but as the basis of a symbolic moral code. This is the intent to be inferred from the section on responsibilities in the Government's 2009 Green Paper *Rights and Responsibilities: Developing our Constitutional Framework*.[136]

PART 10
THE CITIZENS' BRANCH

221. Subject to this Part, the Citizens' Branch shall consist of two men and two women aged 18 or over from each of the constituencies of the United Kingdom. Each serving member shall be selected at random from the electoral register from those who are eligible. No person may be selected who is a serving member of the legislature, the executive or the judiciary under this Constitution or a serving member of the Scottish Parliament, the Welsh Assembly, the Northern Ireland Assembly or the European Parliament. The random selection of members of the Citizens' Branch, who will serve for a period of one year, will take place on an annual basis and no person may serve on the Citizens' Branch more than once unless they are elected as a member of the Citizens' Council. Any member of the Citizens' Branch who is elected to serve on the Citizens' Council may stand for re-election to the Council and is automatically a member of the Citizens' Branch if re-elected.

[136]   Green Paper (n 132) Chapter 2.

222. The Citizens' Branch chosen in accordance with this Part shall elect a Citizens' Council annually. The Citizens' Council shall be elected by the Citizens' Branch from those members of the Citizens' Branch who stand for election. Each member of the Citizens' Branch shall have one vote and the first ten of those standing for election who receive the highest number of votes shall be elected. The Chairman of the Citizens' Council shall be elected by the members of the Citizens' Council by majority vote or, if the number of votes cast is the same, by agreement of the members of the Citizens' Council. Decisions relating to the organisation and operation of the Citizens' Council shall, subject to this Constitution, be decided by majority vote of the Citizens' Council.

223. The Citizens' Council shall be responsible, in accordance with this Constitution, for the discharge of all functions expressly assigned to it by this Constitution on behalf of the Citizens' Branch. The Citizens' Council shall have the general function of promoting and monitoring the fulfilment and implementation of the values of this Constitution, and in particular for promoting education as a process that helps to create better citizenship.

224. The Citizens' Council shall also be responsible for making recommendations to the legislature for amendments to this Constitution or other legislative change or to the executive for inquiries or hearings from time to time and for the organisation of referendums in accordance with this Constitution for the purpose of amending this Constitution, initiating legislation and initiating public inquiries and hearings into public bodies and their senior management.

225. The Citizens' Council shall be fully independent and shall enjoy operative, financial and administrative autonomy. To this end, it shall be allocated from the State budget a variable annual budget appropriation sufficient to enable it to be set up (including the costs of the election of the Council) and to discharge its functions. The budget shall not be less than the budget for the preceding year.[137] Each member of the Citizens' Council shall be remunerated for his or her services at the same rate as a member of the Cabinet. The initial budget appropriation and succeeding budget appropriations shall be determined by the Prime Minister in Cabinet with the agreement of the Citizens' Council once constituted in accordance with this Constitution. If agreement cannot be reached the Citizens' Council may apply to the Supreme Court for the initial budget appropriation and succeeding budget appropriations to be determined.

OBSERVATIONS AND EXPLANATORY NOTES

Overview—rationale for a Citizens' Branch   The term 'Citizens' Branch' is derived from the Venezuelan Constitution. However, the concept of citizens'

---

[137] The term 'preceding year' is defined in Part 14.

power as developed in that Constitution is essentially state orientated and is very different from a muted version of the principle of direct or participative democracy with which Part 10 of this Constitution is concerned.

Direct democracy, in its purest form, is a form of democratic engagement in which sovereignty resides in a citizens' assembly in which all citizens are, at least potentially, eligible to participate (depending on the variant employed) in legislative, executive and judicial decision-making. It may have been practised to some extent in Athens in the fifth century BC and, to a lesser extent, in the Roman Republic as well as in a few other small states.

In a modern industrialised democracy, real, direct democracy is patently unrealistic. The overarching modern principle on which it may be thought democracy is best achieved is that of representative democracy in which the people, in theory, make decisions through elected representatives.

The dangers of a representative democracy being, in fact, thoroughly unrepresentative have been discussed in many sections of this Constitution and in *Setting the Scene*. The key principle underlying this Constitution is that of popular sovereignty, which entails the people having a true voice in political affairs.

In constitutional arrangements designed to give the people effective choice mechanisms, some form of popular participation is needed and this is what is sought to be achieved in Part 10.

Citizens' Branch and Citizens' Council (Articles 221–25)   The idea of a Citizens' Council selected annually by lot (*cf* Article 221) was practised in, amongst other places, ancient Athens. There, the *boule* (as it was called) comprised 500 male citizens but excluded females and slaves. In more modern times, a Citizens' Council of 500 sitting as an Assembly is unrealistic. This Constitution suggests a practical alternative, namely the creation of a Citizens' Branch from which a Citizens' Council of 10 is chosen on an annual basis (see Articles 221–22).

Article 221 requires that an equal number of men and women are selected at random from the electoral register from each of the UK constituencies in order to form a Citizens' Branch. Tenure is ordinarily for one year. Although a year is a short time, any longer might unduly narrow the number of citizens playing a part in political affairs.

However, the Citizens' Branch of well over one thousand people will do no more than select a Citizens' Council of ten persons from those who put themselves forward for election (Article 222). A Chairman is chosen from the newly elected members of the Citizens' Council.

Once elected, the Citizens' Council becomes more than merely symbolic. The work of the Council on behalf of the Citizens' Branch, as envisaged in this Constitution (see Articles 223–24), encompasses three main elements: (i) The undertaking of functions designated elsewhere in the Constitution. The Citizens' Council is therefore—by majority vote—able to seek declaratory relief from the Supreme Court in relation to political parties under Articles 122 and 124 and is also empowered to seek advisory opinions from the Supreme Court under Article 151 on issues of constitutional interpretation. (ii) The undertaking of wider, broadly monitoring and educative functions in respect of the constitutional values so as to ensure (amongst other things) a better appreciation of what citizenship entails.[138] (iii) The taking of organisational steps to initiate legislative change or public inquiries (including where appropriate seeking, under Article 224, to trigger a referendum as provided for in Part 13 of this Constitution).

There is little danger of these powers being abused. The Supreme Court will have the power to refuse to allow the Citizens' Council to apply to it unless the matter in hand raises an issue of constitutional importance (see Articles 159–63). The wider power of education and monitoring will itself be likely to be budget-dependent and the Constitution contains a mechanism for ascertaining the level of the budget (see Article 225). Finally, the power vested in the Citizens' Council to take steps to trigger the initiation of new legislation or public inquiries is no more than laying the ground for a referendum the result of which decides whether new legislation is to be enacted or a public inquiry held.

The reality is, as the Government has recently observed in a Green Paper, that social and economic change has 'encouraged the rise of a less deferential, more consumerist public'.[139] In such a climate, it is unsurprising that the Power Inquiry chaired by Baroness Kennedy made several specific recommendations encouraging more citizen power in the light of its findings that many citizens felt that they did not have enough influence over political decision-making.

A Constitution is an institutional framework rather than a detailed policy document. Thus, this Constitution has not proposed incorporation of all the Power Inquiry's recommendations in respect of greater citizen involvement.

However, under the Constitution, the Citizens' Council itself has power to recommend constitutional amendments and other legislative change. It is therefore able to consider each of the Kennedy recommendations (and suggest whether and how they should be implemented) over all areas of proposed constitutional reform, including reforms which further empower the people (such as citizens' juries) and the recommendation of the Power Inquiry that all public bodies should be required to meet a duty of public involvement in their decision- and policy-making processes.[140]

---

[138] The development of citizenship values may be better achieved by the Citizens' Council than by more formal political policy-making. A Citizens' Council might, for example, seek to promote the English language in a less controversial way than seeking to entrench it at a constitutional or legislative level as the language of the State. In this way the English language could be more subtly promoted to enable anyone resident in the UK to exercise more easily the full rights of citizenship.

[139] Green Paper (n 132) para 2.15.

[140] The Liberal Democrats' proposal for a citizens' convention of 100 citizens to consider proposals for electoral reform (see Nick Clegg, 'Don't Waste our Time ... Bring Forward Real Reform' *The Independent*, 16 November 2009) falls into this category of possible future recommendations, although it would probably be subsumed in the work of the Citizens' Council itself.

Citizen involvement of this kind has been attempted less often in recent times than in ancient times but it is not unknown. For example, in 2004 the province of British Columbia in Canada introduced a Citizens' Assembly on Electoral Reform, members of which are selected at random, which has proved to be extremely successful.[141]

It is likely that persuading responsible members of the public to participate in a full-time role as a member of a Citizens' Council would require considerable incentives. Article 225 proposes a salary equivalent to that of a member of the Cabinet and an appropriate budget. In order to maximise on the experience of those who have already held tenure for a year, Article 221 permits members of the Citizens' Council to stand for re-election.

PART 11
OTHER ASPECTS OF GOVERNMENT

THE CIVIL SERVICE

226. Subject to this Constitution, laws shall make provision for the composition, recruitment and organisation of the civil service, except that this Part of the Constitution does not apply to the Secret Intelligence Service, the Security Service or the Government Communications Headquarters.

227. Such laws must, in particular, provide that recruitment to the civil service shall be solely on merit and on the basis of fair and open competition. They must also contain rules for a code of conduct in respect of members of the civil service and must prescribe as minimum requirements of that code of conduct that civil servants who serve an administration in the United Kingdom must carry out their duties for the administration as it is duly constituted for the time being, whatever its political complexion, and that such persons must carry out their duties with integrity, honesty, objectivity and impartiality.

228. Such laws may also make provision in relation to special advisers who are not subject to the recruitment provisions applicable to the civil service. Any laws made in relation to special advisers shall not affect the other provisions of this Constitution in respect of such special advisers.

---

[141] For further detail see Bogdanor (n 91) 304–05.

THE ARMED FORCES

229. The State shall make sufficient provision to ensure that the armed forces[142] are adequately resourced for the performance of their constitutional function. Laws must make provision for such resourcing of the armed forces and for the regular monitoring of that resourcing which must be required by law to be transparent.

230. Laws may make further provision for the composition, recruitment and organisation of the armed forces.

231. The armed forces shall have the constitutional function of safeguarding the security of the United Kingdom but shall exercise that function only on the direction of the Prime Minister or any Supreme Commander appointed by the Head of State under this Constitution. Any such Supreme Commander shall be subject to the exercise of power by the Prime Minister under Article 92 of this Constitution or pursuant to the exercise by the Prime Minister of emergency powers under Part 6 of this Constitution.

232. The Head of State shall be the nominal Commander-in-Chief of the armed forces but shall remain subject to this Constitution and, in particular, to the powers exercisable in relation to the armed forces by the Prime Minister under Article 92 of this Constitution.

233. The Head of State shall, following any advice of the Prime Minister acting through Cabinet under Article 92 of this Constitution or pursuant to the exercise by the Prime Minister of emergency powers under Part 6 of this Constitution, appoint a Supreme Commander of the armed forces.

THE POLICE

234. The State shall make sufficient provision to ensure that the police are adequately resourced. Laws must make provision for such resourcing of the police and for the regular monitoring of that resourcing which must be required by law to be transparent.

235. Laws shall also make provision for the establishment of police areas and for the maintenance of police authorities throughout the United Kingdom which authorities shall be charged with the constitutional function of securing the effective and efficient policing of their police areas.

236. Laws may make provision for the election of members of the police authorities.

---

[142] See Part 14 for a definition of the term 'armed forces'.

LOCAL AUTHORITIES

237. The State shall encourage by law the progressive simplification of the structure of local government institutions and the progressive strengthening of local government power.

238. To that end, the State shall pass laws with the intention of making local government institutions progressively self-financing and less dependent on central government.

OBSERVATIONS AND EXPLANATORY NOTES

Overview   Part 11 of this Constitution covers a number of controversial constituent elements involved in or associated with the process of government. Each of them has generated recent political debate, with occasional polarisation of views amongst the main parties. For that reason, some care is needed in devising a constitutional mechanism to deal with them.

The civil service (Articles 226–28)   The regulation of the civil service is perhaps the least controversial of the four topics that are addressed in Part 11. This is because it appears not to be seriously disputed that the civil service should be regulated on a statutory basis, that there should be a core statement of values, and that recruitment to the civil service should be merit-based, competitive and transparent.

Stereotypically perhaps, civil servants have been expected to serve the government of the day with independent and objective advice whatever its political complexion. The nineteenth century Northcote-Trevelyan reforms leading to the establishment of a Civil Service Commission in 1855 were designed to achieve just that.

Over the years the neutrality of the civil service has come under fire. Some view the Thatcher era as one in which the willingness of civil servants to challenge ministers' views on policy was weakened by virtue of the Prime Minister's growing influence over senior appointments. But it was the Blair years that witnessed the burgeoning of special advisers and, with the appointment of such persons, the treatment of those pursuing careers in the civil service as 'simple subordinates with little or no recognition that they had a constitutional function of institutional scepticism, of speaking truth to power; of helping ministers to ensure fairness in their decision-making, of legitimating that decision-making; of helping them to achieve objectivity and truth in their public statements and documents'.[143]

The need, in general, for modern reform of the civil service and, in particular, to make special advisers more accountable seems to be common ground amongst all political parties. The 2009 Constitutional Reform and Governance Bill (in this respect essentially repeating provisions contained in the 2008 Constitutional Renewal Bill) includes provisions which set out, amongst other

---

[143]   Christopher Foster, *British Government in Crisis* (Oxford, Hart Publishing, 2005) 218.

things, a statutory code for the civil service and for special advisers, a series of recruitment principles, and a requirement for annual reports to be made to Parliament or the relevant devolved bodies from the relevant minister in relation to special advisers.[144]

This Constitution accommodates these provisions (Articles 226–28) whilst maintaining the entrenched constitutional scheme relating to special advisers (Article 228).

The armed forces (Articles 229–33)   The problem here is lack of adequate funding, and the steadily rising death toll in the armed services, especially in Afghanistan (108 British soldiers were killed in 2009 alone), has caused recent widespread concern that troops are not adequately resourced. This, coupled with the suppressed 2009 report of Bernard Gray, a former senior Ministry of Defence adviser, warning of 'lethal' weaknesses in defence procurement, has led senior personnel to complain about a lack of helicopter support and sufficiently armoured vehicles for troops.

Incontestably, the armed forces require sufficient resources and the Government accepts this. This Constitution therefore creates an express constitutional role for the armed forces (Article 231) and mandates adequate resourcing as well as regular and transparent monitoring of such resourcing (Article 229).

Nothing in the Constitution is designed to interfere with conventional statutory provisions, such as those contained in the Army Act 1955, on the general organisation of the armed forces (see Article 230). However, a new command structure is necessary (see Articles 231–33) because of the diluted role of the monarchy introduced by the Constitution.

The police (Articles 234–36)   In relation to policing, we come up against the difficult question of whether the police force is sufficiently accountable to the electorate. It has even been suggested by some that there should be American-style, directly elected local sheriffs who could make decisions as to how their neighbourhoods are policed.[145] Other suggestions aimed at making the police more accountable involve a requirement that some members of police authorities are directly elected and the creation of a directly elected police commissioner.

The underlying idea is, in whatever form it might be introduced, that electors should be given a greater say in policing in their local areas, with the Home Secretary's power to control police forces' priorities being removed. As voiced by some critics of the present system, the concern is not whether or not *national* crime figures have or have not gone up but, rather, whether *local* crime has risen.

---

[144] For their part, civil servants argue that considerable further reform is needed to ensure that central government has 'a single coherent strategy for government'. See Institute for Government, *Shaping Up: A Whitehall for the Future* (18 January 2010).

[145] See eg Douglas Carswell and Daniel Hannan's self-published *The Plan—Twelve Months to Renew Britain* (2008), available on Google Books.

Although localism in certain areas such as local government (discussed below) is to be encouraged, a rather more complex question arises in relation to the police. It is not at all easy to see how elections for, say, a local sheriff would work in practice. It would be hard to guarantee against extremists standing for office or (perhaps similarly) a far-right party fielding local candidates. As against this, advocates of direct elections point out that policing has become over-centralised with national targets and standards overriding local priorities and that the risk of extremist candidates standing for election is, in principle, no worse than at a general or local election.

There are powerful arguments both ways and it is probably too soon to seek to entrench direct elections into policing or even, perhaps, to introduce such legislation. This Constitution (see Article 236) leaves open the possibility of laws being introduced (which would not be entrenched).

Local authorities (Articles 237–38)   Introducing more localism in local government is a rather different matter. It is hard to deny that the structure of local government has, to say the least, become unnecessarily complicated and that local democracy has all but disappeared. The reason for this is the increasing centralisation of government which has led to the financial expenditure of local authorities being controlled largely from the centre. This started with local authority capping in the 1980s and now some three-quarters of local government finance comes out of the central government purse, often with legal directions as to how it must be deployed.

Articles 237–38 seek to simplify the structure of local authorities and (viewing it as a related matter) to enable local government to be progressively self-financing. The means by which this might be achieved are likely to be highly technical and the detail required is well beyond the scope of any Constitution. This Constitution simply lays down a framework for laws to be passed which achieve both simplification and increased local authority self-financing. However, unlike some other constitutional provisions which *permit* laws to be passed, thus giving a 'steer' to the legislator, Articles 237–38 are mandatory in nature. This is because increased local democracy is one of the most politically 'tangible' elements touching our lives and needs a far greater emphasis than it has been accorded in the past.

PART 12
CONSTITUTIONAL CONVENTIONS

239. Constitutional conventions[146] that are incompatible with this Constitution shall no longer apply. A convention shall be deemed to be incompatible with this Constitution for the purposes of this Part of this Constitution if, amongst other things, its effect is to place any restriction on the exercise of a constitutional power, duty or right.

240. Constitutional conventions existing at the time when this Constitution comes into force shall otherwise continue to apply and form part of this Constitution except that such constitutional conventions shall no longer apply if the convention in question has been codified in this Constitution in whole or in part or if the subject matter of the convention has been provided for by this Constitution.

241. Nothing in this Constitution shall prevent a new constitutional convention from arising after the coming into force of this Constitution and forming part of this Constitution provided that what would otherwise have been a new convention is not incompatible with this Constitution and does not cover matters that have, in whole or in part, been codified in this Constitution or if the subject matter has been provided for by this Constitution.

OBSERVATIONS AND EXPLANATORY NOTES

Constitutional conventions (Articles 239–41)   Articles 239–41 deal with the effect of constitutional conventions in a written Constitution. Their brevity is deceptive, since the problems raised by unwritten 'conventions' arguably go to the analytic integrity of a written Constitution and therefore make drafting this part of the Constitution rather more difficult than the drafting of entirely new and free-standing constitutional provisions.

Conventions, in their broadest sense, are unwritten agreements as to what particular procedures should be followed or as to how certain powers should be exercised in a constitutional arrangement. Where conventions are recognised as having arisen, they are treated in practice as binding. Although such conventions can exist in tandem with a written Constitution they are usually the product of earlier informal arrangements before the Constitution was reduced to writing. In the UK, which has not had a written Constitution since Cromwell, conventions find their place alongside a medley of statutes, court decisions, customary law and other sources of obligations and powers such as the (unwritten) royal prerogative.

---

[146] See Part 14, where the term 'constitutional convention' is defined and given an extended meaning for the purposes of the Constitution so as to include documents such as concordats or memoranda of understanding between government and third parties. This would encompass, for example, the 2004 concordat agreed by the Lord Chief Justice and the Lord Chancellor as to the intended separation of powers as between the government and judiciary.

In order to understand the drafting difficulties entailed in encompassing both substantive conventions and the very concept of conventions in a written Constitution, three things need to be appreciated. First, the entire purpose of a written Constitution is to reduce obligations and sources of power to writing. From that initial perspective, conventions outside the Constitution are both untidy and, worse than that, distort one of the purposes of the Constitution. They should, on this logic, *all* be reduced to writing or discarded. Secondly, however, conventions do not have the force of law. This means that the courts do not normally adjudicate on the meaning or existence of conventions. It follows that the act of reducing a convention to writing in a constitutional provision means that the meaning of what was once a convention but is now a constitutional provision becomes justiciable in the courts. This may (depending on the nature of the convention in question) be a reason *not* to reduce the convention to writing. Thirdly, because of the need to entrench rights in a Constitution rather than enabling them to be taken away by a strong executive, the process of amending a Constitution (see Part 13 below) is intended to be difficult. This is a further argument for retaining at least the possibility of developing some types of conventions over time; otherwise, the vitality of the Constitution may become too dependent on straining the meaning of existing constitutional provisions to cater for new and unforeseen situations.

This Constitution seeks to preserve the fluidity of allowing new conventions to develop whilst, at the same time, not permitting unwritten constraints on power to continue to be exercised or new conventions to develop which could subvert constitutional provisions.

Some existing conventions have been expressly codified in the Constitution. For example, the convention that money bills must originate in the House of Commons is, *mutatis mutandis*, preserved in Article 17. The convention *qua* convention therefore no longer applies (see Article 240) but that is immaterial because it is now an express term of the Constitution.

Where there is no clear transposition of this kind, the first step is to ascertain whether an existing convention not expressly incorporated is incompatible with the Constitution. If so, it no longer applies (see Article 239). A convention is deemed to be incompatible with the Constitution for the purposes of Part 12 if, amongst other things, its effect is to place a restriction on the exercise of a constitutional power, duty or right (Article 239). This has to be read with Article 240, which stipulates that, otherwise, existing conventions shall continue to apply except where the convention has been codified in whole *or in part* in the Constitution or if the subject matter of the convention has been provided for by the Constitution.

A number of existing conventions (if not the majority) will, as a result of these provisions, no longer apply.

A concrete example will illustrate how the Constitution is intended to operate in terms of the incompatibility of current conventions. It would (see the deeming provision in Article 239) be incompatible with the constitutional power of the Houses of the Parliament to legislate for that power to be circumscribed by conventions such as the Sewel Convention, which entails the Westminster Parliament first having to seek the consent of the Scottish Parliament before legislating on devolved (non-reserved) matters. This Constitution therefore prevents such a convention from applying. But that does not mean that it is not still open to the Westminster Parliament to continue to seek consent from the Scottish Parliament before legislating on devolved matters. What it does mean is that any continued practice by Westminster of seeking the consent of the Scottish Parliament before legislating on devolved matters will not, no matter how long-lasting the practice, operate to create a new convention (see Article 241) because the seeking of consent *as a constitutional requirement* is always incompatible with the Constitution. It will therefore always be open to the Westminster Parliament to enact legislation relating to devolved matters without seeking the Scottish Parliament's consent.

Similar principles cover those cases in which the existing convention, whilst not intrinsically incompatible with the Constitution, is nonetheless treated as being subsumed into the Constitution if the Constitution has wholly *or partially* codified it or if the subject matter of the convention has been provided for by the Constitution (see Article 240).

The same principles cover the creation of new conventions. Articles 91–92, for example, set out an express requirement that war may not be declared without a majority vote of the House of Representatives and the Senate sitting as a single Assembly. It follows (see Article 241) that since the Constitution already contains a provision encompassing this subject matter, such a practice involving, say, a higher measure of support from Parliament cannot legitimately develop into a convention.

It can be seen from the above that interpretation issues may arise as a result of these provisions. The process of identifying a convention is itself uncertain and, almost by definition, is fraught with ambiguity.[147] Once a convention has been identified, the further process of deciding whether it is incompatible with the Constitution or whether its subject matter has been provided for by the Constitution may fall to the Supreme Court to decide on a constitutional reference or other application.

There is therefore some scope for debate as to whether the Constitution should seek to encompass constitutional conventions more rigorously, perhaps by itemising them, or whether they should simply not be included at all. The rationale for the drafting underlying the proposed draft Constitution is that given the combination of express codification and wide exclusions in Articles 239–41, few former conventions will remain unscathed and the potential for the development of new ones will be limited though not precluded.

---

[147] A graphic account of the possible difficulties is given in Bogdanor (n 112) 222–24.

PART 13
CONSTITUTIONAL CHANGES AND REFERENDUMS

242. Subject to, and in accordance with, this Part of the Constitution, one or more provisions of this Constitution may be amended following the referendum procedure set out in this Part. Amendments to this Constitution following such procedure include the addition of provisions. Referendums may also be held on matters not affecting this Constitution and this Part shall apply to those referendums as well as to referendums concerning amendment of the Constitution.

243. No fundamental provisions[148] of this Constitution nor rights protected by Article 180 shall be amended, nor shall their amendment be proposed. The nations constituting the United Kingdom as described in Article 1 may only be altered following the referendum procedure set out in this Part applied to the part of the United Kingdom to which a proposed alteration relates.

244. After approval in a referendum by a three-fifths majority of the people, conducted in accordance with this Part of the Constitution, a proposal to amend one or more of the provisions of this Constitution or on any other matter not precluded by this Constitution shall result in an amendment of the provision or provisions of this Constitution approved in the referendum or, as the case may be, adoption of the proposal the subject of the referendum, only with the agreement of the Houses of the Parliament sitting as a single assembly by a three-fifths majority and by a second referendum with a three-fifths majority.

245. Save where, subject to this Constitution, the Executive Government offers a referendum to the people or to the registered voters of part of the United Kingdom in which case the referendum must be organised and funded by the State, a referendum shall only be required to be held, organised and funded by the State where twenty per cent of the registered voters of the United Kingdom (or where the matter principally concerns a part of the United Kingdom, twenty per cent of the registered voters of that part of the United Kingdom) petition the Speaker of the House of Representatives calling for a referendum on a matter not precluded by Articles 242–45 from being the subject of a referendum. A referendum result (whether offered by the executive or otherwise) shall not be valid unless forty per cent of the registered voters of the United Kingdom (or, as appropriate, forty per cent of the registered voters in the relevant part of the United Kingdom) vote in the referendum. A referendum result shall not be binding without a three-fifths majority of those voting in the referendum. Where a referendum is invalid or is not binding, a further referendum shall not be held without a new petition.

---

[148] This term is defined in Part 14.

Save for referendums relating to amendment of this Constitution, no referendum may be offered to the people by the executive Government or proposed by the people on a matter principally affecting a part of the United Kingdom but may only be offered to that part of the United Kingdom principally affected or proposed by the people of that part of the United Kingdom principally affected.[149]

OBSERVATIONS AND EXPLANATORY NOTES

Amending the Constitution (Articles 242–45)   Part 13 is concerned with changing the Constitution and changes affecting the Constitution as well as with the referendum procedure for these and other matters. The proposals relating to referendums treat proposed constitutional amendments and other matters in the same way, on the basis that if a matter is sufficiently serious to require a referendum, a high vote is needed for change to be effected.

In relation to constitutional amendments, a Constitution seeks to *entrench* rights and obligations, as opposed to merely enacting laws, which can easily be changed by different policies of incoming governments. This means that a process of constitutional amendment must make changing the Constitution more difficult than it would be simply to change a law. This is why allowing amendment by majority parliamentary decision (the basis of primary legislation in the UK) would be unacceptable in relation to a written Constitution.

However, this ought not to mean that entrenched provisions can *never* be changed. If that were the position a Constitution, far from being a liberating force, could become a straitjacket.

It is nonetheless suggested that there are certain provisions that should, in principle, be irrevocable.[150] This safeguards against the dangers of tyranny and subversion of the Constitution, as, for example, occurred in Germany in 1933 when a legitimate law—the Enabling Act—passed by majority vote in the Reichstag allowed Hitler to deviate from the Constitution and thereafter to suppress all political opposition.

At first sight there are problems with the suggestion that there may be constitutional principles which are prescribed in advance as irrevocable. The difficulty was expressed succinctly by Thomas Paine in *The Rights of Man* (1791), where he observed that 'Every age and generation must be as free to act for itself, in all cases, as the ages and generations which preceded it. The vanity and presumption of governing beyond the grave, is the most ridiculous and insolent of all tyrannies.' This was part of his stinging rebuke of Edmund Burke, who had suggested that the 1688 Revolution had resulted in a permanent constitutional settlement whereby the people of England submitted themselves and their heirs and posterity 'to the end of time' to the power of the Crown.

---

[149] This latter provision is intended to prevent the UK as a whole from being able to vote on matters that principally affect only part of the UK. Scottish independence is one such issue.

[150] Certain Constitutions (such as that of India) contain such a provision.

Of course, in one sense Paine is right. No government can, in practice, bind another or even itself, let alone a generation. Constitutions that are ostensibly watertight can simply be torn up, as occurred in Fiji in April 2009 when the President of the Republic, dissatisfied with a court judgment declaring his actions to be unlawful under the Constitution of Fiji, simply jettisoned the Constitution and ruled under his own 'emergency' fiat.

Moreover, there is a real danger of hubris in treating any underpinning constitutional 'idea' as irrevocable. If, to take a particularly apposite example, parliamentary sovereignty were to be declared irrevocable, the UK could never, as a matter of constitutional settlement, have a written Constitution. Indeed, that is the subtext of Burke's view of the legal effect of the glorious revolution of 1688.

The difficulty is that the very logic of Paine's position can feed back into a profound relativism which, in political terms at least, is highly dangerous. As suggested in *Setting the Scene*, mankind has no tool other than reason with which to confront prejudice, greed, envy and all the other irrationalities and superstitions that have the potential to destroy us. There is no precise linear reasoning, comparable to a mathematical equation, that will solve the problems of humanity or even point towards a clear solution. But this does not mean that reason is not the underlying principle that should govern our actions and inform how we seek to address our political and constitutional relationships.

An important premise of this Constitution is that whilst reason might get things wrong, it can never be wrong to employ reason. Further, since reason is the antithesis of blind, unquestioning belief yet supports a right to harbour any beliefs one wishes, this Constitution supports as axiomatic a pluralistic society in which mutual tolerance, including religious tolerance, prevails. Finally, consistently with that axiom and with the underlying significance of reason, ultimate constitutional power must reside in the people, whose collective reason is what informs everything in the Constitution.

Philosophically, these may at best be normative statements. But they are, even on that level, statements of practical intent and if the Constitution is to be based on them it is suggested that they should be expressed as permanent values incapable of change. That is why Articles 242–43 prevent the amendment of certain fundamental provisions as defined in Part 14. If they are to be changed, that may only be achieved by abrogating the Constitution itself. Yet that, too, is forbidden (see Article 9). It may, as accepted earlier, be true that ultimately nothing can be done in practice to prevent say a neo-Stalinist from tearing up the entire Constitution and even proclaiming a new one, but there will be a severe price to be paid in terms of loss of legitimacy. Ultimately, as James Madison observed, 'all governments rest on opinion'.[151] The apparent coercive power of the state is only effective if people believe in its legitimacy.

---

[151] 'The Federalist', 49 in Alexander Hamilton, James Madison and John Jay, *The Federalist Papers* (Oxford, Oxford World's Classics, 2008) 251.

Constitutional amendment (where permitted) could be triggered by a large majority of Parliament without recourse to a referendum at all. However, a referendum or series of referendums coupled with a large parliamentary majority is probably more accurately reflective of principles of representative democracy. A referendum is a vote by the whole or a part of the electorate on a specific proposal or proposals. Few countries (there are some exceptions such as Switzerland) currently make extensive use of referendums. Whilst consistent with the doctrine of parliamentary sovereignty, which can never allow a referendum to have legal effect, this is sought to be remedied in this Constitution since referendums are themselves a form of direct democracy of the kind encouraged by it (see Notes on the Citizens' Branch). The UK Government has rarely offered a referendum, and this has sometimes been criticised (take, for example, its failure to do so in respect of the Lisbon Treaty). It did offer a national referendum on the principle of continued membership of the European Community in 1975, and a few local referendums have been held. For example, devolution was made the subject of local referendums in Scotland and Wales.

The referendum procedure (Articles 244–45)   In outline, the referendum procedure set out in Part 13 provides for an initial referendum (if offered by the government or triggered by 20 per cent of the electorate or relevant part of the electorate) which mandates parliamentary consideration if adopted by a three-fifths majority. If Parliament (again by a three-fifths majority) sanctions the proposal it is put out for a second referendum, which will be binding if adopted by at least the same majority as previously.

Articles 244–45 are concerned with the procedure for referendums for constitutional change and other matters. Like a recall referendum (see Articles 41–42) for the recall of elected representatives (albeit usually on a national level save where local interests are involved), it is suggested that the requisite proportion of the electorate needed to trigger a referendum for possible constitutional change in the form of constitutional amendment or relevant legislative change should be quite high. Twenty per cent of the registered electorate is suggested.

Part 13 does not set out a mechanism for organising referendums; this is a matter entrusted to the executive government (see Article 245) or the Citizens' Council (see Article 222). The government may offer a referendum at any time and no constitutional convention can constrain its power to do so (see generally Notes to Part 12). Nor will a prior 'trigger' be necessary for a government referendum to be held.

It is also suggested that—whether offered by the government or triggered by the electorate—there should be a large majority vote in favour of change before further action is required under the Constitution. A three-fifths majority is suggested (see Articles 244–45). Further, a sufficiently high proportion of the registered electorate actually voting in the referendum is suggested as being necessary. Other countries have such a requirement. For example, Poland requires a 50 per cent turnout; in Denmark the threshold is 40 per cent. The size of requisite turnout suggested here is (see Article 242) 40 per cent.

It should be noted that the procedure suggested for referendums (and their legal effect) under Part 13 apply equally to the referendums referred to in other Parts of the Constitution.

Separatism raises particular referendum/amendment issues. If part of the UK (such as Scotland) wished to separate from the UK, Article 245 makes it clear that a petition from 20 per cent of the registered electorate in (say) Scotland will be sufficient to trigger the proposal being debated in the Houses of the Parliament (see also Article 240, which makes it clear that the government can only offer the option of separation to the relevant part, as opposed to the whole, of the UK).

Special considerations may be thought to attach to Northern Ireland. Section 1 of the Northern Ireland Act 1998 requires only a simple majority of the people of Northern Ireland to vote for Northern Ireland to cease to be part of the UK. Parliament would then be required to give effect to that majority wish. Such a provision is incompatible with Part 13 of this Constitution, as currently drafted, which contains stricter criteria for separation to occur; although, if it were considered desirable, an exception could be made for Northern Ireland.

PART 14
INTERPRETATION AND FINAL MATTERS

246. In this Constitution unless the context otherwise requires:

"Appropriate Boundary Commission" is the appropriate Boundary Commission or Commissions established by law for the different nations of the United Kingdom or other body or bodies established by law[152] for those nations to create or review as the case may be constituencies in respect of elections to the House of Representatives and larger regional constituencies in respect of elections to the elected body of the Senate.

"Armed forces" means the Army, the Royal Navy and the Royal Air Force of the United Kingdom.

"Cabinet" means the collective decision-making body of the Executive comprising the Prime Minister and no more than 22 other Ministers occupying the most senior offices of State.

"Child" means every human being below the age of eighteen years.

---

[152] At one stage it was anticipated (see the Political Parties, Elections and Referendums Act 2000) that the United Kingdom Electoral Commission would take over the work of the four Boundary Commissions for England, Scotland, Wales and Northern Ireland. This specific proposal has not been implemented but another body or bodies may, in time, take over the work of the present Commissions.

"Civil list" is the annual sum voted by the Houses of the Parliament for the expenses of the sovereign, the Royal Household and other members of the Royal Family.

"Constituency" is the electoral area electing, as provided for in this Constitution, a member or members to one or other of the Houses of the Parliament.

"Constitutional convention" is a well-established custom or practice that has evolved over time and is widely regarded as a fundamental aspect of government. For the purposes of this Constitution the term shall include documents such as concordats and memoranda of understanding that have been concluded between the government and third parties.

"Declaration of constitutionality" and "Declaration of unconstitutionality" is the name given to the remedies granted by the Supreme Court declaring that a law or other measure or state of affairs (including administrative acts and omissions) is (respectively) in accordance with this Constitution and therefore constitutional or is contrary to this Constitution and therefore unconstitutional with the effects provided for by this Constitution.

"Declaration of incompatibility" is the name given to a remedy granted by a court with the requisite jurisdiction that a law or other relevant measure is incompatible with this Constitution with the effects provided for by this Constitution.

"Fundamental principles" as referred to in Articles 121–22 means the fundamental rights contained in Part 9 of this Constitution, and the values of liberty, democracy and popular sovereignty, fairness, civic duty and the rule of law.

"Fundamental provision of this Constitution" means any of the following provisions of this Constitution: Articles 2–5, 9, 105, 122, 130–32, 176, 177, and 242–43.

"Head of State" shall mean the person or body of persons exercising the functions of Head of State under Part 5 of this Constitution.

"In time of war" as used in Article 113 does not extend to acts of terrorism.

"Larger regional constituency" is the electoral area electing one or, as the case may be, more than one member to the elected body of the Senate.[153]

"Majority vote" means a vote in excess of 50 per cent of the votes cast.

"Multi-member constituency" is the electoral area electing more than two members to the House of Representatives.

---

[153] At a general election there would have to be a minimum of two elected members but at a by-election for one vacant seat only one member would be returned.

"Preceding year" as referred to in Article 225 means the calendar year preceding the day of agreement or determination of the new variable annual budget.

"Primary legislation" means an Act or Acts of Parliament enacted by the Westminster Parliament.

"Royal Acts" means the Bill of Rights 1688, the Coronation Oath Act 1688, the Act of Settlement 1700, the Union with Scotland Act 1707 and the Royal Marriages Act 1772.

"Secondary legislation" means a law made by an executive authority under powers conferred by primary legislation.

"The people" and "the people of the United Kingdom" means throughout this Constitution (including the Preamble) those persons who are, by law, eligible to vote at Parliamentary General Elections in the United Kingdom.

"Two-member constituency" is the electoral area electing two members to the House of Representatives.

"United Kingdom" has the meaning given to it in Article 1.

247. The territories specified in Schedule 1 shall be consulted in relation to, and prior to, the coming into force of this Constitution. Special constitutional relationships may be entered into between the United Kingdom and one or more of those territories which, if proposed to be entered into, shall be the subject of separate provision by law.

248. This Constitution shall come into force at the expiry of 365 days after approval by referendum following the referendum procedure contained in the Constitution of Britain (Referendums) Act. For the avoidance of doubt, the referendum procedure establishing this Constitution shall not be regulated by Part 13 of this Constitution and Part 13 has no application to the referendum procedure establishing this Constitution.

OBSERVATIONS AND EXPLANATORY NOTES

Interpretation and other matters (Articles 246–48) Part 14 is devoted to practical matters relating to interpretation and implementation of the Constitution. Most Constitutions require a section of this kind unless such matters are included in earlier parts of the Constitution as they arise.

As far as interpretation is concerned (see Article 246), general expressions have sometimes been used in the Constitution which, whilst they may trigger associations, may—unless defined more precisely—have the potential to confuse.

For example, a term such as 'the people' could mean anyone living in the UK, or it could have a more restricted meaning. Given that the Constitution represents a conferment of power from the people, and that the people have a certain measure of power under the Constitution (see especially Part 10), it is considered that this term requires precise definition and should be restricted to those persons who are entitled to vote at parliamentary general elections. Currently, these include UK citizens, citizens of the Republic of Ireland aged 18 or over, qualifying Commonwealth citizens,[154] citizens of any EU country who are resident in the UK, and certain UK citizens who live or work abroad.

Importantly, a number of such citizens are not currently entitled to vote at general elections. These include peers entitled to sit in the House of Lords and detained prisoners. In the case of *Hirst v United Kingdom (No 2)*[155] the European Court of Human Rights declared the UK ban on voting by detained prisoners to be unlawful and legislative change to comply with this ruling is expected following the 2010 general election.

Other general expressions of this kind which it is considered require precise definition in order to serve a sensible constitutional purpose are exemplified by 'Cabinet', 'fundamental principles' and 'fundamental provision of the Constitution'. There is obviously scope for debate as to which of these classes of terms need even more careful definition and what such definitions should be.[156] Although in a western liberal democracy the fundamental principles set out in Article 246 are probably uncontroversial, the term 'fundamental provision of the Constitution', from which emergency laws may not derogate (see Article 112), needs to be distinguished from those provisions of the Constitution that may not be amended (see Article 243). Whilst there is likely to be overlap between the two, they are not necessarily co-extensive.

Other expressions requiring definition are those which are terms of art and which are intended to be used in a specialised sense. Examples of these include 'appropriate Boundary Commission', 'constituency' and 'larger regional constituency'.

Articles 247 and 248 conclude the Constitution and deal with (respectively) the future constitutional relationships between the Schedule 1 territories and the UK (see also Article 1), for which separate provision will need to be made, and the date for the coming into force of the Constitution, which, if it is approved, will be dependent on the outcome of the referendum procedure contained in the Constitution of Britain (Referendums) Act.

---

[154] It is possible that different rules would in future attach to citizens of Commonwealth countries that chose to sever constitutional ties with the UK following the coming into force of a written Constitution which altered the position of the monarchy.

[155] (2006) 42 EHRR 41.

[156] For example, although the Constitutional Reform Act 2005 uses the expression 'rule of law' without defining it further, some may think that it should be defined more precisely. The contrary case is that it is fruitless to seek to define broad concepts such as 'rule of law', 'fairness' and 'democracy'.

The Constitution of Britain (Referendums) Act

An Act to make provision for the holding of referendums on the question of whether the United Kingdom should have a written Constitution and, if so, what form the Constitution should take and to make further provision, should the outcome of the referendum be that the United Kingdom should have a written Constitution, for the implementation of the Constitution in substitution for the present constitutional arrangements that prevail in the United Kingdom.

B E IT ENACTED by the Queen's most Excellent Majesty, by and with the advice and consent of the Lords Spiritual and Temporal, and Commons, in this present Parliament assembled, and by the authority of the same, as follows:–

PART 1

REFERENDUM ON A WRITTEN CONSTITUTION

1   A national referendum shall be held on whether there should be a written Constitution for the United Kingdom.

2   The question to be asked in the referendum and the front of the ballot papers to be used for that purpose shall be in the form set out in Schedule 2.

3   An Order under this section shall be laid before Parliament by the Prime Minister and shall:

(1)   appoint a day for the holding of the referendum, and, subject to the provisions of this Act,

(2)   make provision for the manner of holding the referendum, which shall be conducted on the same basis as a Parliamentary Election using the constituencies in existence at the time of the holding of the referendum.

4   An Order made under section 3 may make such further provision as may be necessary or expedient for the carrying out of the referendum including the funding of the referendum from money provided by Parliament and for the provision and funding from money provided by Parliament of a period of public education and debate preceding the holding of the referendum for the purpose of facilitating public understanding of the issues involved in the referendum.

5   No Order shall be made under section 3 unless a draft of the Order has been laid before, and approved by resolution of, Parliament.

6   Those entitled to vote at the referendum shall be:

(1)   persons who, on the date of the referendum, would be entitled to vote as voters at a General Election in the United Kingdom;

(2)   peers who at that date would be entitled to vote as electors at a local government election in any electoral area.

7   The result of the referendum to be held under section 1 of this Act is binding only if at least 60% of the validly cast ballots in the constituencies aggregated together vote the same way on the question that forms the subject of the referendum.

PART 2

SECOND REFERENDUM ON THE CONTENT
OF A WRITTEN CONSTITUTION

8   Part 2 of this Act shall apply only if the outcome of the referendum held under section 1 is binding under section 7 and if it is in favour of a written Constitution for the United Kingdom.

9   If Part 2 applies, a second national referendum shall be held within [ ] of the date of the referendum held under section 1 of this Act, in which the question to be asked in the referendum and the front of the ballot papers to be used for that purpose shall be in the form set out in Schedule 3, and the draft Constitution in the form set out in Schedule 1 shall be attached to the ballot paper.

10   An Order under this section shall be laid before Parliament by the Prime Minister and shall:

(1)   appoint a day for the holding of the referendum, and, subject to the provisions of this Act,

(2)   make provision for the manner of holding the second referendum which shall be conducted on the same basis as a Parliamentary Election using the constituencies in existence at the time of the holding of the referendum.

11   An Order made under section 10 shall make such further provision as may be necessary for the carrying out of the second referendum including the funding of the second referendum from money provided by Parliament and for the provision and funding from money provided by Parliament of a period of public education and debate preceding the holding of the second referendum for the purpose of facilitating public understanding of the issues involved in the second referendum.

12   No Order shall be made under section 10 unless a draft of the Order has been laid before, and approved by resolution of, Parliament.

13   Those entitled to vote at the second referendum shall be:

(1)   persons who, on the date of the referendum, would be entitled to vote as voters at a General Election in the United Kingdom;

(2)   peers who at that date would be entitled to vote as electors at a local government election in any electoral area.

14   The result of the second referendum is binding according to the choice of a simple majority of the validly cast ballots in the constituencies aggregated together.

PART 3

IMPLEMENTATION OF THE SECOND REFERENDUM

15   If the outcome of the referendum in Part 2 is that the Constitution set out in Schedule 1 is approved, that Constitution shall come into force in accordance with Article 248 of that Constitution and from that date the provisions of that Constitution shall apply in their entirety.

16   If the outcome of the referendum in Part 2 is that the Constitution set out in Schedule 1 is not approved, then within three months of that binding outcome an Order under this section shall be laid before the House of Commons by the Prime Minister and shall make provision for the drafting of a Constitution for the United Kingdom and for its implementation in accordance with this Act.

17   An Order made under section 16 shall make provision for the following matters:

(1)   the process by which the Constitution is to be drafted which must include full public consultation by those entrusted with the responsibility for drafting the Constitution;

(2)   (without prejudice to the general need for public consultation) arrangements for citizens' councils and assemblies to participate in the process of drafting the Constitution;

(3)   the persons or bodies to be entrusted with the responsibility for drafting the Constitution (including any necessary appointment process) which should include, in a proportionate manner, a mixture of persons qualified by reason of expertise and experience including one or more members of the Law Commission but which should also contain a small number of citizens of the United Kingdom without such expertise or experience;

(4)   the time within which the Constitution is to be drafted which shall not be later than [ ] years after the making of the Order.

18   An Order made under section 17 shall make such further provision as may be necessary for the implementation of the second referendum including the funding of such implementation from money provided by Parliament.

19   No Order shall be made under section 17 unless a draft of the Order has been laid before, and approved by resolution of, each House of Parliament.

20   A Constitution drafted in accordance with the process contained in an Order made under section 17 shall come into force in accordance with the provisions of that Constitution and from that date the provisions of that Constitution shall apply in their entirety.

Part 4

Supplementary

21   No court shall entertain any proceedings for questioning the numbers, as certified by the Chief Counting Officer or any counting officer, of any ballot papers counted or answers given in a referendum under this Act.

22   The preceding provisions of this Act shall come into force on such day as the Prime Minister may order made by statutory instrument appoint.

23   This Act extends to England and Wales, Scotland and Northern Ireland.

24   This Act may be cited as The Constitution of Britain (Referendums) Act [ ].

SCHEDULES

SCHEDULE 1

[THE CONSTITUTION]

SCHEDULE 2

FORM OF BALLOT PAPER

Are you in favour of a written Constitution for the United Kingdom?

Put a cross (X) in one box:

YES ☐

NO ☐

SCHEDULE 3

FORM OF BALLOT PAPER

Do you approve the Constitution attached to this Ballot Paper in its entirety?

Put a cross (X) in one box:

YES ☐

NO ☐